Risky Rivers

Arizona Studies in Human Ecology

Editor

Robert McC. Netting (University of Arizona)

Associate Editors

Peggy F. Barlett (Emory University)

James F. Eder (Arizona State University)

Benjamin S. Orlove (University of California, Davis)

Risky Rivers

The Economics and Politics of
Floodplain Farming in Amazonia

Michael Chibnik

The University of Arizona Press / *Tucson & London*

The University of Arizona Press
Copyright © 1994
The Arizona Board of Regents
All rights reserved

♾ This book is printed on acid-free, archival-quality paper.
Manufactured in the United States of America

99 98 97 96 95 94   6 5 4 3 2 1

LIBRARY OF CONGRESS CATALOGING-IN-PUBLICATION DATA
Chibnik, Michael, 1946–
   Risky rivers: the economics and politics of floodplain farming in Amazonia /
   Michael Chibnik.
      p.   cm. — (Arizona studies in human ecology)
   Includes bibliographical references and index.
   ISBN 0-8165-1482-8 (cloth)
   1. Floodplain agriculture—Peru—Iquitos Region.   2. Floodplain agriculture—
   Economic aspects—Peru—Iquitos Region.   3. Farmers—Peru—Iquitos Region.
   I. Title.   II. Series.
S475.P42I673   1994   94-28792
307.72′0985′43—dc20   CIP

British Cataloguing-in-Publication Data
A catalogue record for this book is available from the British Library.

*Publication of this book is made possible in part by a grant from the Office
of the Vice President for Research of the University of Iowa.*

For Joan and Sheldon Chibnik

Contents

Preface   xi

Acknowledgments   xix

1   The Political Ecology of Amazonia   1

2   Regional Geography   16

3   Regional History   26

4   Regional Economy   51

5   Ribereño Villages   72

6   Porvenir, Santa Sofía, and Tapirillo   94

7   Food and Income Sources   111

8   Agricultural Labor Organization   134

9   Economic Strategies   152

10   Agricultural Credit   173

11   Campesino Unions   192

12   Prospects for Sustainable Development   219

Appendix 1: Household Socioeconomic Surveys   227

Appendix 2: Cost-Benefit Analyses   229

Glossary   231

References Cited   235

Index   251

Figures

2.1 The research area   18

2.2 Floodplain landforms   22

4.1 Peru's geographical zones   52

4.2 Prices in the Iquitos market for corn, manioc, and plantains   68

4.3 Prices in the Iquitos market for tomatoes, papayas, and chickens   69

6.1 The number of males and females of various ages in Porvenir, Santa Sofía, and Tapirillo, March 1986   103

8.1 A flowchart model of extrafamily labor recruitment   145

Tables

4.1 Population of Regions of Peru, 1940–1989   55

4.2 Average Annual Immigration and Emigration Rates in Tropical Forest Departments, 1976–1981   55

4.3 Products on a Tapirillo-Iquitos Colectivo, February 8, 1986   64

4.4 Average Yearly Consumer Price Index in Iquitos, 1975–1989   71

5.1 Previous Residences of Adult Men in Porvenir, Santa Sofía, and Tapirillo   82

6.1 Characteristics of Porvenir, Santa Sofía, and Tapirillo   96

6.2 Number of Households of Various Types in Porvenir, Santa Sofía, and Tapirillo   104

6.3 Ethnic Origins of Surnames of Men and Women 21 and Older in the Three Villages   108

6.4 Ethnic Origins of Paternal Surnames of Husbands and Wives in the Three Villages   108

6.5 Ethnic Origins of Maternal Surnames of Husbands and Wives in the Three Villages   109

7.1 Rice Production in Barreales, 1985: Cash Outlays and Labor Demands for 4 Hectares Yielding 8 Metric Tons   117

7.2 Rice Production in Barreales, 1985: Cash Outlays and Labor Demands for 2 Hectares Yielding 4 Metric Tons   118

7.3   Percentage of Households That Planted Various Crops
        in Porvenir, Santa Sofía, and Tapirillo, 1984 and 1985   123

7.4   Mean Area in Hectares of Various Crops Planted by Households
        in Porvenir, Santa Sofía, and Tapirillo, 1984 and 1985   124

7.5   Percentage of Major Crops Grown on Various Land Types
        in Porvenir, Santa Sofía, and Tapirillo, 1984 and 1985   125

7.6   Estimated Gross Household Income in Intis from Various
        Sources in Porvenir, Santa Sofía, and Tapirillo, 1985   132

8.1   Characteristics of Santa Rosa, Tamshiyacu, and Yanallpa   136

8.2   Characteristics of Exchange Labor Groups in Various
        Communities   141

8.3   Characteristics of Various Forms of Extrafamily Labor   143

8.4   Flowchart Predictions for Four Important
        Agricultural Tasks   148

9.1   Crop Mix of Panduro-Piña Household, 1984 and 1985   160

9.2   Crop Mix of Ahuanari-Manuyama Household, 1984
        and 1985   161

9.3   Crop Mix of Flores-Montes Household, 1984 and 1985   163

10.1   Economic Characteristics of Borrowers and Nonborrowers
        in Porvenir, Santa Sofía, and Tapirillo, 1985   183

Preface

The rivers of the midwestern United States ran wild in the summer of 1993. Floods ruined crops, closed roads, swamped water-treatment facilities, and forced thousands of people to leave their homes and close their businesses. Desperate efforts by volunteers to erect walls of sandbags often failed to hold back the rising water. Feeble jokes were made about new Great Lakes.

Many people were surprised by the extent of the damage caused by the flooding. The Army Corps of Engineers had constructed an elaborate system of levees, dams, reservoirs, and floodwalls to prevent rain-soaked rivers from changing course and inundating valuable farmland. After much of this system failed in 1993, some people questioned the effort to harness rivers such as the Mississippi. Perhaps it would be better, they said, to abandon efforts to build on certain parts of the floodplains.

Iowa City, where I live, was hit hard by the floods of 1993. I followed the news stories of raging rivers, heroic volunteers, devastated entrepreneurs, and unhappy farmers with even more interest than most of my flood-obsessed neighbors. I had spent much of the past decade thinking about how people in the lowland Peruvian tropics reacted to the rise and fall of enormous unharnessed rivers. My anthropological fieldwork in the 1980s near the city of Iquitos in the Peruvian Amazon had focused on the ways in which river movements affect economic strategies, political conflicts, and settlement patterns.

My decision to conduct research in the Peruvian Amazon was a combination of design and happenstance. Although my doctoral thesis had concerned the economic strategies of English-speaking rural Belizeans, I found myself regularly teaching courses and advising students about all parts of Latin America. I decided to carry out my next research project in a Spanish-speaking part of South America. During the period when I was considering potential fieldwork sites, Christine Padoch suggested that I visit Iquitos.

Christine and I have been friends ever since we were graduate students at Columbia University in the 1970s. She is an ecological anthropologist who works for the New York Botanical Garden. Christine's principal task in the mid-1980s was to examine the economic use and commercial potential of various tropical plants. When I first went to Iquitos in July 1984, Christine and her colleagues from the Botanical Garden were examining the production and marketing of certain fruits raised in agroforestry systems in communities near Iquitos. The Botanical Garden was establishing institutional ties with Peruvian organizations and cooperating closely with local scientists.

One of Christine's projects examined the social and economic relationships among fruit growers, boat operators, wholesalers, processors, and vendors. She wanted to talk to me about what economic anthropologists had to say about marketing chains. I was pleased to have the opportunity to visit Iquitos. Amazonia, with its complex tropical lowland ecology, was an exciting research area. If I did eventually work near Iquitos, informal ties with the Botanical Garden would help me learn about the region.

Iquitos was not at all what I had expected. I had thought that the area would be affected by the revolutionary movements and cocaine trade that were so important in other parts of Peru, but I discovered that the Sendero Luminoso (the Shining Path) and other guerrilla groups were not operating around Iquitos. Some coca trading networks had included Iquitos in the late 1970s, but most of them had shifted elsewhere by 1984. Furthermore, the most noteworthy aspects of the Iquitos area seemed only tangentially related to the principal Amazonian themes of environmental destruction, small-scale colonization, large-scale development projects, and relations between settlers and indigenous peoples. I was intrigued instead by the region's ethnic makeup, land tenure systems, cooperative work groups, credit programs, and grassroots political movements.

Nobody I talked to could give me a very clear account of the ethnic origins of the people living in the riverine villages near Iquitos. These *ribereños* were said to be of mixed European and Amerindian descent. Some had Spanish surnames; others had surnames that apparently were typical of certain Amerindian groups. Many rural people had parents or grandparents who spoke indigenous Amazonian languages, yet most of these same people openly disdained Amerindians and identified themselves as ribereños. I was unsure whether the ribereños should be regarded as a distinct Amazonian ethnic group.

The economic lives of the ribereños revolved around the rise and fall of local rivers. The annual flooding of low-lying areas had interesting implications for land tenure in ribereño communities. Some very fertile lands were underwater most of the year. Such *barreales* were impermanent. Every year deposits of silt created new barreales, and old barreales disappeared when rivers changed course. My introduction to floodplain ecology made me curious about rights to land. How did farmers gain access to new barreales? What did farmers do when their barreales disappeared? What kinds of disputes arose concerning access to new barreales? How were these disputes resolved? Did cooperative work groups have property rights in barreales?

My interest in cooperative work groups stemmed from a trip I made to the small town of Tamshiyacu with Wil de Jong, a Dutch forester then working for the Peruvian Ministry of Agriculture. We spent some time visiting a large work party of men and women clearing undergrowth. Wil said that in Tamshiyacu groups of rural households took turns helping each other with agricultural tasks. These cooperative work groups adopted names, elected officers, and had written rules. They seemed to be an important feature of the local social organization. I wondered about their origins, prevalence, and economic advantages.

Wil told me that government credit programs were enabling some farmers to rely more on hired labor and less on cooperative work groups. The state-run Agrarian Bank provided credit to both large-scale entrepreneurs and small-scale farmers. Prosperous rural residents obtained credit for water buffalo, boats, motors, and various enterprises. Small-scale farmers used credit mainly to hire labor to help with the production of rice, jute, and corn. Credit programs clearly had the potential to affect rural economic strategies and class relations.

When I asked people about agricultural development programs in the Iquitos area, they inevitably began by telling me about credit. When I asked if credit was ever given to agricultural cooperatives, I was told that credit was offered only to individuals and that there were no cooperatives of any importance in rural areas. The most active rural grassroots development organizations were peasant (*campesino*) unions. I did not find out much about these unions on my first visit to Iquitos, but I could see that they were an important part of the social landscape.

Setting Up a Project and Establishing Ties with Local Institutions

Christine suggested that I explore the possibility of establishing an affiliation with the Centro Amazónico de Antropología y Aplicación Práctica (CAAAP). This organization, which receives financial support from the Catholic church and various European groups, sponsors research in the Peruvian Amazon and carries out small-scale rural development projects concerning agriculture, education, and public health. During the late 1970s and early 1980s, CAAAP worked closely with the campesino unions to help ribereños and Amerindians in their conflicts with entrepreneurs over access to land and other natural resources.

I talked about possible research projects with Miguel Pinedo, one of the workers at the CAAAP office in Iquitos. Miguel said that CAAAP was very interested in the effects of market penetration on rural villages and suggested that I study the effects of government credit programs. He thought that arranging affiliation would not be a problem.

In December 1984 I submitted a research proposal to the National Science Foundation. The general aim of the proposal was to examine how ribereños were changing household economic strategies in response to agricultural credit programs and improvements in marketing conditions. My theoretical focus was on the willingness of ribereños to take risks in order to improve their material circumstances; my practical focus was on the impact of credit and other development programs on land use patterns and socioeconomic conditions in ribereño communities.

My grant proposal was approved, and in July 1985 I returned to Iquitos for a year of research. I immediately discovered that my initial plans for institutional affiliation would not work. Most of the Iquitos staff of CAAAP had quit after the central administration in Lima had urged them to avoid confrontations with local elites in land tenure disputes. Some ex-CAAAP staff continued to work as advisers to the campesino unions. A few obtained support for this work from European organizations or the unions' meager funds, but most helped as volunteers.

Miguel Pinedo, who had married Christine Padoch in early 1985, was one of the unpaid advisers to the unions. Although Miguel was busy with his union activities and long-postponed university work in forestry, he was seeking paid employment. I arranged to hire him as a research assistant, with the understanding that his work with me would be juggled with his multiple obligations as union adviser, student, husband, and member of a large family. The term *research assistant* is really a misnomer for what Miguel did for me; a better characterization of our relationship would be to say we were research associates. Miguel's ideas and schedule influenced our research activities as much as did my own initiatives. Miguel was remarkably knowledgeable about the economics, politics, and ecology of the Iquitos area. Despite a lack of formal anthropological training, he had well-developed, theoretically motivated ideas about the social structure of riverine communities.

Miguel quickly arranged an affiliation between two campesino unions and me. Our written agreement was quite simple. The unions said that they supported my credit research, and I promised to tell them what I found out. I eventually included some of the results of my research in reports to the unions and presented other results at a meeting in 1986.

My affiliation with the unions proved to be very useful when I worked with residents of ribereño communities. Most villagers supported the activities of the unions, and very few opposed them. The union affiliation, however, would be of no help in my dealings with government officials. Many regional bureaucrats disliked the unions' role in land tenure disputes between campesinos and members of the local elite. Thus my affiliation with the unions could not be used to gain access to data in government offices or to justify my activities to the police and immigration officials. The only other possible disadvantage of the union affiliation involved my relations with the Agrarian Bank. The head of the bank knew of my ties with the unions and was unwilling or unable to give me much help with my research. I do not know, however, if he would have been more helpful if I had not been associated with the unions.

After some negotiation, I obtained an affiliation with the Centro de Investigación de la Amazonía Peruana (CIAP), part of the Universidad Nacional de la Amazonía Peruana (UNAP) in Iquitos. Even though the terms of affiliation were spelled out in numerous detailed clauses, the principal part of the agreement was straightforward. CIAP provided me with a letter of affiliation, and I agreed to provide CIAP with interim and final reports on my research activities. I eventually showed my letter of affiliation with CIAP to a few government officials and wrote the reports, but I never set foot in UNAP (my negotiations took place with one of the directors of CIAP at his house), and the affiliation had little effect on my day-to-day research.

Working with Miguel Pinedo and the Campesino Unions

I conducted fieldwork in the Peruvian Amazon between July 1985 and June 1986 and in July and August 1987. This research was profoundly affected by my ties with Miguel Pinedo and the campesino unions. Miguel was then in his early thirties. He is an energetic and talented man who was born and raised in the small town of Dos de Mayo on the Ucayali River and who knows people from all strata of society in the Iquitos area. After studying at UNAP and working for oil companies for several years, he had taken a large cut in salary to join the staff at CAAAP. Miguel, now a doctoral student at the Yale School of Forestry and Environmental Studies, continues to work with the campesino unions around Iquitos.

My association with Miguel Pinedo and the campesino unions had many advantages. I was able to visit a village where Miguel knew people, and I could begin conducting research almost immediately. I also met farmers from many different communities when they came to union headquarters in Iquitos and visited Miguel at his home. They were quite willing to tell me about their economic plans and problems.

My connections with Miguel and the unions led to rather unusual research conditions. On our trips to riverine communities, Miguel had the double agenda of helping me and conducting union business. His diverse union activities included informing people about changes in government credit regulations, advising communities involved in land tenure disputes, and telling people about agricultural innovations and public health measures. When we visited a community for several days, Miguel would inevitably arrange a village meeting in which he advised people and answered questions.

My travels with Miguel gave me an extraordinary opportunity to learn about union activities and a diversity of village problems. However, I was not perceived as an impartial observer of events. In the eyes of the villagers, I was working for the unions, and in fact I strongly supported the goals of campesino organizations. Furthermore, most people's initial reactions to me were influenced by their relations with Miguel. Fortunately, he was very well liked by many people living along the rivers.

Despite Miguel's far greater knowledge of the area, much of the research we carried out was at my suggestion. The ways I looked at risk taking, ethnicity, and cooperative work groups came from my anthropological training and were unfamiliar to Miguel. The systematic socioeconomic surveys we carried out were entirely my idea. Nonetheless, there can be no question that Miguel greatly influenced how I initially thought about many of the issues we examined. He was especially instrumental in drawing my attention to the importance of agricultural credit programs, campesino unions, and struggles over access to land and other natural resources. Although Miguel is not responsible for anything I say here, this book would have been very different without his generous help.

Acknowledgments

I have been working in and writing about the Peruvian Amazon since 1984. Several organizations and countless individuals have helped me in diverse ways over the past decade. Here, I can briefly mention only the most important of my many debts.

Grants from the National Science Foundation, the Midwest Universities Consortium for International Activities, and the University of Iowa supported my research and writing. While conducting fieldwork I was affiliated with Centro de Investigación of the Universidad Nacional de la Amazonía Peruana, the Federación de Campesinos de Maynas, and the Comité de Productores de Arroz de la Provincia de Maynas. These institutional connections were invaluable when I attempted to explain my often mysterious activities to farmers, boat operators, wholesalers, vendors, and government bureaucrats.

Christine Padoch and Wil de Jong were wonderful colleagues and friends during fieldwork. Christine introduced me to many people in the Iquitos area and aided me immensely in my initial efforts to find food, shelter, and institutional affiliation. I continue to be astonished by Christine's encyclopedic knowledge of tropical ecology and her vast network of friends and acquaintances. Wil, a Dutch forester who lived in Iquitos for most of the 1980s, was always willing to discuss the complexities of local farming systems. His patient, lucid, and often amusing explanations encouraged me on days when I thought I would never figure out what was going on.

My debt to Miguel Pinedo is apparent on every page of this book. The preface explains our unusual research relationship in detail. I have profound respect for Miguel's dedication, energy, knowledge, and fortitude. I was incredibly lucky to have had the opportunity to work with him.

Holly Carver and I have been together happily since the fall of 1987. I cannot overstate how much her unwavering support and steadfast good humor meant to me as I wrote and rewrote this book. But Holly's contribution to my first sole-authored book consists of much more than this. She is an editor with a university press who has improved the prose of many anthropologists. Holly was able to give me professional advice about such arcane matters as manuscript submission, artwork, design, and production. She also copy edited and proofread several chapters before they were sent off to reviewers.

I am also most grateful for the help given me in Peru and the United States by the following individuals: Shirley Ahlgren, Santiago Arévalo, Bella Bouaziz, Katharine Chibnik, Howard Clark, Kate Clark, Beth Conklin, Patricia Conrad, Karen Copp, Joan Crowe, Teresa Faden, Jürg Gasche, Samantha Havel, Mário Hiraoka, Leif Jonsson, Andorra Katz, Marcela Mendoza, Nemesio Montes, Robert Netting, Teodora Nuñez, Francisco Ochovano, Lisa Parker, Charles Peters, Paige Peterson, Beverly Poduska, Juanita Schaper, Alan Schroder, Paul Spragens, Christine Szuter, John Unruh, and the late Jan Vogelzang.

My most important debt, of course, is to the people of the Peruvian Amazon. I remain overwhelmed by their kindness and good cheer in response to my incessant questions about the most mundane aspects of everyday life.

1. The Political Ecology of Amazonia

The destruction of the Amazonian rain forest may be the best-described ecological calamity of our time. Newspapers, magazines, and television programs report the environmental damage resulting from road construction, colonization projects, cattle ranches, mining operations, and unsuitable agricultural practices. Books aimed at both scholarly audiences (e.g., Anderson 1990b; Browder 1989; Foresta 1991) and the general public (e.g., Cowell 1990; Revkin 1990) warn that deforestation reduces biological diversity and may lead to global warming and changes in rainfall patterns. Anthropologists and human rights activists note that many Amazonian Amerindian groups have been devastated by disease, forcibly relocated, and deprived of their cultural identity.

The tropical lowlands around Iquitos, Peru, differ in many ways from the portrayal of Amazonia in most scholarly and popular publications. Even though the Iquitos area is the most densely populated part of the lowland Peruvian Amazon, there is little deforestation. The region has few large-scale extractive enterprises and no huge cattle ranches. Most rural inhabitants are neither recent settlers nor self-identified Amerindians. Many are floodplain farmers who use agricultural methods well suited to the local ecology.

This book is about the household economies, cultural ecology, political struggles, and grassroots organizations of people living in riverine villages near Iquitos. A close examination of these communities can tell us something about the potential for, and obstacles to, sustainable, equitable agricultural development in Amazonia. Despite their use of environmentally appropriate agricultural methods, most farmers have been unable to improve their material circumstances over the past two decades. Despite the vastness of the tropical forest, peasant farmers and small-scale entrepreneurs bitterly compete for access to certain pieces of land.

Because of the absence of spectacular deforestation, ambitious business enterprises, and violent political confrontations, the Iquitos area has been ignored by most environmentalists, human rights advocates, and academics writing about Amazonia. The region is nonetheless typical of large parts of the rain forest. Much of Amazonia has not experienced the effects of road building and colonization projects. Many rural Amazonians are locally born non-Amerindian peoples living in small floodplain communities along major rivers and their tributaries.

The Uneven Exploitation of Amazonia's Resources

Although entrepreneurs have regarded Amazonia as a potential source of wealth ever since the first Spanish and Portuguese explorers came to the area in the sixteenth and seventeenth centuries, the region's difficult terrain and its distance from major ports and population centers prevented the exploitation of the rain forest for hundreds of years. The economic isolation of the tropical lowlands of South America persisted until rubber became a valuable commodity in the industrial countries of Europe and North America. A seemingly insatiable demand for "black gold" in the late nineteenth century transformed Amazonia. Fortune seekers poured into the jungle and set up companies to collect, process, and market rubber. The cities of Manaus, Brazil, and Iquitos, Peru, became prosperous trading centers.

When the rubber boom ended around 1912 because of competition from Asian plantations, the Amazonian parts of Brazil and Peru once again became economic backwaters. Most of the attempts of entrepreneurs to make money from forest products in the interwar period were unsuccessful. Some enterprises failed because of a failure to understand tropical ecology and local politics; others foundered when industrial countries developed synthetic substitutes for particular forest products.

In recent years Brazil has made a concerted effort to exploit the resources of Amazonia. The government's investment in the rain forest increased greatly after a military takeover in 1964. State policies such as tax abatements and low-interest loans encouraged investors to seek land titles, and an elaborate road building program eased colonization.

These Brazilian development programs have led to the first massive, irrevocable environmental destruction of the rain forest. Some of this damage is related to technological change. New kinds of machinery have made it easier to log out large tracts of land or clear them for pasture. Improvements in construction techniques, communication devices, and methods of transportation have spurred road building. The resulting Amazonian highways have increased the flow of people, machines, and products in and out of the tropical lowlands. Much of the destruction of the Brazilian Amazon, however, can be attributed to government policies that favor cattle ranching (Fearnside 1987a; Hecht 1985). Establishing a pasture was for many years the cheapest way to obtain the right to occupy land. The military regime gave easy credit to would-be ranchers and excused them from excise duties and corporate income taxes for ten to fifteen years. Even though Amazonian pastures are usually productive immediately after clearing, soil fertility quickly declines and weeds invade. Ranchers often found that clearing new pastures was economically more advantageous than maintaining old ones, so they left behind a succession of abandoned degraded pastures usually invaded by scrubby vegetation.

Unlike Brazil, Peru did not dramatically increase its investment in Amazonia in the 1960s. The proportion of the government's budget allocated to the tropical lowlands ranged from 10 to 15 percent between 1960 and 1980 (Wilson and Wise 1986:98). This comparatively small investment did not indicate a lack of interest in Amazonia among the government's leaders. Two-time president Fernando Belaúnde Terry (1963–68, 1980–85) devised complex plans for roads that would integrate the jungle into the national economy and provide transportation links with the tropical lowlands of neighboring countries (Belaúnde Terry 1965). Many other political leaders and planners discussed the economic potential of the Peruvian Amazon as well. But Peru is poorer and smaller than Brazil. The per capita gross national product of Peru in 1987 was U.S.$1,470, compared to $2,020 for Brazil. Similarly, between 1965 and 1987 the per capita gross national product of Peru increased by 0.2 percent, compared to 4.1 percent in Brazil (Webb and Fernández Baca 1990:4). Finally, because Peru has only one-seventh of Brazil's population, there are far fewer investors able to afford the cost of large projects.

The geography of Peru also slows the colonization of the rain forest. The Andes separate Peru's tropical lowlands from its major population centers, making the movement of people and products to and from Amazonia more difficult than in Brazil. The lowland Peruvian Amazon has remained a backwater; its only transportation links to the rest of the

world are airplanes and riverboats. Most of Peru's Amazonian development has taken place in the high jungle on or near the eastern slope of the
Andes. Roads now connect this region to the rest of the country, and
numerous settlers from the Peruvian highlands have migrated to the
Andean foothills over the past three decades (Aramburú 1986; Collins
1989; Renard-Casevitz 1980; Shoemaker 1981). Because coca grows well
on the lower eastern slopes of the Andes, the high jungle has become the
center of Peru's thriving illicit narcotics industry, and drug-related profits
finance various legal enterprises.

Sustainable, Equitable Development

Some conservationists (e.g., Foresta 1991) have argued that the only way
to maintain the biological diversity of Amazonia is to set aside large parts
of the rain forest as nature reserves. But plans for such reserves have been
harshly criticized both by proponents of large-scale development and by
human rights activists. Entrepreneurs and business-oriented politicians
argue that impoverished South American countries cannot afford to ignore the valuable economic resources of much of Amazonia, while members of indigenous Amazonian groups and their supporters point out that
plans for national parks can threaten the livelihood of the peoples who
farm, fish, and forage in the proposed reserves.

Recently, many researchers have been examining various sustainable
development strategies in Amazonia. Such strategies have been characterized as "innovative technologies or approaches that permit simulta-
neous use and conservation of the rain forest, and that have the potential
to provide a better way of life for people than do the land uses that
currently predominate in the region" (Anderson 1990a:11). Advocates
of sustainable development in Amazonia (e.g., Anderson 1990b; Browder
1989; Clay 1988; Goodman and Hall 1990) have been especially interested in the subsistence activities of Amerindians and other longtime inhabitants of the rain forest. These practices have been tested over many
years and are likely to be better adapted to a tropical forest environment
than methods imported from temperate zones. The subsistence methods
of longtime Amazonian residents rarely lead to significant environmental
damage.

Stephen Bunker asserts that many advocates of sustainable development pay insufficient attention to political economy. According to Bunker, they are often "not talking about development at all, but are rather

comparing the balance sheets between returns to land and labor in different land uses without considering how these local uses fit into or conflict with larger systems" (1991:486). Bunker suggests that local subsistence systems are unlikely to remain autonomous when people are living on lands that are desired by governments and business enterprises. He goes on to question whether sustainable development can even be considered in Amazonia except "in those remote corners not affected by road and rails built around large mineral and electric projects that can create opportunities for large capitals." Bunker also contends that many proposals for sustainable development would be attractive only to the very poor.

While I agree with Bunker that advocates of sustainable resource management sometimes neglect political economy in their analyses, I think that he may underestimate the feasibility and attractiveness of small-scale development in much of Amazonia. More than half the land area of Peru, for example, consists of a sparsely populated tropical rain forest that has been largely unaffected by roads, railroads, and mineral and hydroelectric projects. Most of the rural people of the lowland Peruvian Amazon are poor enough that the diverse land use systems proposed by advocates of sustainable development might well be appealing.

Amazonian development has been inequitable. Only a small number of the region's people have prospered from ranching, mining, lumbering, or land speculation. Development incentives such as agricultural credit and tax abatements have favored large-scale entrepreneurs more than peasant farmers, impoverished colonists, and Amerindians (Bunker 1985; Hecht and Cockburn 1989; Moran 1981). The enterprises of wealthy investors have driven many poorer Amazonians off their land. Amerindian groups have been forced to resettle in reserves; rubber workers have lost access to the trees they once tapped.

Most advocates of sustainable development are concerned about economic equity. Some are motivated primarily by considerations of social justice. Others think that small-scale development projects that are beneficial to many people are less environmentally destructive than large-scale enterprises that benefit only a few.

Many recent plans for sustainable, equitable development involve the creation of extractive reserves for rubber tappers, peasant farmers, and even small-scale miners. In some ways, these reserves resemble those that have been set aside for Amerindian groups in Amazonia. Local populations would obtain long-term leases on land from the state and would make communal decisions about land use and access. The eagerness of some development agencies to promote the idea of reserves may reflect a desire to shunt problem populations into enclaves. Nonetheless, the enthusiasm with which the concept of extractive reserves has been embraced by many peasant unions in both Brazil and Peru demonstrates the vulnerability of the rural Amazonian poor to land grabs by the wealthy. Although a few extractive reserves have been established in various parts of Amazonia, there are none in the area around Iquitos.

Misleading Impressions of Amazonia

By focusing on dramatic events, the outpouring of popular and scholarly literature on Amazonia has fostered several misleading impressions among both the general public and many academics. These erroneous ideas, which have had considerable influence on discussions of sustainable development strategies, are the following:

1. Much of the rain forest has already been cut down, and irrevocable environmental damage has occurred or is imminent in most of Amazonia.

2. Sustainable agricultural development in Amazonia is virtually impossible because of poor soils.

3. Most Amazonians are either recent settlers or members of indigenous groups.

The Extent of Deforestation

The extensive environmental destruction that is now occurring in parts of Brazil and that has already occurred in many other tropical areas has led some outsiders to overestimate the proportion of Amazonia that has been deforested. Anyone who has flown over the lowland South American tropics knows that vast areas of jungle remain. The exact amount of deforestation has been disputed. Estimates for Brazil range from 5 to 20 percent, with a range of 8 to 12 percent often cited (Hecht and Cockburn 1989:232; Moran 1993:156). There has also been environmental damage to a lesser degree in most other parts of Amazonia. Deforestation is a serious problem and is likely to continue at an alarming pace, but the luxuriant rain forest is not yet lost.

The major causes of deforestation in Amazonia have been cattle ranching, logging, mining, road building, and tax breaks for investors (Moran

1993:58–59; Schmink and Wood 1992:100–101; Schwartzman 1989: 151). These preconditions for environmental destruction are not yet present in much of the region. Most parts of the Brazilian and Peruvian tropical lowlands are far from roads, and tax incentives for cattle raising and extractive industries have not been offered everywhere. Deforestation has taken place mainly in "development poles" such as the state of Rondônia in Brazil and the eastern slope of the Andes in Peru.

The Practicality of Agricultural Intensification

Discussions of sustainable Amazonian development usually focus on the uplands, which comprise most of the rain forest. Intensive agriculture is not practical on many upland soils. Researchers and development workers who have written about upland areas with poor soils have therefore discussed various alternatives to continuous cultivation. They have considered the commercial potential of tropical fruits (e.g., Prance 1989), the merits of agroforestry (e.g., Peck 1990), and the political desirability of extractive reserves (e.g., Schwartzman 1989). They have also debated the feasibility of using chemical fertilizers to improve the agricultural potential of upland soils (e.g., Cochrane and Sanchez 1982; Fearnside 1987b). The rural population of Amazonia, however, is concentrated in river valleys where intensive agriculture has been practiced since precolumbian times. Several writers (Denevan 1984; Eden 1978; Hiraoka 1989; Roosevelt et al. 1991) have suggested that sustainable agricultural development in Amazonia may be most feasible in these wide floodplains.

As Thomas Park (1992:91–93) observes, definitions and theoretical discussions of agricultural intensification do not always exactly fit floodplain farming. Ester Boserup, perhaps the best-known writer on this topic, defines agricultural intensification as an increase in the frequency with which a particular piece of land is cropped. According to Boserup, agricultural intensification in nonindustrial farming systems is associated with greater inputs of labor and greater returns per unit of land. On a given piece of land, however, returns per unit of labor decrease as cropping frequency increases (Boserup 1965, 1981). Boserup's theory of agricultural intensification thus assumes that farmers are able to increase yields per hectare by shortening fallow periods. Because much floodplain agriculture depends on the annual rise and fall of a river, yields per hectare in some land types cannot be increased this way. Agricultural intensification in such places must therefore be defined as obtaining higher yields per hectare as a result of increased expenditures of labor and capital.

The river valleys of the tropical forests of Amazonia differ greatly in the extent to which agricultural intensification is possible (Eden 1990: 165–66; Moran 1993:84–115). Soil fertility and the range of annual flooding vary considerably from place to place. Floodplains contain a diversity of land types that differ in their soil composition and susceptibility to inundations. The agricultural methods that can be used in floodplains in the Iquitos area are quite different from those appropriate to the estuaries near the mouth of the Amazon, and agricultural methods that are suitable on seldom-flooded natural levees cannot be used on annually inundated mud bars. Much agriculture in river valleys involves crops being sown as annual floods recede. Park points out that in such flood-recession agriculture "top-quality soils in good years can yield superlative returns per unit of labor as well as per hectare" (1992:93). These yields can be sufficiently high that they may seem to undermine Boserup's theory. For example, a study in Thailand (Hanks 1972:54–64) showed that, for some years, the returns per unit of labor for fields of flood-recession rice were considerably higher than those from fields of rice grown using shifting cultivation methods. However, Hanks's appendix on data sources (1972:165–67) does not indicate whether the crops of flood-recession and shifting-cultivation rice were grown on land that had similar soil qualities.

Park (1992:93) notes that returns per unit of labor in flood-recession agriculture can vary greatly from year to year. The inherent unpredictability of floods can make farming in river valleys riskier than tropical shifting cultivation. In some years the returns per unit of labor (and even per hectare) from flood-recession agriculture are likely to be much lower than those from shifting cultivation. It is not uncommon for rising waters to destroy almost all of a farmer's crops.

Population Groups

Inhabitants of Amazonia can be broadly classified into three groups: Amerindians, recent settlers from other areas, and locally born non-Amerindians. Most Amerindians, the smallest of these groups, live in Peru and Brazil. There are about 200,000 self-identified Amerindians in the Peruvian Amazon (Stocks 1984:35), about 15 percent of the population of lowland tropical Peru. About 190,000 Amerindians live in all of Brazil (Ramos 1984:83). Contemporary Amerindians are at least partially descended from precolumbian indigenous peoples, but current groupings differ considerably from those of precolumbian times. Groups have moved, merged with other peoples, or disappeared. The self-defining features of particular groups have changed over time as they incorporated the customs of Europeans and other Amerindians into their cultures.

The colonization of Amazonia has proceeded rapidly in the past several decades. Settlers of tropical forests are mostly migrants from more densely populated highland and coastal regions. Their principal motivations for migration are the greater availability of land and other perceived economic opportunities. Migrations usually follow roads that governments construct in order to increase access to the resources of Amazonia. Colonists ordinarily self-identify both as members of a national population and as migrants from a particular place. The proportion of colonists varies greatly in different parts of Amazonia. In some regions, such as Rondônia, they are the majority; in the Iquitos area and many other places, they are an insignificant minority.

Most recent writings on Amazonia have focused on settlers and Amerindians. Tropical biologists, geographers, and anthropologists have noted the problems settlers have in adapting to unfamiliar environments and the often adverse effects of colonization on the local ecology (e.g., Moran 1981; Schmink and Wood 1984). Anthropologists and human rights advocates have been concerned about the ways in which the colonization of Amazonia has affected the well-being of Amerindians (e.g., Kroeger and Barbira-Freedman 1988; Price 1989). Despite some notable exceptions (e.g., Coomes 1992; de Jong 1987; Hiraoka 1985b, 1985c; Nugent 1993; Pace 1992; Padoch 1988c; Padoch and Pinedo-Vásquez 1991; Parker 1981, 1985; Wagley 1953), relatively little has been written about the majority of people whom Padoch and de Jong have labeled the "forgotten Amazonians" (1989:103), who are neither Amerindians nor recent settlers. These people are called by various terms, including *ribereños* (Peru), *caboclos* (Brazil), and *cambas* (Bolivia). These terms often have rural, lower-class connotations and may be associated with particular occupations and regions (see Chibnik 1991).

Sustainability, Equity, and Economic Development in the Iquitos Area
Farmers in the riverine communities near Iquitos practice sustainable agriculture. Some of their crops have been raised by Amerindians since precolumbian times; others have been successfully imported into the area in recent years. Most ribereño villages, moreover, exhibit only minor socioeconomic stratification. The few wealthy inhabitants of rural areas

live away from villages on separate estates in the countryside, but they own much less land than their Brazilian counterparts. Nonetheless, ribereño communities can hardly be regarded as models of sustainable, equitable Amazonian development. Infant mortality is very high, with about 15 of every 100 children dying before the age of two. Villages lack electricity and running water. Latrines and outhouses are uncommon. Most children end their education with primary school. The most desired consumer goods—radios, boat motors, and sewing machines—are owned by only a minority of households. Many ribereños have shown their dissatisfaction with rural economic opportunities, public health facilities, and schools by migrating permanently to Iquitos, the only sizable city in the region.

Riverine villages have remained poor for several reasons. The rural area near Iquitos could be used as a textbook example of a peripheral zone. Profits from various economic booms have been siphoned away to entrepreneurs in Lima, Europe, and the United States. The geography of the region also hampers economic development. Ribereños living in small, dispersed communities in a large, sparsely populated area have difficulty transporting their produce to market, and despite good soils, farmers' agricultural livelihoods are periodically threatened by major floods.

The Peruvian government's most important attempts to stimulate small-scale agriculture have involved the provision of credit and guaranteed prices for certain crops. The state wants to increase the production of crops such as rice, jute, and corn in order to reduce agricultural imports and promote domestic self-sufficiency in foodstuffs. Credit and guaranteed prices are incentives for farmers to grow more of particular crops. Even when guaranteed prices are comparable to or slightly lower than those on the open market, efficiently run state buying centers should stimulate production by reducing risk. Farmers know that they will be able to sell all of what they produce at a set price (Zavaleta et al. 1984).

The state's provision of credit and guaranteed crop prices has not transformed the rural economy. Campesinos who attempt to improve their standard of living still encounter many obstacles, including difficulties in obtaining access to land, a chaotic marketplace, poor schools, inadequate medical facilities, and expensive, infrequent transport. Some of these problems are inevitable for a rural population inhabiting the interior of a poor nation. The debt-burdened Peruvian government cannot afford to spend much on improving conditions in rural areas. Other campesino problems, however, are the direct result of regional socioeconomic stratification in the tropical lowlands. Members of rural and urban elites profit from a sociopolitical system in which campesinos have little power. Entrepreneurs can obtain government credit more easily and in larger amounts than campesinos; moneylenders can require high interest rates; owners of commercial estates can pay low wages; and boat operators can impose high shipping fees.

In the past two decades, campesinos have formed several grassroots organizations having the general goal of increasing the political power and economic well-being of the rural poor of the Peruvian Amazon. These unions, which have received some financial and technical aid from nongovernmental international development agencies, pressure the state to improve marketing conditions and to provide individual ribereños and rural communities with clearly defined, legally protected rights to land and other natural resources. Although most of this pressure takes the form of demonstrations, publications, and meetings with government officials, on several occasions the unions have persuaded farmers to refuse to take their products to market for brief periods. The unions also provide campesinos with technical and legal aid and information about government policies. Although at times they have been strongly opposed by government bureaucrats and members of the rural and urban elites, the unions have become an important political force in the Peruvian Amazon, with local chapters in most rural villages, a voice in many government organizations, and some legal recognition.

Regional Analyses in Anthropology

My research focused on three riverine villages but also involved considerable fieldwork in other communities, on boats traveling along the river, and in the city of Iquitos. A regional study like this has certain drawbacks. Much anthropological research has focused on the activities of a single community for a year or two. This enables researchers to gain the confidence of the people they work with, check and recheck hypotheses using different types of evidence, and examine the relationships between cultural norms and actual behavior. Community studies also allow ethnographers to offer concrete examples of cultural phenomena and present multiple insider accounts of particular events.

Even proponents of regional analysis, such as William Roseberry, acknowledge that when we conduct such an investigation we may be "more removed [than traditional researchers] from the daily lives, hopes, and feelings of the people we study, which will rob our accounts of a distinctly anthropological focus" (1989:152). Nonetheless, I chose a regional approach because I agree with many contemporary anthropologists that community studies of economic activities have two fundamental limitations. First, because communities are not autonomous, one cannot understand their economies without reference to their connections with the outside world. Second, because regions often exhibit considerable internal variability, focusing on any one community may give a misleading picture of the area as a whole.

Connections Between Rural Communities and the Rest of the World

The lack of isolation of the rural communities studied by many anthropologists had become obvious by the 1960s and 1970s. Hamlets, villages, and towns were being transformed by changing agricultural technology, improved transportation, political upheavals, and the fluctuating prices of products on the world market. Anthropologists working in Latin America and elsewhere recognized that a failure to emphasize ties between particular communities and the wider world was a shortcoming of much past research. Although intensive examinations of particular communities are still common, a growing number of anthropologists—especially those interested in economics, ecology, and politics—have conducted regional studies in Latin America (e.g., Durham 1979; Gill 1987; Orlove 1977; Roseberry 1983; Smith 1975).

The contemporary marketing systems, ethnic identity, population distribution, and social structure of the riverine villages near Iquitos have been influenced by both the region's position in the world market system and local political, ecological, and economic circumstances. Not long after Spanish explorers first entered the area, Jesuit missionaries began gathering Amerindians into nucleated settlements along rivers. Many indigenous Amazonians died from various diseases; others fled into interfluvial zones. After the Spanish government expelled the Jesuits from the Peruvian Amazon in 1767, the region was fairly isolated from the rest of the world for almost a century. The rubber boom then brought many settlers to the area and forged new ethnic boundaries, occupational groups, and class relations. Since the rubber era, there have been numerous minor booms and busts as the demand for various Amazonian products has fluctuated on the world market. Transportation improvements in the past half century have lessened the isolation of the Iquitos area, and even the most remote villages have been affected by Peru's high inflation and mounting national debt.

Despite these historical connections with the outside world, ribereño villages are self-contained in some ways. Villagers grow or catch almost everything they eat, and they build their houses, furniture, and boats using local materials. Ribereños spend most of their time in their community, and most people find their mates in their own community or one nearby. Riverine villages nonetheless cannot be regarded as bounded and isolated. Most adult ribereños have lived in several places, and many have spent several years in urban centers. Almost every resident of a riverine village in the study area has close relatives in Iquitos. The livelihood of a ribereño farmer is affected by fluctuating prices in the Iquitos marketplace and by the government's decisions about land tenure and credit. Finally, villagers are involved in complex social and economic relationships with entrepreneurs—such as owners of large commercial estates and boat operators—who do business with merchants in Iquitos, Lima, and Brazilian cities.

Intercommunity Variability

Although anthropologists have long been aware of intercommunity variability, most single-place ethnographies include only brief descriptions of the typicality of the research site. Some ethnographers refuse to make generalizations about regions based on a close observation of one community. Others assume, without much supporting evidence, that the cultural patterns they describe can also be found in nearby communities. Ribereño villages, however, exhibit considerable economic and ecological variability. Some have access only to uplands, others only to floodplains, and still others have access to both. Some communities have many inhabitants who work for and borrow money from owners of commercial estates; others have fewer connections with members of the rural elite. Villages differ markedly in their cash crops, access to markets, use of government credit, and methods of recruiting extrafamily agricultural labor. Thus a detailed examination of subsistence production and cash cropping in any one village would provide limited information about the regional economy of the Iquitos area.

To gain a sense of regional economic variability, I visited numerous riverine communities and carefully examined the economic activities of three villages in particular: Porvenir, Santa Sofía, and Tapirillo. In these communities I conducted socioeconomic surveys, collected credit histories, did ethnohistorical interviewing, and talked informally with people about their lives and problems. Many of my activities in these hot and humid villages were similar to those of anthropologists doing classic participant observation. I did not, however, attempt to make a careful ethnographic study of any one community, because I considered that the advantages of a regional perspective outweighed the loss of thick description that greater concentration on one community would have made possible.

Although I have not changed the names of the villages I worked in, I have given pseudonyms to the campesinos whose lives are discussed. All other names mentioned here are real.

Risky Rivers

This book's title refers most directly to the various threats to floodplain farming posed by the rise and fall of the Amazon, Marañon, and Ucayali rivers. Farmers who grow rice on mud bars may lose their crops when annual floods cover their fields before harvests can be completed. Manioc (*yuca*), plantain (*plátano*), and corn fields in natural levees may be inundated in years in which the river is unusually high. Villagers who lose their subsistence crops may be forced to move in temporarily with relatives in Iquitos. Cultural ecologists have traditionally described how subsistence techniques and social organization allow groups and individuals to adapt to their particular physical environment. Ribereño agricultural practices, land tenure systems, and cooperative work groups, however, can be only partly understood as attempted adaptations to the risks of farming on a floodplain. Economic factors like everchanging crop prices, rural credit programs, and inflation rates are also part of the farmers' "environment" and are thus also part of the complex of influences on floodplain farming.

Much of this book is about the political ecology of floodplain farming in the Peruvian Amazon. The economic and environmental risks that ribereños face are inextricably intertwined with local, regional, and national politics. The land tenure system in the Iquitos area has been affected by protracted struggles between campesino unions and rural elites. State agricultural policies in the lowland tropics have changed greatly over the past several decades, with some governments providing guaranteed prices for certain crops and giving low-interest loans to farmers and others allowing the market to determine prices and offering hardly any agricultural credit.

2. Regional Geography

In March 1986 everybody in the Iquitos area was talking about the river levels. The rapid rise of the Amazon, Ucayali, and Marañon rivers threatened many farmers' crops and houses. Residents of floodplain villages were frantically harvesting plantains and converting sweet manioc into a storable cereal. Jute cutters in Santa Sofía were slogging their way through widening streams. A footpath in Tapirillo that had been dry at the end of February was covered with waist-high water by the second week of March. People living in the riverfront port of Belén in Iquitos had to take boats when traveling to other parts of the city.

The annual floods are a staple of conversation in the Peruvian Amazon every March and April. Longtime inhabitants tell stories of past disasters and give detailed descriptions of how the rivers have changed course. Reports of water levels upriver spread rapidly as villagers speculate about what will happen in their own community. In 1986 ribereños were worried that river crests were going to be exceptionally high. Farmers in floodplain communities have adopted agricultural practices that ordinarily enable them to cope well during March and April. Rice farmers in mudflats, for example, attempt to time certain tasks so that they are completed just before water covers their fields. But every five years or so the rivers rise so much that fields are swamped and many subsistence crops are lost. When this happens, rural families may need assistance from the state or from relatives living elsewhere.

The ribereños' fears turned out to be well-founded. When I visited Tapirillo in April, I was forced to use a boat to get around the village. Men and women who usually spent much of the day in their fields were idly chatting in their houses. Some people had left the community and were staying with relatives in Iquitos. Others were seeking wage work on commercial estates or attempting to take advantage of occasionally good fishing conditions. Most residents of Tapirillo, Santa Sofía, and other floodplain villages, however, were patiently—if not altogether happily—waiting for the rivers to fall so that they could resume their normal activities.

The annual rise and fall of the rivers is the most dramatic and variable climatic feature of the tropical lowlands of Peru. The average monthly temperature in Iquitos ranges between 24° and 27°C. The mean annual rainfall is about 2,800 millimeters (Webb and Fernández Baca 1990: 86–87). Even the driest months—July, August, and September—average more than 150 millimeters of rain (Hiraoka 1985b:248).

The steamy hamlets where I conducted my research are 3,600 kilometers west of the Atlantic Ocean and 500 kilometers east of the Andean foothills (see Figure 2.1). This hot, wet area is in the western part of the Amazon Basin. Geographers usually divide Amazonia into two ecological zones: floodplains (*várzea*) and uplands (*terra firme*). Near Iquitos, the floodplains—the valleys in which the rivers swing back and forth over annually deposited sediments—are 15 to 25 kilometers wide. The uplands, locally called *alturas,* comprise all areas that are not part of the river valleys. Typical alturas in the Peruvian tropical lowlands are about 20 to 40 meters above the river level (Hiraoka 1985b:246). Although most Amazonians live in floodplains, about 98 percent of the region is in uplands.

Some archaeologists (e.g., Meggers 1971, 1988) and sociocultural anthropologists (e.g., Gross 1975) have used the upland/floodplain distinction in their attempts to explain Amazonian settlement patterns. These ecologically oriented scholars argue that poor soils and limited faunal resources permit only small, scattered settlements in terra firme. The floodplains' richer soils and greater availability of fish and game allow denser populations. However, many writers (e.g., Denevan 1976, 1984; Moran 1982, 1993; Sponsel 1986) have noted that the upland/floodplain distinction ignores significant variability within each of these zones. Furthermore, ribereños commonly exploit both floodplains and uplands. Most rural villages in the Iquitos area are close to major rivers and their tributaries. Some communities have access to agricultural land in both river valleys and alturas. Residents of villages with fields only in alturas often fish in floodplain rivers and lakes, and residents of villages with fields only in floodplains sometimes hunt and collect forest products in alturas.

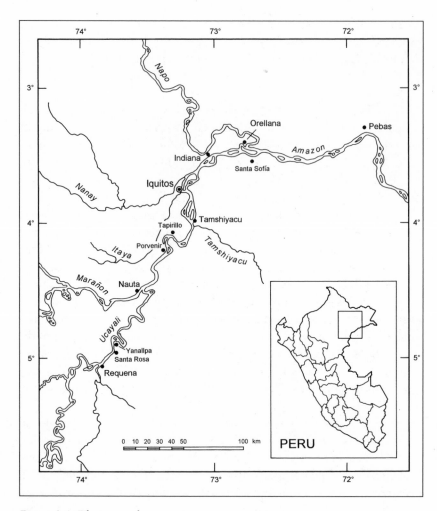

Figure 2.1. The research area

Uplands

When Europeans first explored the Amazon Basin, they were astonished by the lush vegetation and diversity of species, which led many to see the land as having great agricultural potential. They soon discovered, however, that the intensive methods of seed crop farming used in temperate zones did not work in much of the rain forest. After several years of planting in a field, soil quality deteriorated, yields dropped, and weeds flourished.

The fertility of a particular patch of soil depends partly on the age of the rock from which it is formed. Younger soils tend to be more fertile than those formed from ancient rock masses, or shields. Much of the Amazon Basin developed between the Guiana and Brazilian shields, which are several billion years old. Furthermore, most of the nutrients in tropical rain forests are in the biomass, humus, and litter. Short-fallow agricultural methods such as those employed in many temperate zones may lead to declining soil fertility.

Scientists have not reached a consensus about the proportion of upland soils with low fertility. Several decades ago most researchers (e.g., Gourou 1966; McNeil 1964) thought that the great majority of tropical upland soils were acidic, lacked horizons, and had been leached of important materials. Many argued that these soils were suited only to extensive agricultural systems with long fallow periods. Anthropologist Betty Meggers (1954, 1971, 1988) continues to be a forceful proponent of this view. In a typical passage, she writes,

> The combination of great geological antiquity, warm temperature, and heavy rainfall accounts for the remarkable infertility of the Amazonian soil. In contrast to temperate regions, where physical weathering is the primary source of soil formation, chemical weathering predominates in the tropics. Warm rainwater percolating through the ground dissolves soluble materials and carries them through the subsoil and ultimately into the rivers. The longer the process continues, the more the upper soil layers become impoverished until only insoluble ingredients remain. (Meggers 1971:12)

Most contemporary researchers consider that this view of the infertility of upland soils an oversimplification. According to Emilio Moran (1982:6; 1993:65–68) and Stephen Beckerman (1987), agronomic research has shown that the soils of the Amazon are highly diverse. Because of the interaction of many environmental variables and the differing chemical

composition of parent rocks from which soils are derived, tropical upland soils exhibit differential degrees of weathering. Moran states that
"relatively good soils with good drainage" occur over about 8 percent of
the Amazon basin (1993:66).

Some agronomists contend that intensive agriculture is now possible
in many parts of upland Amazonia. During the 1980s, researchers from
North Carolina State University and Peru's National Institute for Agricultural Research and Promotion conducted well-publicized experiments
with continuous cropping in Yurimaguas, Peru. They found that, "with
adequate fertilization . . . moderately high yields of [rice, corn, and soy-
beans] under continuous production can be achieved and sustained on
some of the most infertile soils of the Amazon Basin. . . . These systems
are as economically feasible as they are agronomically productive" (Nicholaides et al. 1984:347, 349).

These conclusions have been challenged by Philip Fearnside (1987b),
who points out that many costs of the Yurimaguas experiments were
underwritten by North Carolina State and the Peruvian government.
Farmers were given subsidies for the rental of agricultural machinery
and for transportation costs. They also received free seeds, fertilizer, pesticides, and herbicides from the experiment station. Fearnside observes
that, even with the subsidies, no farmer in the Yurimaguas area has been
able to adopt the recommended technology on a commercial basis (1987b:
212). This debate over the Yurimaguas experiments is clearly relevant to
the economic and agricultural possibilities in ribereño communities that
do not possess land rights in river valleys. Villagers with access to floodplains, however, are unlikely to have much interest in expensive ways to
increase the soil quality of uplands.

Fauna

Anthropologists have been arguing for more than two decades about the
extent to which the availability of faunal resources in upland Amazonian
forests limits population size (for analyses of the debate, see Johnson
1982; Sponsel 1983). Writers who emphasize resource shortages (Gross
1975; Harris 1984; Roosevelt 1980; Ross 1978b) note that poor soils
prevent seed crops from growing well in tropical forests in interfluvial
zones. Forest residents therefore obtain most of their calories from root
crops, which have little protein. They must satisfy their protein needs by
exploiting local faunal resources. Food for mammals, reptiles, and birds
in upland areas is scarce, however, because of the low overall level of

nutrients in the ecosystem and the mechanisms by which the forest cycles these nutrients (Roosevelt 1980:82–83). Since faunal resources are thinly dispersed over large areas, human population densities are also low.

Although most anthropologists, geographers, and biologists acknowledge that faunal resources are sparse in upland forests, many reject the conclusion that this limits human population density. Those opposing the arguments of Gross, Harris, Roosevelt, and Ross say that human protein requirements are often overestimated (Diener et al. 1980), that there are abundant wild plant sources of protein (Beckerman 1979), and that faunal resources are sufficiently available to meet the needs of Amazonia's forest population (Chagnon and Hames 1979).

Whichever argument is correct, the controversy has only limited relevance to the population distribution of riverine villages near Iquitos. Because most upland residents can fish in floodplains, they are easily able to obtain sufficient protein. Moreover, some residents of villages and towns in alturas earn considerable income from the sale of fruits and other forest products (Padoch et al. 1985). Such income can be spent on food purchases. The protein debate does, however, have certain implications for ribereño subsistence strategies. If upland faunal resources are sparse, ribereños are unlikely to be able to rely on hunting in alturas as a major food source.

Floodplains

Floodplains contain several distinct landforms (see Figure 2.2). Mud and sand bars are formed by soil deposits associated with annual changes in water level; natural levees and backswamps are the result of the lateral movement of river channels.

In the Iquitos area, the Amazon is at its lowest from July through September. It begins rising in October but often remains quite low through January. Peak floods occur during the "wet season," or "winter" (*invierno*), in April and early May. After that the river rapidly falls. Flooding patterns are determined by rainfall in the distant Andes. The average annual range in water level is about 8.5 meters (Hiraoka 1985b:249), but the difference between the high and low points varies considerably from year to year (Gentry and López-Parodi 1980).

The Amazon is a whitewater river characterized by low transparency, slightly alkaline pH, and a heavy load of dissolved minerals and suspended soil particles. The sediments of the whitewater rivers of Amazonia

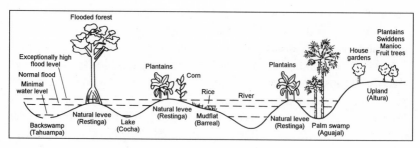

Figure 2.2. Floodplain landforms

are more fertile than those of the clearwater and blackwater rivers. Whitewater sediments, which originate in the Andes mountains and their foothills, come from parent materials that are much younger than those of much of the uplands. As the Amazon flows through dense tropical forests, organic materials are incorporated into the water.

The mineral- and nutrient-rich mixture carried by the Amazon is deposited along its main channel in areas with low water speed and along the river's margins when banks overflow during floods. These deposits of mud (*barreales*) and sand (*playas*) appear when the river falls in June and are ordinarily above water for four to six months of the year. Playas are usually lower than barreales and are above water for less of the year. Because barreales and playas follow the ever-changing course of the river, they are impermanent. Each year new ones form, and land that was once barreales and playas remains underwater.

The Amazonian floodplain is extraordinarily flat, falling only 100 meters between Iquitos and the Atlantic Ocean. This flatness results in the meandering of the Amazon back and forth within its valley. As the river swings, it deposits large amounts of sediment, and former inner banks become natural levees. These *restingas,* which can extend for several kilometers, often parallel the river. The higher parts of restingas stay above water during most flood seasons, but the lower parts are frequently inundated. High restingas have sandier soils than low restingas. Restingas in the Iquitos area can disappear within a generation as the river's meandering cuts them away.

Classifying floodplain landforms is not an altogether straightforward process. Indigenous classification systems sometimes differ from those of ecologists, geographers, and anthropologists; villages differ in their classification systems; and even within communities, ribereños may disagree about the meaning of particular terms. Some classifications are based on how soils are deposited, while others depend on susceptibility to flooding or on plant associations.

There are numerous floodplain landforms besides restingas, barreales, and playas. Two important local land classifications involve plant associations: *aguajales* and *ceticales*. *Aguajales* are shallow swamps dominated by aguaje palms (*Mauritia flexuosa*). *Ceticales* is the term that ribereños in some communities use to refer to lands associated with the cetico tree (*Cecropia latifolia*), which is common in areas that flood frequently, such as low restingas.

Tahuampas are backswamps that are penetrated by river water during the annual flooding. These mostly forest-covered lands form both between restingas and between restingas and alturas. Although tahuampas are agriculturally unimportant, ribereños use them for fishing, hunting, and obtaining construction materials. Other floodplain landforms include islands, oxbow lakes (*cochas*), side channels (*caños*), and ravines (*quebradas*) draining backswamps.

Although the definitive study of ethnoecology of landforms in the Peruvian Amazon has not yet been carried out, it is already clear that there is considerable intercommunity variability. For example, Hiraoka (1985b: 252–53) provides a lengthy list of terms people in the Peruvian community of San Jorge employ to classify floodplain lands. In addition to using the terms *restinga alta* (high restinga), *restinga baja* (low restinga), *barreal*, and *playa* to classify natural levees and mud and sand bars, some residents of San Jorge use terms such as *barreal de orilla alta, playa de orilla baja, barrizal alto,* and *barrizal bajo*. Many ribereños, however, do not make such fine distinctions.

Soils

The soils of the floodplains of the Amazon Basin vary in fertility depending on the amount and type of sediment carried by particular rivers. Sediments derived from some geological areas are highly acidic and infertile, while those derived from other places have higher pH values and are more fertile. Most alluvial soils near Iquitos are quite fertile. The annual siltation of the Amazon replenishes them with clayey material rich in salts with basic pH. These clays hold large amounts of water, which is released gradually to plants (Hiraoka 1985b:250).

Despite the generally high quality of alluvial soils near Iquitos, there is considerable variability. When levees become sufficiently elevated to remain above water in normal years, the soil becomes susceptible to leaching. Low restingas are therefore somewhat more fertile than high restingas. When they overflow their banks, rivers deposit coarse sediments first and finer ones farther away, which can result in restingas having sandier soils than backswamps. Heavy clay soils of relatively low fertility are sometimes found in locations distant from a river (Denevan 1984:318).

Fish

The geographical distribution of fish is affected by the seasonal rise and fall of the rivers. When water levels are low in the "dry season," or "summer" (*verano*), fish populations are small and concentrated. Food for the fish is scarce during the dry season, and this is also when nonhuman predators do their most intensive harvesting. As the rivers rise, fish migrate inland to forage and spawn in oxbow lakes and flooded forests. During this wet season, fish are less accessible to predators. The lessening of predator pressure, the production of young, and an increased food supply result in increased fish biomass (Roosevelt 1980:101–2).

As a result of the annual cycle, fishing returns in the Iquitos area vary over the course of the year. The best times are when mixed groups of fish migrate upstream. These *mijanos* usually occur two or three times a year. One migration takes place in October and November, when the Amazon starts to rise and fish go upriver and inland to lay eggs. In years in which floods are especially high, there is a second mijano in March or April. Fish that are seeking food then move from oxbow lakes through flooded forests into the river, migrate upstream, and leave the river again to enter other oxbow lakes and flooded forests. The third mijano occurs when the Amazon recedes after the flood crests and fish are forced to abandon the oxbow lakes and flooded forests and go back to the river.

Ordinarily, fishing is best when the river is low, though good catches can be made during the wet season if mijanos accompany exceptionally high floods. Most fishing in the dry season takes place in side channels of the river and along the shore. In years of normal flooding, most fishing during the wet season is in oxbow lakes and flooded forests. In years of high floods, ribereños also fish in the river during mijanos.

Other Fauna

Researchers disagree about the availability of land fauna in Amazonian whitewater floodplains. Hiraoka (1985a:211) states that the floodplains have supported an abundant and varied faunal population of birds, reptiles, rodents, and primates. Roosevelt (1980:98), in contrast, argues that a low overall level of primary productivity has always limited the ability of whitewater rivers to support animals.

Some of the disagreement between Hiraoka and Roosevelt may derive from different notions of what constitutes abundance. Whatever the availability of land fauna in floodplains has been in the past, their contemporary distribution is greatly affected by human activity. Hunters' principal catches are those animals that thrive on crops, secondary growth, and semimanaged agroforestry areas. These include armadillos (*Dasypus novemcinctus*), agouti (*Dasyprocta variegata*), paca (*Myoprocta* spp.), and birds (Hiraoka 1992:144). Hunting is best when the river is high and nonarboreal mammals take refuge on strips of high ground. Other animals, such as the capybara (*Hidrochoerus hidrochaeris*) and cayman (*Caiman sclerops*), are hunted from canoes in flooded forests (Hiraoka 1985a:211–12). Game meat is highly prized by ribereños and is often consumed on special occasions. The rates of return from hunting, however, are usually much lower than those from fishing, so land fauna comprise only a minor part of the diet in most floodplain communities.

3. Regional History

Few books and articles about contemporary Amazonia place much emphasis on events prior to the rubber boom of the late nineteenth and early twentieth centuries. Most writers assume explicitly or implicitly that previously the region was an isolated backwater. While this assumption is in some ways correct, massive population shifts, complex political struggles, and a series of economic booms and busts took place in the Iquitos area before 1870. The ethnic identity, economic situation, and class relations of present-day ribereños must be understood with reference to colonialism, missionary activities, and early commercial enterprises. Irrevocable changes took place long before the rubber boom transformed the Peruvian Amazon.

Precolumbian Floodplain Societies

Although many groups lived in the river valleys of the present-day Peruvian Amazon during the period of European exploration and missionization, the two most important floodplain societies were the Omagua and the Cocama. Neither group had been in the area for many years. At the time of the conquest, both groups were migrating into the region from farther down the Amazon. The Omagua occupied long stretches along the upper Amazon (Meggers 1971:122–24; Myers 1992:91–92), and the Cocama, who apparently fissioned from the Omagua "not too long" before the fourteenth century (Stocks 1978:77), lived in the upper Amazon and along the Ucayali.

All of our information about the Omagua, Cocama, and other precolumbian groups comes from archaeological investigations and the accounts of travelers and missionaries in the years immediately after Europeans first entered the area. Both of these sources have severe limitations.

Few archaeological sites in floodplains of the Peruvian Amazon have been carefully investigated. Environmental conditions hamper archaeological research in tropical lowland South America. Before pottery was adopted in Amazonia, the absence of suitable stone resulted in almost everything being made of wood, bone, plant fibers, feathers, or other perishable materials. Artifacts made of such materials are unlikely to be preserved in a hot, humid climate. Also, because of the meandering of rivers and annual alluvial deposits, the sites of floodplain settlement several thousand years ago may not be accessible to contemporary archaeological researchers. Finally, in many places dense vegetation conceals any artifacts that may be lying on the ground (Meggers 1971:35; Meggers 1988:55).

The payoff for Amazonian archaeology may not justify the investment in time and money that such work requires. Considerable logistical difficulties arise in mounting archaeological expeditions to tropical areas far from major population centers, and preservation problems can lead to months of research with few tangible results. Despite these difficulties, several research teams (Meggers 1971, 1985; Meggers and Evans 1983; Roosevelt 1980, 1987, 1989, 1991; Roosevelt et al. 1991) have been able to conduct detailed archaeological studies in the Brazilian Amazon. In the Peruvian Amazon, some important archaeological work has been carried out by Donald Lathrap (1970) and his students (Allen 1968; Myers 1973). Nonetheless, we do not know much about precolumbian cultural ecology in this region. In a recent lengthy review article about Amazonian resource management before the European conquest, Roosevelt (1989) was able to present only a few pages about lowland Peru.

Much of our knowledge of floodplain societies at the time of first contact with Europeans is based on several descriptions by explorers and missionaries written between 1542 and 1692 (see Toribio Medina 1988 [1894] and Cohen 1975). Meggers characterizes these accounts as "fragmentary and sometimes biased" and notes that the data they contain are often vague and inconsistent (1971:121). She pointedly observes that "the accuracy of specific information must be evaluated in the light of our knowledge that few observers kept notes during their travels, that impressions were often engraved on their memory under the stress of battle, and that the temptation to embroider or exaggerate for personal glorification may have been strong" (Meggers 1971:122).

Estimates of precontact populations of the upper Amazon (including the eastern Andean foothills) range between one and four million (Beckerman 1987; Denevan 1976; Dobyns 1966; Grohs 1974; Stocks 1987). Sizable populations were located along the floodplains of major rivers such as the Marañon, Ucayali, Huallaga, and Amazon, with the first European explorers reporting a narrow band of almost continuous settlement along the rivers (Carvajal 1988). Although even the biggest villages had fewer than ten thousand inhabitants (Stocks 1987:2), political units could be quite large. The domains of some chiefs in the upper Amazon extended for hundreds of kilometers (Roosevelt 1980:256).

Amazonian floodplain societies were constantly at war with one another and with their interior neighbors. Warfare over land and slaves among riverine peoples often resulted in the losers migrating upriver to less populated areas (Lathrap 1970). Although precolumbian Amazonian floodplain societies have been characterized as "small states" (Roosevelt 1987:165), they almost certainly lacked the large public works, elaborate bureaucracies, legal codes, and writing systems of riverine civilizations in Egypt, India, and China.

Explorers, Missionaries, and Colonists, 1541–1824

The first lengthy European-led trip through the present-day Peruvian Amazon took place in 1541–42. This conflict-ridden expedition, directed by Gonzalo Pizarro and Francisco de Orellana, had both economic and political objectives. The Spanish had heard rumors of gold in the jungle regions and wished to establish military control over the vast Amazonian lowlands. Pizarro and Orellana found little of value to Europeans, but this did not stop several other Spaniards from returning to Amazonia to explore it in the sixteenth century.

Most of the explorers' descriptions of Peruvian lowland Indians concern the Omagua (Carvajal 1988 [1500s]) and the Cocama (Regan 1983: 44; Stocks 1978), though they encountered numerous other indigenous groups as well. Grohs (1974) lists 56 tribes contacted by the Spanish in one part of the Peruvian Amazon. Only 16 of them still exist today.

Spanish colonists did not settle the Peruvian Amazon rapidly. Most attempts to set up communities in the sixteenth and seventeenth centuries were unsuccessful. In many parts of Latin America the Spanish established an *encomienda* system, in which indigenous peoples were forced to spend some of their time working for the colonial government or particular colonists. This system never took root in Amazonia. Because there was little of economic value in the tropical lowlands, the Spanish had no reason to compel Indians to work on commercial enterprises. Furthermore, transporting products out of the jungle was time-consuming and expensive. The round-trip between Quito and the most important Peruvian jungle settlements took six months (San Román 1975:65). The only significant attempt to set up encomiendas in the Peruvian Amazon occurred in the early 1600s near the new town of Borja in the high jungle of the present-day department of San Martín. Indians living along the Marañon River were carried off to work for landowners in Borja. The Indians, however, soon rebelled successfully (Stocks 1984:38–40).

The upper Amazon was one of several areas where Spain and Portugal were competing during the 1600s. In order to establish a stronger military and political presence in the upper Amazon, colonial Spanish governments encouraged the Catholic church to establish missions, which they hoped would pacify the indigenous population and recruit natives for local militia. Because of the weak colonial government and the great distance between the Peruvian Amazon and the centers of power, the missions had tremendous influence in the area in the latter part of the seventeenth century and the first two-thirds of the eighteenth.

The Jesuits and the Franciscans, the most important missionary groups, controlled different areas. The Jesuit zone comprised the lower Huallaga River, the upper Amazon, the lower Marañon, and all the rivers flowing into the Marañon from the north (Stocks 1984:39). This region was called Maynas (or Mainas) after one of the local Indian groups. Although three Jesuit communities were founded by Padre Rafael Ferrer in 1604, large-scale missionization did not begin until 1635, when the governor of Maynas requested that the order enter the area. The governor's stated reason for his request was a desire to spread Christianity to indigenous groups, but his real motivation was to pacify the Indians and extend his domain (Regan 1983:48; San Román 1975:44). After 1580, Franciscans were sent from the highland town of Huánuco to work along the upper Huallaga River, and by 1631 they had founded seven communities. During the first half of the seventeenth century, other Franciscans based in Quito were working along the Napo River, but after 1657, Franciscan work was concentrated along the Ucayali (Regan 1983:34).

The Jesuit and Franciscan areas met where the Amazon splits into the Marañon and the Ucayali near the present-day town of Nauta. Most of the communities discussed in this book (including Iquitos, Tamshiyacu,

Porvenir, Santa Sofía, and Tapirillo) are located in the Jesuit zone, though a few (including Requena, Santa Rosa, and Yanallpa) are in the Franciscan area on the Ucayali.

The priests, especially the Jesuits, tried to keep their missions as separate as possible from Spanish colonial society (Marzal 1984:13), gathering Indians into small communities (*reducciones*) along the rivers. Most missions were in alturas because periodic inundations made floodplains less desirable locations for nucleated communities. While most inhabitants of the reducciones were from the densely populated floodplains, some forest Indians were also brought into mission settlements.

Many Indians migrated voluntarily to the missions. Some were attracted by the availability of steel axes and machetes, which greatly reduced the time needed to perform agricultural tasks such as clearing fields and weeding. Others were seeking refuge from hostile neighbors or Portuguese slave raiding expeditions. There is some controversy over the amount of force used to gather Indians into reducciones in the Amazon. Accounts of the period often note that inhabitants of reducciones frequently fled into the forest without being pursued. Stocks, however, writes that "those who did not voluntarily move to mission sites, insofar as they could be located, were rounded up by armed soldiers in expeditions called *entradas*" (1984:39).

Mission settlements were small. The population of San Joaquín de Omaguas, the largest Jesuit mission, never exceeded 600 (San Román 1975:52). The founder of Omaguas was Samuel Fritz, a Bohemian (sometimes described as a German) priest who worked in the area from 1686 until his death in 1723 (see Fritz 1922). The first site of Omaguas was on some islands near where the Ampiyacu and Amazon rivers meet, but the community moved several times during the late seventeenth and early eighteenth centuries. The final site was established in 1726 on the Amazon close to the present-day village of Porvenir.

By 1760, 22 Jesuit missionaries had gained control of more than 12,000 Indians in 34 communities (Regan 1983:50). Many other Jesuit communities had been founded and later abandoned. Fritz alone is said to have established 33 communities among the Omaguas, and more than 40 settlements were taken from the Jesuits by a Portuguese expedition in 1710 (San Román 1975:48–50). Besides the mission at Omaguas, there were at least three other Jesuit settlements in the general area of my research. San Miguel de Ucayali de Yameo was upriver from Omaguas at present-day Nauta. San Juan Evangelista de Miguianos was a two-and-a-half-hour trip downriver from Omaguas, and San Pueblo de Nuevo Napeanos was still farther downriver at present-day Iquitos (San Román 1975: 74–81).

The Jesuits tried to establish self-sufficient communities. The economy of the region was centrally planned, with each missionary in a pueblo subordinate to a superior in Lagunas and vice-superiors in Omaguas and on the Napo River. Inhabitants of the reducciones farmed both their own fields and community land. Products grown on the communal fields fed the priests and the children residing at community schools. The missionaries introduced cattle to the region and encouraged Indians to raise domestic animals such as chickens, ducks, doves, and pigs. Men living at the missions went on lengthy communal searches for turtles and their eggs. Residents of the missions also caught fish using barbasco (*Lonchocarpus utilis*), a poison (San Román 1975:51–67).

The Jesuit schools placed great emphasis on teaching Quechua, a language spoken in highland Peru that was used as a lingua franca throughout the Jesuit and Franciscan zones. Many contemporary place names in the Peruvian Amazon are Quechua. Although Quechua has not been spoken around Iquitos since the nineteenth century, ribereño Spanish includes many words of Quechua origin (Castonguay 1987).

Using the famous reducciones of Paraguay as a model, the Jesuits also taught the residents artisan skills such as carpentry, sculpting, weaving, and painting. Educated Indians became cultural brokers between the missionaries and the non-Christians living outside of the reducciones, which began a longstanding division of Indians into two classes—Christians (*reducidos*) and non-Christians (*infieles* or *salvajes*).

Despite their efforts at self-sufficiency, the missionaries in Maynas had to trade with distant towns and cities such as Yurimaguas and Quito. The missions bought tobacco, cloth, sugar, poison, blankets, iron, needles, fishhooks, axes, machetes, knives, wine, and flour. Wax was the principal export from Maynas, but hammocks and other items were also sent from the jungle. Because the value of imports exceeded the value of exports, the Jesuit order was forced to subsidize the mission's purchases (San Román 1975:64–66).

The activities of missions greatly affected the demography, ethnicity, and economy of the Peruvian Amazon. Old World diseases such as smallpox, measles, and yellow fever decimated Jesuit communities. Although epidemics occurred in all Amerindian populations, they were especially devastating in densely populated riverine areas. Missions contributed to the spread of disease by concentrating populations into nucleated settlements and by promoting contact between different Indian groups. Fifty percent of the Cocamas in mission settlements are reported to have died between 1644 and 1652 (Regan 1983:49).

The floodplain population of the Peruvian Amazon dropped dramatically between 1540 and 1700, and by the end of the period, rivers were no longer continuously occupied by the Cocamas, Omaguas, and other groups. Instead, small mission communities were separated from one another by many kilometers. Large numbers of Indians moved from the floodplains to the forest to escape disease, missionaries, and Portuguese slavers.

Jesuit settlements included members of several tribal groups. Omaguas, Yurimaguas, Mayorunas, Cocamas, and Cocamillas all lived at San Joaquín de Omaguas at one time or another (San Román 1975:52). Little mestizoization occurred during mission times. Nonetheless, there were striking changes in local ethnicity as a result of disease and intermarriage. With each passing year there were fewer self-identified Omaguas.

Mission records are usually not very helpful with respect to changing ethnic patterns. Jean-Pierre Chaumeil's attempt (1981) to unravel the history of the Yagua (a group important around Santa Sofía) shows how even the most diligent research can have only limited results. Contemporary Yaguas appear to be descended from earlier groups called Zavas, Caumares, Pevas, and Covaches. Although missionaries distinguished among these groups, their records contain little information about their origins. We do know that the language they spoke was closely related to that of the present-day Yagua.

Eric Ross, writing primarily about the Brazilian Amazon, has argued that the missions transformed the riverine ecology and economy:

> In their effort to organize the Amerindian population and to civilize it, by which was implied the creation of an available wage-labor force, the missions wholly restructured the relationship of their "congregations" to the ecology of the valley, preparing the basis for the shift of strategic resources away from subsistence exploitation to commercial development and wrenching the Amerindians out of their traditional patterns of interaction with the environment to place their labor at the disposal of an increasing number of settlers and entrepreneurs. (1978a:202)

Actually, while the missions of the Peruvian Amazon clearly had a major effect on the demography and political and social organization of indigenous groups, the groups' *ecological* relationship with the environment was probably not "wholly restructured." Unfortunately, accounts of mission Indians provide little information about their agricultural techniques. The introduction of steel tools and new domestic animals substantially changed subsistence patterns, but there is no evidence that indigenous methods of raising the staples of manioc and corn, or other agricultural, hunting, and fishing techniques were abandoned during the mission period. Nevertheless, the indigenous *economy* was dramatically transformed. Residents of mission settlements became part of a large-scale, centrally planned economy with well-developed ties to highland areas.

The Jesuits were expelled from all Spanish territories in 1767. Their first replacements in Maynas were secular clerics from Quito, but most of them found they were unsuited for missionary work and quickly left Amazonia. Some Franciscans from Quito began working in Maynas around 1770, but they abandoned the region in 1774. The Franciscans returned to take control of the missions in 1790 (Regan 1983:69–70). In 1802 the king of Spain created the diocese of Maynas, transferred control of the region from Quito to Peru, and established a Franciscan bishopric at Ocopa. These actions had been requested by Francisco Requena, the governor of Maynas, who was worried about Portuguese incursions from Brazil and thought that Peru could protect Maynas better than Quito.

After the Jesuits left the Peruvian Amazon, fewer priests worked in Maynas. As a result, the missionaries' influence waned and the government's power increased. The Jesuits had been able to restrict white and mestizo immigration to Maynas and had ruled their settlements without serious challenge from the colonial governments. Their replacements, who had little control over immigration, found their activities monitored and influenced by new settlers and by representatives of the government.

The Jesuits' expulsion changed the lives of the floodplain Indians. Many Indians who lived at missions fled to regions away from rivers. The population of 36 mission settlements halved between 1767 and 1799 (Regan 1983:93). Power over the Indians passed from religious hands to military and civilian hands, and the government forced Christianized Indians to provide agricultural products and game for its military forces (Stocks 1984: 41).

Little information is available about commercial activities in Maynas during the period immediately after the Jesuits' expulsion. Since trade increased in neighboring areas in Brazil, a similar growth of commerce may have occurred in the Peruvian Amazon (San Román 1975:96). The Jesuits had traded mostly with their mission headquarters in Quito. When they left, new avenues of commerce with Brazil were established along the rivers, and traveling merchants began visiting riverine communities to buy and sell products.

Changing Political and Economic Conditions, 1824–1870

Peru gained independence from Spain in 1824. The new government suppressed missionary activity and converted the Franciscan convent at Ocopa into an educational center. Although the Franciscans were permitted to return to Ocopa in 1838 (San Román 1975:112), the influence of missionaries in the Peruvian Amazon remained low during the remainder of the nineteenth century and the beginning of the twentieth. Most schools had closed when the Jesuits departed, and priests gradually lost rights over Indian labor.

Not long after independence, the government passed a series of laws designed to protect members of indigenous groups. Indians were made citizens of the state and given the lands they occupied. The practice of forcing Indians to work as laborers for the state or private individuals was outlawed (Stocks 1984:42). The new laws were rarely enforced, however, because Indian labor was needed in commercial trade in Maynas. The principal merchants were the provincial governors, who coerced or induced Indians to obtain and transport salted fish, sarsaparilla (a plant whose roots are used as a flavoring), and wax. A small but increasing number of colonists also used Indian labor in their enterprises.

The debt peonage system that characterized Amazonian labor relations for many years began in Peru around the time of independence. Indians living in or near mission settlements had developed a desire for tools and other consumer goods, and merchants gave them goods on credit in return for fish and forest products. Because rates of exchange were often unfair, many Indians found themselves saddled with enormous debts. When they died still owing work to the merchants, their debts were assumed by their families.

The merchants and traders made great use of alcohol in gaining the use of Indian labor. Indians and merchants would drink *aguardiente* (cane liquor) or *chicha* (corn liquor) together before making agreements about credit terms. Relations between the two groups ranged from paternalistic to directly exploitive. In response to abuses, Indians occasionally attacked colonists and government officials. Others attempted to improve their conditions by asking white and mestizo merchants to be godparents of their children.

Because of the great distance between Maynas and the large commercial centers, the amount of trade in the region was quite small in the first half of the eighteenth century. Balsam, copal, salt fish, turtle fat, hammocks, and tar were exported, and iron, steel, crockery, tools, and cloth were the most important imports (San Román 1975:99). Government officials were involved in trade and demanded kickbacks from local merchants (Stocks 1984:43).

During the first part of the nineteenth century, Nauta, Omaguas, and Iquitos were the most important communities in the area of my research. Much of our scant knowledge of what these villages were like comes from the accounts of two travelers: the artist and writer Laurent Saint Cricq, who used the pseudonym Paul Marcoy and who was a member of a French-Peruvian expedition in 1846, and William Herndon, who visited these villages in 1851 on a trip sponsored by the U.S. government (see Marcoy 1875 and Herndon 1952 [1854]).

Nauta, which had about a thousand inhabitants in 1851, was the principal administrative center of the region and the main trading connection between Maynas and Brazil. Marcoy was less than enthusiastic about the community:

> The mud huts, erected at all angles, buried in the brushwood, and apparently playing at hide-and-seek—the naked hill with its bare heavy outline leaning against the sky—the absence of trees around the dwellings—and altogether the sickly, mean poverty of the place—had so far cooled my enthusiasm as a traveling artist, that when the time came to make a sketch of the place it took me twice the usual time to prepare my pencils. (1875:249)

The population of Omaguas had declined after the Jesuits left. Marcoy described the population as "mongrel" descendants of Omaguas and Cocamas (1875:261). Herndon counted 232 inhabitants "of the tribes [called] Omaguas and Panoas" and observed ethnocentrically that "they are peons and fisherman, cultivate chacras [small fields cut out of the forest using slash-and-burn methods] and live in the usual filthy and wretched condition of all these people" (1952 [1854]:129–30).

After independence was proclaimed, various small communities near the juncture of the Amazon and the Itaya consolidated to form Iquitos. Indigenous groups living there included Mayorunas, Pevas, Omaguas, and Yameos (Rumrrill 1983:16). Although Iquitos became a center of artisan production and trade in the 1830s, its population remained small during the first part of the century, numbering only 150 inhabitants by 1847 (Rumrrill 1983:18). Three white families obtained hammocks, beeswax, honey, copal, and sarsaparilla from Indian residents of Iquitos (San Román 1975:104). When Herndon (1952:132) visited the Peruvian Amazon in 1851, he described Iquitos as a fishing village of 227 inhabitants. Of these, 98 were whites and mestizos from the town of Borja in the department of San Martín. They had been driven from their homes by an Indian rebellion in 1841. According to Marcoy, most "Indian" residents had "the blood of four distinct tribes [Cocamas, Omaguas, Iquitos, and Ticunas] mingled in their veins" (1875:263).

The introduction of steamboats to Amazonia in the 1850s stimulated commerce and allowed the region to become increasingly incorporated into the Peruvian state. In 1853 the Peruvian government passed a law providing free passage, tools, and land for nationals and foreigners wishing to settle along the Amazon and its tributaries (San Román 1975:120). The state also increased the number of military units in the tropical lowlands and established municipalities and mail service. As a result, colonists slowly moved into the area. During two trips to Maynas in the 1850s and 1860s, the Italian-Peruvian geographer Antonio Raimondi (1929 [ca. 1874], 1942 [1862]) observed numerous tiny settlements of whites and mestizos along the rivers. Towns were divided into white/mestizo and Indian sections, with the Indian section being larger and poorer.

The relative importance of the region's communities changed after steam transport came to Maynas. Omaguas was economically insignificant after 1850, and Nauta also declined. The capital of Loreto, as a large part of the Peruvian Amazon was now known, moved in 1857 from Nauta to Moyobamba in the high jungle. Nauta's population had dropped to 821 by 1862 and remained under a thousand for the rest of the nineteenth century. Iquitos, in contrast, prospered because of its status as the farthest point upriver that steamships could travel.

Loreto became an official department of Peru in 1861. It included the present-day departments of Loreto, Ucayali, San Martín, and Amazonas. The principal products imported into Loreto from Brazil during the 1850s and 1860s included iron objects, wheat flour, alcoholic beverages, woolen and cotton goods, clothing, and munitions (Regan 1983:76). The most important exports during this time were sarsaparilla, straw ("Panama") hats, salt fish, and wax. Other exports included balsam, copal, turtle fat and eggs, hammocks, tobacco, and quinine. Such exports produced the first noticeable depletion of the Peruvian Amazon's resources. The local government found it necessary in 1859 to establish rules limiting the production of sarsaparilla and later banned its export. The sarsaparilla laws were ignored, however, as the price at the mouth of the Amazon at Pará was five times greater than that in Loreto (Raimondi 1942 [1862]: 123).

White and mestizo merchants and traders relied heavily on Indian labor. Most of the laborers were Christians, but there was some trade between merchants and infieles as well. We have no reliable counts of the Indian population at this time. Raimondi (1929 [ca. 1874]:96) estimated that in 1869 there were 50,000 Christianized Indians in Loreto and no more than 30,000 to 40,000 infieles. However, a census of Loreto in 1862 reported a total population (including whites and mestizos) of only 52,688 (Rumrrill 1983:19).

Raimondi observed (1942 [1862]:85–86) that a large proportion of the Christianized Indians spoke Quechua and that a few understood Spanish. These Indians worked as rowers and carriers of cargo in towns and as extractors of forest products in the countryside. Relations between merchants and traders and Indian laborers became firmly established in the form that persisted through most of the Peruvian Amazon well into the twentieth century and that still exists in remote areas today. The key figures were the *patrones* and the *regatones*. Patrones, based in either rural or urban areas, operated extractive and agricultural businesses. Debt peonage relations became established when patrones gave advances of goods or money to their employees in exchange for future work. Wages were low. Some Indian laborers, for example, worked a month in exchange for an axe (Raimondi 1942 [1862]:72–73). The role of the other key figure, the regatón, or trader, became established in the early and middle 1800s when the patrones' practice of traveling to small communities along rivers to buy and sell goods expanded and long-distance trading became an occupational specialty. The *regatones* received goods from urban merchants in exchange for the promised delivery of products bought in rural areas.

Agriculture in the Peruvian Amazon appears to have steadily lessened in importance in the years after the Jesuits left. By 1870 the extractive industries placed so much demand on Indian labor that food had to be imported into the lowland jungles (Stocks 1984:43–44). According to Raimondi, plantains and manioc were the most important crops in 1859, though farmers also raised sugarcane, coca, tobacco, cotton, coffee, cacao, bombonaje (*Carludovica palmata*, used in hatmaking), and fruits such as pijuayos (*Bactris gasipaes*), aguajes, lemons, avocados, lúcumas (*Lucuma obovata*), breadfruit, and pineapples (1942 [1862]:102–3). Although Raimondi commented on the scarcity of domestic animals in Loreto, he noted that all the Indian communities raised chickens. Christianized Indians also raised pigs (Raimondi 1942 [1862]:110).

In his second visit to Loreto, in 1869, Raimondi observed that rural Indians were beginning to sell plantains and corn in Iquitos and that the prices for these crops were rising because of a growing demand for food for the urban population. Raimondi made no mention in either visit of crops like rice, cowpeas, tomatoes, onions, peanuts, and melons, all of which are important in contemporary Amazonian agriculture.

The Rubber Boom, 1870–1912

The rubber boom permanently changed the social landscape of the Peruvian Amazon. Thousands of fortune-seeking settlers poured into Loreto. Floodplain and forest Indians were coerced or induced to work in the rubber trade. The offspring of colonists and Indians formed a large mixed group of Spanish-speaking rural residents. These ribereños soon outnumbered Indians and whites in the floodplains. The typical riverine community during the rubber boom was a commercial estate (a *fundo*) owned and operated by a white or mestizo patrón, who gave goods to ribereño and Indian residents in exchange for their labor in the rubber trade and other enterprises. Residents of fundos farmed and fished using many of the methods of indigenous Amazonians.

Even after the Amazon rubber industry collapsed around 1912, the region's commercial estates continued as an important form of floodplain social organization. Some fundos concentrated on extracting forest products for export; others raised cattle and sugarcane for local markets.

The Rubber Industry

The indigenous residents of Amazonia had long known of rubber and its uses. The Omaguas made rubber pouches, bags, syringes, and shoes in precolumbian times (Furneaux 1969:147; San Román 1975:126). But rubber became commercially valuable only in the first part of the nineteenth century. The Brazilian city of Belém, for example, exported 450,000 pairs of rubber shoes in 1839 (Dean 1987:9).

Rubber's greatest drawback was its tendency to become soft and sticky in hot weather and brittle in cold weather. In 1839 Charles Goodyear discovered that rubber becomes stronger, more elastic, and more resistant to hot and cold weather when it is mixed with sulfur and heated. This process, known as vulcanization, led to many new industrial applications. The volume of rubber imported into Great Britain rose from 211 kilograms in 1830 to 58,710 kilograms in 1874 (Dean 1987:9). The demand grew even more over the next forty years as rubber came to be used for bicycle and automobile tires.

The quality, yield, and abundance of the rubber found in the Amazon (*Hevea brasiliensis*) were extraordinary. Rubber already had a prominent place among the exports of eastern Peru in the 1850s, when trade statistics for the region were first compiled, and as the demand for rubber grew, the amount produced in the Amazon increased greatly. Loreto exported 2,088 kilograms of rubber in 1862; 58,584 in 1870; 540,529 in 1884; 1,095,625 in 1890; 2,246,967 in 1900; and 4,500,000 in 1910 (San Román 1975:130–31). Rubber ranked second among Peru's exports between 1902 and 1906 (Werlich 1978:122). The price per kilogram remained stable at about thirty-five cents until the early years of the twentieth century. It then rose markedly, reaching $1.35 per kilogram in 1910.

The origins of Amazonia's loss of the world market to Asian rubber are recounted in the oft-repeated story that the Englishman Henry Wickham used bribery and deceit to smuggle rubber seeds out of Brazil in 1876 despite a prohibition on their export. Wickham sent the seeds to botanists in England, and they were later transported to British estates in Asia (Chirif and Mora 1980:287; Collier 1968:32–37; San Román 1975:131–32; Smith 1990:277–83). The tales of Wickham's daring exploits are probably exaggerated, however, because laws against the export of rubber seeds were not adopted in Brazil until well into the twentieth century. Wickham's transfers of rubber seeds to Great Britain were not, in fact, strongly opposed by Brazilian authorities (Dean 1987: 13–23; Furneaux 1969:155–56).

Amazonian rubber was collected from trees scattered throughout the jungle. The British took several decades to develop reliable methods of raising rubber in plantations. As late as 1906 only 464 metric tons of rubber (less than 1 percent of the world's production) were grown on plantations. Exports from rubber plantations then took off. Worldwide output of plantation rubber increased to 7,270 metric tons in 1910 and 64,880 metric tons in 1914, exceeding wild rubber for the first time. By 1928 twenty times more plantation rubber was being produced than wild rubber (Furneaux 1969:157–59).

As plantation production increased, the price of a kilogram of rubber on the world market fell to 30 cents in 1915 and 9 cents in 1923 (Ross 1978a:215). Although Amazonian rubber collection was not profitable after about 1912, Asian plantations continued to make money, for various reasons. Rubber production, whether in the rain forest or on a plantation, entails cutting slits in trees, placing cups under the incisions, and collecting liquid rubber (latex) in cups. But to get to the trees, tappers in Amazonia spent much time moving around in the jungle, while Asian plantation workers could cultivate large clumps of trees in easily accessible areas. Large quantities of Asian latex were coagulated rapidly using chemicals, while small quantities of Amazonian latex were coagulated slowly on poles over fire. Finally, plantation trees grew faster and yielded more.

Attempts to grow rubber in plantations in Amazonia have failed partly because of problems with ants and leaf fungi (Coomes 1992:33–117 discusses other reasons for the absence of plantations). The dispersed distribution of rubber trees in Amazonia represents the densest mass possible in the presence of the pests and parasites that have coevolved with *Hevea brasiliensis* and other types of rubber. Asian plantations owe their success to the absence of rubber-specific plants and parasites.

Labor Recruitment

Rubber entrepreneurs needed a large, dispersed workforce and preferred laborers who were familiar with tropical forests. Amazonian rubber companies, which were often foreign-owned or financed, recruited workers in a variety of ways (Coomes 1992:78–83). Two important labor recruitment methods were *habilitación* and *correría*. Habilitación was most common along the major rivers; correrías were used in interfluvial zones.

Habilitación was an extension and intensification of pre-existing feudal relations. Patrones borrowed money from banks or merchants in Iquitos or elsewhere in order to set up a fundo along the river or in the forest. While land titles were not hard to get, would-be patrones often fought bitterly over promising groups of trees. The focal part of a fundo was a main house, which served as the patrón's residence, the operation's accounting center, and a general store. Workers lived in nearby huts and left the fundo for extended periods of rubber collection.

Rubber tappers involved in habilitación were Christianized Indians and poor mestizos, who usually began rubber collecting voluntarily because of their desire for consumer goods. Because rubber tappers spent much of their time dispersed in the forest, they also had to obtain food and other necessities from the patrón's store. All these goods were provided in advance in return for the promised delivery of rubber. This was the final link in a long chain of credits and debits. The river traders, or regatones, provided the patrones with goods on credit in exchange for rubber. The regatones received their goods on credit from rubber merchants in Iquitos. Boats used by regatones belonged to Iquitos companies. As Michael Taussig has astutely observed, "It was not the rivers that tied the Amazon basin into a unit but these countless bonds of credit and debit wound round people like the vines of the forest around the great rubber trees themselves" (1987:68).

The credit chain resulted in workers receiving low prices for their rubber and paying high prices for goods purchased at the patrón's store. These poor rates of exchange forced rubber tappers to accept more and more goods on credit. Most soon found themselves hopelessly in debt. As in the earlier debt peonage system, when workers who owed money to patrones died, their debts were assumed by the nearest relative (the wife or oldest son). The debt peonage system had always resembled slavery in some respects. Patrones giving up fundos would "sell" their indebted workers, with tappers' debt obligations transferred from the former patrón to the new one.

It was the second form of worker recruitment, the correría, that made the Peruvian Amazon infamous. The Peruvian government gave companies title to large tracts of land away from the rivers. Overseers rounded up entire tribes of non-Christianized Indians and compelled them to work as rubber gatherers, sometimes forcing them to move hundreds of kilometers. Reports of correrías sometimes say that the Indians incurred debts to the companies because of their desire for consumer goods. However, the forest Indians did not have the option of refusing advances. They were forced to accept goods on credit and then to work as rubber tappers to pay off their debts (Taussig 1987:66–74).

Many Indians died under the brutal working conditions, and those who survived received little or no compensation for their labor. When the practices of the rubber companies of the Peruvian Amazon were publicized (Casement 1912; Hardenburg 1912), there was an international uproar (Collier 1968; Taussig 1987). Few entrepreneurs were punished, however. By the time the scandalous working conditions became widely known outside of Amazonia, the rubber boom was over.

Demographic and Ethnic Change

The rubber boom permanently changed the demographic and ethnic composition of the Peruvian Amazon. Settlers flooded the tropical lowlands, with the greatest number coming from San Martín in the high jungle east of the Andes (San Martín, once part of Loreto, became a separate department in 1906). Most colonists were males who moved around the jungle, having multiple unions with Indian and mestizo women. The offspring of these unions and their descendants became the ribereños, the dominant population of the riverine Peruvian Amazon in the twentieth century. They adopted mestizo and white customs of dress and religion but farmed, fished, and hunted using indigenous Amazonian methods.

Between 1870 and 1910, many fundos were established along the Amazon and other major rivers (San Román 1975:133–36). Although most were devoted primarily to rubber tapping, some raised cattle or produced aguardiente. The majority of patrones came from San Martín, coastal and highland Peru, and Brazil, although a few Europeans and native Loretanos owned commercial estates. Most fundo residents were Christianized Indians and ribereños. Non-Christian forest Indians and settlers also lived on commercial estates.

Numerous languages were spoken along the rivers. Although Quechua had ceased being used as a lingua franca by 1870, many indigenous Amazonians in the floodplains spoke lowland Amerindian languages. Most settlers were monolingual in Spanish, and many ribereños could converse in both Spanish and an Amerindian language. Colonists from Brazil, Italy, Great Britain, France, Germany, China, and other places spoke the languages of their home countries.

Some mestizoization occurred away from the major rivers, where indigenous groups with different languages and cultures were forced to work together. The offspring of members of different indigenous groups often became Spanish-speaking ribereños. Many indigenous groups in interfluvial areas, however, were able to maintain their ethnic identity despite their brutal treatment and involuntary relocation. In the interior, the proportion of settler-Indian unions was much lower than along the rivers. Moreover, some indigenous groups were able to avoid correrías by moving around in the vast jungle.

During the rubber boom, the city of Iquitos grew rapidly and became more cosmopolitan. There were about 10,000 people living in the city in 1905, including 60 Germans, 187 Asians, 127 British, 100 Spanish, 35 French, 50 Italians, 514 "Portuguese" (probably mostly Brazilians), 14 Colombians, 24 Ecuadorians, 5 U.S. citizens, 36 "Moroccans" (probably a term for Arabs), and 4 Russians (San Román 1975:138–39). The population had reached 14,000 by the end of the rubber boom (Rumrrill 1983:55). With oceangoing steamers as large as a thousand tons calling regularly from New York and Liverpool, Iquitos was the second most active port in Peru and had resident consuls from ten foreign countries (Werlich 1978:122). The city included several elaborate tiled buildings designed by European architects. Because of the expenses associated with transporting luxury goods up the Amazon, the cost of living for wealthier residents was said to be two to four times that of New York, London, or Paris.

An Economic Backwater, 1912–1940

The collapse of the rubber industry devastated the economy of the Peruvian Amazon. The fortune seekers who had rushed into the jungle had the choice of returning to their places of origin, emigrating somewhere else, or remaining in Amazonia. Most large-scale entrepreneurs left Loreto, but many other immigrants, lacking economic opportunities elsewhere, stayed in the region. Iquitos-based merchants, desperately hoping that one of several forest products would replace rubber as a major source of income, hired ribereños and Indians to extract timber, gums, resins, essential oils, natural insecticides, medicinal plants, and ornamentals. The scale of these operations, however, never approached that of the rubber companies. A number of forest products briefly appeared promising, but each eventually declined in profitability because of resource depletion or competition from synthetics.

Although timber companies had operated in Loreto since about 1880, lumber was not exported from the region until a sawmill was constructed in Iquitos in 1918 (Kuczynki-Godard 1944:11). Cedar and mahogany were the woods with the most commercial value. Between 1925 and 1940 the volume of wood exported yearly from Iquitos ranged from six to ten thousand metric tons (San Román 1975:172). One commentator (Delboy

1942:24) described the timber industry as "sordid and speculative" and remarked on the miserable prices woodcutters received per meter of cedar or mahogany. As the most accessible trees were chopped down, timber cutting became less profitable.

The most important non-timber forest products were balata (*Manilkara bidentata*), leche caspi (*Couma macrocarpa*), and tagua (the fruit of the yarina palm, *Phytelephas macrocarpa*). Balata, a gum used in belting and golf balls, was first exported from the Peruvian Amazon around 1910. Trees were cut with the goal of bleeding them to the last drop. As a result, balata became less profitable as trees near rivers were destroyed and importers found cheaper substitutes. Leche caspi, a latex used in chewing gum, was extracted in large quantities between 1935 and 1945. This boom ended when synthetic gums destroyed the market. Tagua is a vegetable ivory used in buttons and game pieces. The market for tagua was good immediately after World War I but fell in the mid-1920s, when buttons made from synthetic products became more common. Nonetheless, a button factory was operating in Iquitos as late as 1942. At that time, two thousand metric tons of tagua were being exported annually from the Peruvian Amazon, mostly to Brazil (Delboy 1942:28).

Amazonian entrepreneurs earned substantial sums of money from the collection and cultivation of barbasco. The roots of barbasco contain rotenone, a chemical used in insecticides. Exports of barbasco began in 1931 and grew rapidly, but the development of DDT in the 1940s and the synthesis of rotenone in 1953 ended the barbasco boom.

Economic conditions in the tropical lowlands were so bleak during World War II that some Peruvians thought that the only hope for the region was the rehabilitation of the rubber industry (see, e.g., Delboy 1942:10). Because the Allied Powers lacked access to Asian plantations, Amazonian rubber production did increase between 1940 and 1945, but the end of the war and the development of synthetics brought a final end to dreams of rubber wealth in the Peruvian Amazon.

From a long-range perspective, the most important extractive activity in the period between the wars was the discovery and initial exploration of petroleum. Oil exploration in the Peruvian Amazon began around 1938 and had few immediate economic effects. Petroleum operations continued, however, and important finds were made after World War II.

Rural Economic and Social Organization

The people stranded by the end of the rubber boom varied considerably in wealth. More-prosperous colonists continued to operate commercial estates, with some fundos concentrating on extracting export products such as tagua and lechi caspi and others raising cattle and sugarcane for local markets. Factories on the fundos made sugarcane into aguardiente, which was sold in Iquitos and along the rivers. Since most fundos made little money, rural residents were forced to rely more on their small plots of maize, plantains, and manioc. These crops were grown primarily for home consumption. Agricultural production for the regional and national markets was minimal because of poor transport and the distance between most rural communities and the city of Iquitos.

Regatones, who continued to travel along the rivers, selling goods and plying their customers with aguardiente, were important rural figures. Máximo Kuczynki-Godard, a Loreto doctor, provided a vivid description of a regatón:

[He] goes from house to house along the river selling or trading essential articles for products of the field or forest; chickens, eggs, manioc, turtles, skins, rubber, and anything the colonist can offer. This of course works out better for the regatón than the colonist. [The regatón] has been compared to a mushroom that goes wherever there is no resistance; he is ubiquitous and imperturbably patient, he knows what he has and what he lacks, he gives credit, he is the life of these regions. . . . [He] makes his money providing necessities to all that live in the indescribable solitude of a hamlet far from the city, in the midst of the jungle on the bank of a river or stream; his specialty is his knowledge of the people and his lack of altruistic scruples. He is truly an ambulatory store. . . . [T]he owner and master accompanied by two or three boys . . . goes along the river from hamlet to hamlet carrying cloth, soap, kerosene, candles, aguardiente, gunpowder, tobacco and cigarettes. A dictator of prices and values in the loneliness of the tropical jungle. A judicious man who knows how to distinguish between his customers. (1944:38, my translation)

Most ribereños, however, lacked even the meager resources needed to establish themselves as patrones or regatones. They worked on fundos and set up humble households along the banks of the principal rivers. Many of their households included adopted children, who sometimes were almost servants. *Caserios* (small communities attached to fundos) grew up as colonists' children and adopted children reached adulthood and formed their own households. The various households in a caserio were usually tied together by webs of kinship and *compadrazgo* (ritually prescribed relationships, usually between a child's parents and godparents).

In the period just after the rubber boom, most settlements along the principal rivers were fundos. Over the years independent communities, usually without clear land titles, slowly replaced fundos. These villages formed in several ways. Many patrones abandoned commercial estates because they were no longer profitable. In other cases, when fundo owners died, their urban heirs had little incentive to move to, or even maintain control over, their remote jungle outposts. Sometimes they even neglected to sell their property. As a result, workers on fundos occasionally moved to the unoccupied areas and established their own villages.

Ribereños in the independent communities adopted indigenous methods of farming, fishing, hunting, and cooking. Housing conditions were similar to those of today. Palm strips covered hardwood floors and walls of houses, and palm leaves formed the roof. Houses were elevated a meter or two above the ground for protection from floods and mud. They usually included a principal room, which served the entire family as a dormitory, and a second room, which was used as a storehouse. The kitchen was ordinarily separated from the house, to which it was connected by a bridge. Kuczynki-Godard's description of sleeping arrangements in the 1940s still fits most ribereño villages:

> Under the same mosquito net sleep two, three or more persons, a couple and children, a mother and two children. . . . In a room they put three or four or more beds or mosquito nets, filling it completely. . . . The beds are put on the floor. . . . They move these during the day; but only to roll them up in a corner without sun and air. . . . The bed is a piece of crude cloth, . . . perhaps a sheet and a mosquito net. (1944:50–51, my translation)

Ethnicity

The process of ribereñoization continued after the rubber boom ended. White or mestizo colonists often established small commercial estates using Indian laborers. The patrones entered into multiple sexual unions with women living on their fundos, and the offspring of these unions identified themselves as ribereños. Over several generations, such communities became ribereño villages. By the middle of the twentieth century, Indian ethnic identity had died out in many communities along the major rivers.

Padoch's detailed discussion of ethnicity in the village of Santa Rosa (1986) indicates the recentness and complexity of some ribereñoization. She notes that the residents are former members of at least four and probably five native groups or are mestizos with no recognized tribal background. Many Santa Rosinos or their parents previously lived in far distant parts of the Peruvian Amazon. In the early and middle years of this century, entrepreneurs brought laborers to commercial estates in the Santa Rosa area. The fundos are gone, but the descendants of the people brought into the area remain. Most contemporary Santa Rosinos are reluctant to talk about their tribal background, and Spanish is the language of the community. During disputes, however, ethnic backgrounds are frequently mentioned. Padoch concludes that "[t]he commonly held view that the native element in ribereño communities consists entirely of local riverine groups, acculturated in centuries past by missionary efforts, is not true in the case of Santa Rosa and many other villages of the area. Mestizaje, cultural and physical, has occurred within the lifetimes of many Santa Rosinos" (1986:4).

Despite the steady process of ribereñoization, many people identified as Indians apparently lived in rural communities around Iquitos as late as 1940. According to the Peruvian census of that year, the district of Iquitos included 43,294 whites and mestizos and 11,361 Indians. The population of the city of Iquitos was 31,828. While the census does not provide an ethnic breakdown of the city's population, the great majority were doubtless whites and mestizos. In rural areas around Iquitos, whites and mestizos therefore only slightly outnumbered Indians. For example, in the mostly rural district of Fernando Lores, which includes the town of Tamshiyacu and the village of Tapirillo, there were 7,312 whites and mestizos and 4,110 Indians. The population of all of Loreto (including the present-day department of Ucayali) was 180,000, of which 61 percent were classified as whites or mestizos, 38 percent as Indians, and 1 percent as "other" (Censo 1940).

These census figures should be regarded with considerable skepticism. The census does not indicate what criteria were used to place people into the categories of "white and mestizo" and "Indian." I suspect that urban-based census takers may have classified some ribereños or "quasi-ribereños" as Indians because they had some knowledge of an Amerindian language. During the process of ribereñoization, many Amazonian people do not fit easily into the census categories. Even anthropologists disagree among themselves about the best ways to classify culturally mixed Amazonian peoples (Gow 1991; Padoch 1986, 1988c; Stocks 1978). For instance, Peter Gow (1991:294) seems surprised by Padoch's description of people as "ex-Ashaninka" and "ex-Cocama" and says that he has never heard anyone in the Peruvian Amazon use terms of this sort. Gow speculates that "the only meaning I can think of for terms like 'ex-Ashaninka' or 'ex-Cocama' is in situations where 'kinds of people' are located in the parental generation or higher: where 'kinds of people' operate as identities in ascendant generations, but not as the personal identities of living people" (1991:296). Although I find Gow's comments about "kinds of people" less than crystal clear, his remarks about generational differences in identity in the Iquitos area seem well-taken. In some places, Indian identity was more relevant in the recent past (such as at the time of the 1940 census) than it is now. In such cases, people of "ascendant generations" sometimes might well be categorized by others as having belonged to a particular indigenous group. The great majority of contemporary people, however, would be unequivocally categorized as ribereño or mestizo.

Integration of the Peruvian Amazon into the National Economy, 1940–1970

Economic and political connections between the Peruvian Amazon and the rest of the country were tenuous before the 1940s. Most products were exported by boat down the Amazon through Brazil to the Atlantic Ocean. Transportation links between Loreto, Lima, and the Peruvian highlands were rudimentary. The Peruvian Amazon was a sparsely populated, economically unimportant backwater of little concern to government policymakers in Lima.

The tropical lowlands became more closely connected with the rest of Peru during World War II. When the United States and other Allied Powers wanted to ensure access to the raw materials of Amazonia, they supported regular air service between Iquitos and other parts of Peru.

The Peruvian army has been active in the Amazon since the late 1930s, when Peru and Ecuador clashed in a number of border skirmishes. Ecuador claimed large parts of the lowland tropics, including the city of Iquitos. An undeclared general war, won by Peru, was fought in late 1941 and early 1942, but Ecuador has never accepted the outcome, which transferred the more navigable lower portions of several tributaries of the Amazon to Peru. These border disputes led the Peruvian government to set up many military outposts in the Amazon in the 1940s, and flights of soldiers into and out of the jungle increased.

Many rural Amazonian men, who have the detailed understanding of the tropical forest environment necessary for jungle warfare, have been drafted to serve in the army since the beginning of the Peru-Ecuador conflict. As draftees are transferred around the jungle and to other parts of Peru, they identify more with the nation. After they complete their military service, many men migrate temporarily or permanently to urban areas.

The establishment of primary schools in the Amazon has also strengthened ties between the small riverine communities and the nation. Only five primary schools operated in the vast areas along the Amazon and Napo Rivers before 1940, but twelve more schools were set up in the 1940s, an additional 38 in the 1950s, and another 63 in the 1960s (San Román 1975:222). The schools, which teach Peruvian history and geography, inculcate loyalty to the nation.

The completion in 1943 of a road between Lima and Pucallpa, the major city of the high jungle, accelerated the integration of the Amazon into the national economy. Amazonian products were shipped up the Ucayali to Pucallpa and were then transported overland to the rest of Peru. For the first time, Loreto's products could be exported more easily through Lima than via Brazil. In the high jungle, production between 1940 and 1965 became oriented toward the internal markets of the coast, though the lowland tropics remained primarily an extractive enclave, with most products exported to other countries. Wood and ornamental fish were important exports from Loreto during the 1950s and 1960s. There was also a short-lived boom at this time in rosewood oil (from *Aniba roseadora*), used to scent soaps.

After World War II, agriculture replaced wage labor in extractive industries as the most important source of income for many ribereños. Rice was first grown commercially in the early 1940s, and jute was sold in substantial quantities after 1955. Sales of plantains, manioc, fish, and other staples in the Iquitos area also increased. The rapid growth of the city's population—from 32,000 in 1940 to 110,000 in 1972—provided a rapidly expanding market for food crops (Webb and Fernández Baca 1990:110).

Transportation improvements and new government agricultural policies stimulated cash cropping in the 1950s and 1960s. More boats cruised the rivers in the years after World War II, and by about 1960 motorized craft were common. Ribereños could now sell their crops directly in Iquitos at higher prices than the patrones and regatones offered. The state guaranteed prices for rice and jute and gave credit to farmers to raise these crops.

The improved market for agricultural products encouraged some ribereños to leave the fundos. The typical riverine settlement was now an independent ribereño village. Nonetheless, many fundos continued to operate along the rivers, especially in remote areas. The owners of commercial estates were often unwilling to cede part of their holdings to ribereños who wished to establish their own communities. Even those ribereños who succeeded in setting up independent villages sometimes worked temporarily or semipermanently on commercial estates because their agricultural income was not always sufficient to cover expenditures for medical care, education, clothing, kerosene, and other necessities.

4. Regional Economy

Miguel Pinedo and I were trying to get from Tapirillo to Iquitos one morning in early April 1986. After waiting around for several hours, we were picked up by a boat operated by some brothers from a village near Nauta. They were going into the city to sell game meat and turtles, and their small craft was so crowded with people and produce that we had difficulty finding a place to sit. Miguel ended up next to the motor, and I was able to squeeze in between a bag of sugarcane and the side of the boat. Four chickens pecked enthusiastically at my neck, and a little girl in a swinging hammock above me bumped my head every few minutes. The man steering the boat was drinking aguardiente, and the engine operator was puffing away on a cigarette.

Farmers in floodplain villages near Iquitos often take their crops to market on such crowded, uncomfortable, and unsafe boats. When these men and women arrive in the city, they must cope with a dispersed, confusing marketplace where prices fluctuate wildly. Although farmers complain about the obstacles they encounter, they nonetheless say that transporting and selling their crops have gotten easier in the past several decades.

The Economic Geography of Peru

Geographers usually divide Peru into three zones: the tropical lowlands (the *selva*), the Andean highlands (the *sierra*), and the Pacific coast (see Figure 4.1). The selva includes the departments of Loreto, San Martín, Ucayali, and Madre de Dios, most of the department of Amazonas, and part of the departments of Junín, Ayacucho, Cuzco, and Puno. Even though 58 percent of Peru's land is in the selva, the country's population

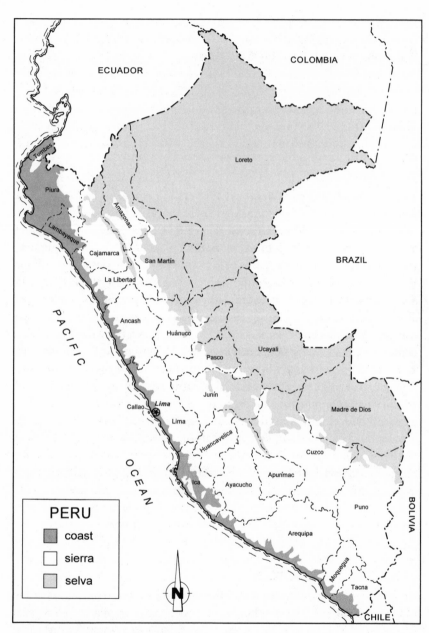

Figure 4.1. *Peru's geographical zones*

is concentrated along the coast and in the sierra. In 1989, 2.5 million people lived in the selva, 7.9 million in the sierra, and 11.4 million on the coast (Webb and Fernández Baca 1990:29).

Government publications rarely provide much economic data on the selva as a whole. For analytical purposes, the National Institute of Statistics of Peru divides the country into twelve regions, each consisting of one or more departments. For each of these regions, the institute calculates the gross domestic product (GDP), a figure that does not include crops grown for home consumption (Chibnik 1978), the enormous illegal cocaine trade, and the large, well-developed informal sector (Babb 1989; de Soto 1989). Because some regions include areas in two or three geographical zones, the institute's statistical publications do not allow direct comparisons of the GDP of the coast, sierra, and selva.

The overall contribution of the lowland selva to the nation's economy has been low in the past several decades. The departments of Loreto and Ucayali accounted for only 2.5 percent of Peru's GDP in 1975 and only 5.0 percent in 1988 (Webb and Fernández Baca 1990:297). The institute's figures on per capita GDP indicate that the selva is neither the wealthiest nor the poorest part of Peru. For every year between 1970 and 1988, the region consisting of the coastal provinces of Lima and Callao had the highest per capita GDP. The three poorest regions during this period were Inca (the departments of Apurímac, Cuzco, and Madre de Dios), Chavín (the department of Ancash), and Los Libertadores–Wari (the departments of Ayacucho, Huancavelica, and Ica). The per capita GDP in 1988 in these three regions was about one third that of Lima and Callao (Webb and Fernández Baca 1990:299). In all three regions, well over half the population lived in the sierra (Webb and Fernández Baca 1990:29). The two regions with more than half of their population in the selva were relatively prosperous. Amazonas (the department of Loreto) had the second highest per capita GDP in 1988 (89 percent that of Lima and Callao), and Ucayali (consisting of the department of that name) had the fourth highest per capita GDP (52 percent that of Lima and Callao).

Peru's economic and political situation has worsened since 1980, and the departments of Loreto and Ucayali have received little government aid in recent years. The country has had to cope with a mounting debt to international banks, sometimes horrendous inflation, a steadily falling GDP, and revolutionary movements in the sierra, coast, and high selva. The government has expended most of its scarce financial resources on repaying debts, repressing guerrillas, and attempting to improve living conditions in the densely populated sierra and the rapidly growing city of Lima. The sparsely populated and relatively peaceful lowland jungle has placed less pressing demands on the state's meager funds.

The lowland selva's geographical isolation has sheltered the region from Peru's most difficult political problems. Despite occasional rumors about the presence of the Sendero Luminoso, guerrilla groups have not been active. While government officials sometimes call their opponents terrorists or communists, martial law has not been declared, and violent repression of antigovernment leaders has been uncommon. The most important regional political issues involve the drug trade near the Peru-Colombia-Brazil border and continuing territorial disputes with Ecuador. Government actions concerning these problems have little effect on the daily life of most ribereños near Iquitos.

Population Structure

According to government publications, the population of the department of Loreto grew from 475,000 people in 1981 to 638,000 in 1989 (Webb and Fernández Baca 1990:99). These figures probably underestimate the actual population. Census takers cannot possibly make an exact count of either the mobile, dispersed rural population or the many residents of squatter settlements (*pueblos jovenes*) in Iquitos. A sophisticated analysis indicates that the population of Loreto in 1981 was about 514,000, 8.2 percent higher than the census count (Ferrando 1985:38). If the 1989 government figure (not based on a census) is a similar underestimate, the actual population of Loreto in that year was about 690,000. The lowland selva has grown no faster than the rest of Peru in the middle and latter parts of the twentieth century (see Table 4.1). The officially recorded population of the present-day departments of Loreto and Ucayali increased from 321,000 to 862,000 between 1940 and 1989, while the population of the rest of Peru grew from 6,702,000 to 20,930,000.

Immigration and emigration have had little effect on the population of the department of Loreto in the past several decades. The most recent figures on migration patterns cover the years 1976 to 1981. The annual rate of immigration to Loreto between 1976 and 1981 was only 10 per thousand inhabitants; the annual rate of emigration was 13 per thousand. These rates were higher in other jungle departments (see Table 4.2).

Since immigration to and emigration from Loreto have been approximately equal in recent years, the department's rapid population growth

Table 4.1. Population of Regions of Peru, 1940–1989

Year	Loreto and Ucayali	Sierra	Other Parts of Peru
1940	321,000	3,741,000	2,145,000
1961	411,000	5,129,000	4,367,000
1972	541,000	6,052,000	6,946,000
1981	694,000	7,017,000	9,294,000
1989	862,000	7,900,000	13,030,000

SOURCE: Webb and Fernández Baca 1990:98–99.

Table 4.2. Average Annual Immigration and Emigration Rates in Tropical Forest Departments, 1976–1981

Department	Immigrants per 1,000 Inhabitants	Emigrants per 1,000 Inhabitants
Amazonas	23	22
Loreto	10	13
Madre de Dios	65	21
San Martín	43	14
Ucayali	26	17

SOURCE: Webb and Fernández Baca 1990:120.

must be attributed primarily to births exceeding deaths. Although birth rates have been declining, they remain high. The number of births per thousand inhabitants was 47.5 in 1972, 43.5 in 1981, and 40.0 in 1989. The total fertility rate was 7.5 children per woman in 1972, 6.5 in 1981, and 5.3 in 1989 (Ferrando 1985:42; Webb and Fernández Baca 1990:118). Death rates dropped from 14.8 per thousand inhabitants for 1967–72 to 12.4 for 1981–82. Life expectancy increased only from 53 to 55 during this period, mostly because many people continued to die at early ages. Infant mortality, which was 131 per thousand births for 1967–72, dropped only to 120 in 1981–82 (Ferrando 1985:42). The National Institute of

Statistics claims that mortality rates decreased sharply in the 1980s (Webb and Fernández Baca 1990:118). The institute's estimate for the death rate per thousand people in 1989 was 9.0, the estimated rate of infant mortality was 83, and the expected life span was reported to be 62 years. These estimates, which are not based on censuses, should be regarded with considerable skepticism.

The urban centers of Loreto are growing faster than the rural areas. Between 1972 and 1981, the proportion of residents of Loreto who lived in urban areas rose from 47.8 percent to 52.9 percent (Ferrando 1985:55). This difference was almost entirely the result of population trends in the province of Maynas, which includes Iquitos. The rural population of Maynas dropped from 82,000 to 78,000 between 1972 and 1981, while the urban population grew from 121,000 to 186,000 (Ferrando 1985:54). In 1981, 70.5 percent of the residents of Maynas lived in urban areas, a jump of 10.9 percent since 1972. This trend has continued in recent years, and the population of Iquitos is now around 300,000.

Not much has been written about rural-urban differences in fertility and mortality rates in Loreto, but some fragmentary evidence (Censo 1972) suggests that such differences were not great in the early 1970s. The data on fertility and mortality rates in rural Loreto, while woefully incomplete, are nonetheless sufficient to show that the lack of significant population change in rural Maynas can be attributed almost entirely to extensive outmigration. Birth and death rates would otherwise lead to rapid population growth.

Both the rural and the urban areas of Loreto have very young populations. The median age of the entire department in 1981 was 15.1, a figure that is very close to that of rural areas in the late 1960s and early 1970s (Censo 1981:xxix; San Román et al. n.d.:117–19). The median age in rural communities such as Porvenir, Santa Sofía, and Tapirillo remained around 15 in the mid-1980s.

One of the most striking demographic features of Loreto is the bifurcation of the population into one large city and many small communities. Iquitos had a population of 176,175 in 1981. The next biggest place was Yurimaguas, a town with a population of only 22,902 located far away from Iquitos on the Huallaga River. The largest town within a day's boat trip of Iquitos is Requena, with a population of 8,000. Iquitos, Yurimaguas, and Requena were the only urban places with more than 5,000 people in 1981. Five towns had between 2,000 and 5,000 inhabitants; ten towns had populations between 1,000 and 2,000. About 195,000 residents of Loreto lived in villages with fewer than 1,000 people.

Sources of Income

The two most important economic booms in Loreto in recent years have involved petroleum exploration and the drug trade. Although some lowland Amazonians have earned large amounts of money from oil and cocaine, these products play no part in the economic lives of most contemporary ribereños.

In the 1960s and 1970s, North American companies stepped up their oil exploration in Loreto. Helicopters and motorized barges made drilling in remote lowland areas more feasible than previously, and the use of aerial photography and magnetic surveys made it possible to locate oil reserves more accurately (Davis and Mathews 1976:53–55). Petroperu, the state-owned oil company, signed contracts with several North American and Japanese corporations, and during the peak of the oil boom between 1972 and 1975, more than $750 million was invested in oil exploration (Davis and Mathews 1976:61). A small but significant portion of this money was paid to ribereño laborers. The oil exploration met with only limited success, however, and in 1976 the foreign companies pulled out of the Peruvian Amazon. While there was some renewal of foreign interest in Amazonian oil in the 1980s, petroleum companies did not hire many local people as laborers. The only time most rural Amazonians had contact with the petroleum industry was when they saw an oil barge traveling along a river.

During the late 1970s and early 1980s, some residents of Iquitos earned substantial amounts of money transporting and processing coca-based products. The narcotics traffickers occasionally hired campesinos to help in their enterprises. By the time I began my research, however, the illegal drug trade was only a minor factor in rural economies, as delivery routes had shifted away from the Iquitos area. Rural and urban Loretanos often gossiped about the alleged drug-related income of patrones, but they generally agreed that campesinos were too poor to be involved in the narcotics traffic. Few rural villagers had unexplained sources of wealth. Their illicit trade was limited to some minor smuggling of goods in and out of Brazil.

Statistics on the relative importance of the various sources of income in Loreto are scattered and difficult to locate. Those available are often dated and of dubious validity. The figures presented here are intended to give a broad picture of economic activity in Loreto and should not be regarded as precise.

Forest products have continued to be economically important in Loreto. The lumber industry constituted about 45 percent of the industrial gross national product in the department in 1975 (Villarejo 1979:283), and currently there is some trade in gums, resins, wild fruits, and medicinal plants (Padoch 1988b). Agriculture, however, is now the Peruvian Amazon's most important income-producing activity. Agricultural and forestry activities together constitute about 60 percent of the gross national product of the Peruvian Amazon (Aramburú 1986:332). Few tropical lowland farmers raise many crops for export to other parts of Peru or abroad. Except for jute, commercial agricultural products grown in Loreto are sold almost exclusively to urban consumers in Iquitos and other towns in the department.

Rice is Loreto's most important commercial crop, though yields are below the national average. Farmers in Loreto averaged 2,500 kilograms of rice in husk per hectare in 1985, whereas the average yield in all of Peru was 4,361. Although 10.7 percent of the land devoted to rice in Peru was in Loreto, the department accounted for only 6.1 percent of the national sales (Comité Nacional de Productores de Arroz 1986).

Corn and jute are the next most important cash crops of Loreto. Although many ribereños sell small quantities of plantains and manioc, these crops are not raised commercially by large-scale growers.

Transportation

Commercial airlines make several daily round-trips between Iquitos and Lima. Air routes also connect Iquitos with other Peruvian cities and parts of Brazil. Direct flights to Miami ceased in 1984 because of a complicated dispute between Peru and the United States concerning airport fees, but they resumed in the late 1980s.

Because very few rural Amazonians can afford the cost of air passage, most Loretanos take boats on the rare occasions when they travel long distances. Large boats (*lanchas*) make regularly scheduled trips along the Amazon, Ucayali, Marañon, and Huallaga rivers, picking up passengers and cargo in towns and cities. Lanchas are crowded, noisy, and picturesque, with hammocks, machinery, animals, merchandise, luggage, and hundreds of people crammed together on two decks. Boats rarely leave on schedule, and lengthy unexplained stops in port are common. The speed of a lancha depends on whether the boat is going upriver or down. For example, the upriver trip from Iquitos to Pucallpa takes seven to ten days; the downriver journey from Pucallpa to Iquitos lasts a mere five days.

Ribereños who live less than about eighty kilometers from Iquitos ordinarily travel to the city on river buses, or *colectivos*. These are small motorized boats that can carry up to fifty people and that have a tin or thatched roof to shelter passengers and cargo. Most colectivo owners, or *transportistas,* have two houses, one in a rural community and another in Iquitos. Many transportistas make two or three weekly round-trips between their village and Iquitos. Colectivos typically go to Iquitos one day and return the next. The colectivo owner spends the night at his house (I heard of no female transportistas) while an assistant stays with the boat. Most passengers find lodging with relatives in the city.

Colectivos are slower than lanchas and make many more stops. A forty-kilometer trip by colectivo may take four hours downriver and six or even seven hours upriver. The same trip by lancha might take two and a half hours downriver and four hours upriver. Lanchas pick up passengers only at specific sites, while colectivos stop for anyone who signals from the shore. The closer one is to Iquitos, the easier it is to find a colectivo. Villagers living near the city can usually get a ride within a few hours by waiting along the river. Ribereños living more than forty kilometers or so from Iquitos must rely more on regularly scheduled boats, as some days pass without a single colectivo going by.

Colectivos also connect some riverine villages to the towns of Loreto. Residents of villages on major rivers far from Iquitos may be able to get to the city by taking a colectivo to the nearest town and then boarding a lancha. People living away from the Amazon, Ucayali, Marañon, and Huallaga rivers, however, often have considerable difficulty finding passage to Iquitos.

Some rural Amazonians own motorized boats or canoes, which they occasionally use for travel to towns and the city. These boats are rarely taken on routine trips to market crops or visit relatives. Their owners worry about balky motors and the cost of gasoline.

In addition to lanchas, colectivos, and campesino-owned boats, an astonishing variety of private and commercial boats runs up and down the Amazon and its tributaries. The operators of these craft are usually willing to give rides to paying passengers. Finding a ride on such a boat is easy near Iquitos but can be difficult even in communities as close to the city as Porvenir. The rides can be an adventure, as a trip that Miguel Pinedo and I took between Porvenir and Iquitos on a long Sunday in November 1985 illustrates. Even though no colectivo was expected to pass Porvenir that day, Miguel and I were determined to find passage to the city. At eleven in the morning we saw a barge filled with cargo pull into a cantina in the commercial estate adjoining Porvenir. The captain of the barge, which belonged to the state oil company, agreed to take us to the city after he had finished drinking. Miguel and I waited on the barge with some of the crew as the captain and a few oil workers talked with friends from other boats. At four in the afternoon the drinkers staggered out of the bar, and the oil barge took off at a rapid clip. (Fortunately, the engine operator had stayed on the boat.) After about two hours of pleasant cruising, the engine stopped. We drifted aimlessly for about thirty minutes and came to rest on a sandbar. The crew was able to restart the engine an hour later, and we got into Iquitos not long before midnight. Miguel and I ended our voyage with a long, muddy climb from the port into town.

Despite the unpredictability of travel along the river, many ribereños enjoy the trips. They talk with friends and relatives from other villages and observe the ever-changing, always fascinating scene on the water and at the ports. One never knows who or what will get on or off a boat.

Marketing Crops at Government Buying Centers

During the period of my fieldwork, ribereños could sell rice, corn, and jute at guaranteed prices to government buying centers. Peru had several national-level organizations that bought crops from farmers at the fixed prices and worked closely with the Agrarian Bank, which loaned money to many farmers for growing crops. In ordinary circumstances, farmers who delivered a crop to a buying center received the value of the sale minus any outstanding debts on that crop owed to the Agrarian Bank.

Six rice buying centers, operated by the Empresa de Comercialización de Arroz (ECASA), played an important role in the economy of Loreto. ECASA did not operate exactly the same in all buying centers. The centers in Nauta, Requena, Lagunas, Pevas, and Caballococha, for example, included state-run storehouses and mills, but the one in Iquitos contracted with private enterprises for these services. Here I will describe the Iquitos center, which was by far the largest in Loreto.

Farmers were responsible for arranging the transportation of rice from their community to Iquitos. The cost of transport by boat or truck depended on the amount of rice shipped and the distance. Ribereños who arrived in Iquitos by boat also had to arrange and pay for trucking their rice to one of several mills. At the mills, rice was dried, cleaned, and weighed, and the farmers were given a receipt indicating the dry weight of their rice. They took the receipt to ECASA's central office, where they were paid. The guaranteed price at ECASA was usually about one and a half times that offered on the open market.

ECASA sold the rice to wholesalers in large quantities. The price ECASA charged depended on the retail price in the stores and markets of Iquitos. But the Peruvian government established maximum retail prices for rice and other essential consumer items in each department. ECASA's Iquitos center had to sell rice to wholesalers for less than the maximum retail price permitted in Iquitos. Because government rice policies subsidized both farmers and urban consumers, ECASA incurred losses every year. The difference between ECASA's buying and selling prices was insufficient to cover its operating costs.

The government also operated a corn buying center in Iquitos. Because this office was not always open in the mid-1980s, farmers who planted corn never knew whether they would receive a guaranteed price for their crop. For example, the office was closed for more than a year before it reopened in February 1986. Even when the center was open, the price it offered was often little better than that of the open market.

Farmers in the Iquitos area had received credit and price supports for jute since the 1950s, but the attractiveness of jute as a cash crop dropped during the 1980s when selling prices did not keep pace with inflation. During 20 months in the middle of the decade, the general indices of consumer prices quadrupled, but jute prices remained the same. When the selling price of a kilogram of first-class jute went from 1.5 to 5.5 intis per kilogram in early 1986, farmers' interest in the crop revived somewhat.

Peru's increasing national debt during the 1980s led to periodic calls from some free-market economists to end agricultural subsidies and instead to allow the forces of supply and demand to determine wholesale prices of rice, corn, and jute. These proposals were strongly opposed by ribereño farmers, but the economists' recommendations prevailed in 1991 when the government led by Alberto Fujimori instituted a series of austerity measures. The state-operated buying centers were closed, and all crops had to be sold on the open market.

The Open Market

During the 1980s most crops in the Iquitos area were sold at open markets, where prices vary from day to day. The small markets of Loreto's towns are insignificant in comparison to those in Iquitos, with its six markets and many traveling vendors. The largest market is in Belén, an impoverished port area. Belén includes retail stores, wholesaler's storehouses, and a two-story covered market built and maintained by the municipal government. Much of Belén's trade, however, is carried out by several thousand vendors in outside stalls that cover more than twenty city blocks. The vendors, who are mostly women, exhibit their small stocks of food products and herbal medicines on cloths or blankets on the ground near their stalls. Often several family members take turns tending a stall.

The Belén market seasonally changes its size and location. When the Amazon rises from March to June, the lower parts of Belén are covered with water, and residents move around by boat (the port areas of Iquitos are sometimes jokingly compared with Venice). At these times, the market is concentrated on the higher ground.

In the 1980s, most corn, some rice, and a little jute was sold on the open market. One reason was that the buying centers sometimes ran out of money and had to delay payments to farmers selling crops to the state. As a result, farmers who needed cash immediately were forced to sell their crops in city markets. Another reason was that rice and corn growers who were in debt to the Agrarian Bank often preferred to sell their crops on the open market because their proceeds for such sales could be used for any purpose, whereas some or all of their proceeds from sales to buying centers had to be used to pay off their debts.

Intermediaries

Crops take diverse pathways and can pass through the hands of various intermediaries between the farmers' fields and the markets and stores of Iquitos. Contractors (*habilitadores*) and subcontractors (*subhabilitadores*) lend money to rural Loretanos in exchange for exclusive rights to buy their forest products, agricultural crops, and fish. These moneylenders, based in both rural and urban areas, pursue a variety of enterprises: owners of commercial estates lend money to farmers unable or unwilling to borrow from the Agrarian Bank; regatones on lengthy buying and selling trips lend money to Amerindians and ribereños living in remote villages without colectivo service; traveling merchants working as subhabilitadores for Iquitos wholesalers buy fish from campesinos; and entrepreneurial women in Iquitos finance the production of aguaje, which is used to flavor ice cream sold on street corners (Padoch 1988a).

Farmers who live on major rivers send their products to market on regularly scheduled colectivos or lanchas. Colectivos charge less for shipping and passage, but lanchas are better able to carry large quantities of produce. Although ribereños often accompany their crops to market, they sometimes ask transportistas to sell their products. Such *encomienda* agreements usually stipulate that boat owners are not to sell the crops for less than a certain price, and if they sell the products for more than this agreed-upon price, they can pocket the difference. Many transportistas do not charge extra for encomiendas. Ribereños also contract with boat owners to buy consumer goods in the city. Transportistas charge a small fee for this service.

The number of passengers and the amount and type of produce carried on colectivos vary seasonally, though boats almost always carry plantains, manioc, fish, and a remarkable assortment of fruits and vegetables. Table 4.3 shows the products taken to market on a typical colectivo trip. Farmers who arrive in Iquitos by colectivo or lancha cannot easily sell their products to retailers. Carrying produce from a boat to land can be a daunting task, as passengers usually must clamber through several other boats and over narrow wooden planks before reaching shore. After farmers get to the port, they must find someone willing to buy their produce, which can be equally daunting because most retailers do not need what the farmer is selling and vendors' stalls and stores are scattered over a wide area.

The chaotic port and dispersed retail outlets create a niche for men and women working as small-scale wholesalers, or *rematistas,* who meet boats in Iquitos or at collection points outside the city. Their activities at the port are a remarkable spectacle. To get a jump on their competitors, rematistas row small boats into the Amazon and jump onto colectivos and lanchas as they approach the port. Many try to grab products from passengers without ascertaining whether they are for sale. Some hapless farmers, worried about losing their produce, sell to the first rematista they encounter, but the rematistas' tactics lead many farmers to disdain them as "pirates" or "lizards."

Rematistas have several outlets for the produce they buy, including stores, vendors, and larger-scale wholesalers (*mayoristas*). Both rematistas

Table 4.3. Products on a Tapirillo-Iquitos Colectivo, February 8, 1986[a]

Product	Amount Taken by Passengers	Amount Sent by Encomiendas
Manioc	50 paneros[b]	30 paneros
Fariña[c]	128 kgs	none
Plantains	9 racimos[d]	1 racimo
Corn	3 sacks[e]	800 ears
Tomatoes	112 cajitas[f]	440 cajitas
Salt fish	4 bandejas[g]	83 fish
Fresh fish	206 fish	none
Fowl	7 chickens, 2 ducks	1 rooster, 1 duck
Fruit	147 papayas	80 papayas
	400 grapefruit	200 grapefruit
	1/2 sack of cocona[h]	1 1/2 sacks of cocona
	26 zapallos[h]	1 roll of pijuayo
	20 melons	62 palm hearts
	9 watermelons	5 sacks of aguaje
Firewood	2 bundles	none
Other	1 sack of onions	1 bag of cucumbers

[a]There were 11 passengers with products and 22 encomiendas.
[b]A panero (a measure of volume) is about 20 kgs.
[c]Fariña consists of granules of toasted manioc flour.
[d]A racimo is a bunch of 40 to 150 plantains.
[e]A sack of shelled corn weighs about 25 kgs.
[f]Each cajita (little box) has 7 to 10 tomatoes.
[g]Each bandeja (dish) has 50 to 60 fish.
[h]Cocona, a native fruit, is *Solanum sessiflorum*; zapallo, a squash, is *Cucurbita* spp.

and mayoristas hire men to carry the cargo to its destination. The cargo carriers would not be out of place in a medieval painting of hell: small, muscular men hauling enormous loads on their backs through mud, crowds, and torrential rains. Mayoristas also hire trucks to carry produce to storehouses.

Social and Economic Relationships in the Marketing Chain

In many parts of the world, members of a marketing chain are linked by long-term trading partnerships (Davis 1973; Katzin 1960; Plattner 1989:212–14; Swetnam 1978; Trager 1981). A seller promises to deliver certain products to a particular buyer, who promises in return to pay agreed-upon prices. Such arrangements reduce risk for both sellers and buyers but are sometimes disadvantageous for one or both parties. Sellers may get less than the prevailing market price; buyers may pay more than the prevailing market price or be forced to acquire products they do not want.

Long-term trading partnerships are common in certain links of the Iquitos marketing chain. Regatones buy the products they sell from particular habilitadores, who buy their products from particular subhabilitadores. Both buyers and sellers are powerful in these partnerships and are wealthy by local standards. In the third important marketing link in which long-term trading partnerships are common, buyers are much better off than sellers. Habilitadores and subhabilitadores give loans to rural producers in return for the guaranteed delivery of a crop at a fixed price. The terms of these arrangements are almost always more beneficial to the buyer than the seller: a campesino needs the loans of a particular habilitador more than the habilitador needs the products of a particular campesino.

Trading partnerships are rare among other members of the Iquitos marketing chain. A colectivo owner usually sells his encomiendas to one of several rematistas, but no one is offended if he sells to someone else. Transportistas selling encomiendas get the prevailing market price from both their regular customers and other rematistas. Mayoristas may buy regularly from particular rematistas but do not offer them special prices. Farmers and rematistas sometimes establish regular trading relationships with close relatives who are vendors; otherwise they sell to anyone willing to buy their products.

The absence of long-term trading partnerships among small-scale producers, intermediaries, and retailers in Iquitos can be attributed partly to transport conditions and partly to the geographical layout of the market. Since boat schedules are unreliable and communications between the countryside and the city are largely limited to infrequent radio messages, rematistas cannot predict when particular boats or customers will arrive. Incoming passengers cannot easily find particular rematistas in the crowded, sprawling port. Thus the logistics of the port make many trading partnerships impractical. In addition, the economics of the market make such arrangements unnecessary and undesirable. Because the profit per unit is very low for most wholesale transactions, buying and selling prices offered by the various rematistas usually do not vary much. The amount of money rematistas make depends almost entirely on how quickly they can turn over their stock. Trading partnerships would slow down rematistas' turnover because they would have to search for their customers in the busy marketplace while ignoring hordes of other producers and retailers eager to buy and sell. Farmers have little trouble selling their products and do not need the protection of a guaranteed outlet from rematistas or vendors. Vendors rarely need a guaranteed supply of a particular product; their major problem is finding customers willing to buy their offerings.

Selling Prices

Although the Peruvian government does not collect information about wholesale prices in Iquitos, the Regional Office of Statistics of the department of Loreto compiles monthly lists of retail prices in the city. Since retail and wholesale prices parallel one another for many products, this information could theoretically be used to make inferences about prices farmers get from intermediaries at open markets, and indeed the government's price data for consumer goods such as soap and kerosene seem reasonably accurate. But the figures that the office gives for the retail prices of agricultural products such as manioc, plantains, and native fruits are questionable. Prices are given per kilogram even though most crops are sold by the unit, and government publications say nothing about the assumptions used in converting units to kilograms. Furthermore, government statistics on most crops show steady monthly retail price rises that closely parallel the rate of inflation. Anyone who spends a little time in the Iquitos market quickly learns that both retail and wholesale prices fluctuate greatly from month to month according to seasonal variations in the supply of the various products.

I was able to obtain reliable information from a nongovernment source about prices that farmers receive from rematistas in the Iquitos market. The Voz de la Selva is a radio station affiliated with the Catholic church which aims its broadcasts at Loreto's rural population. One program, *El Chacarero* (The Farm Worker), includes a report on wholesale prices in the Iquitos market. Announcers give information collected by the station on a range of prices offered for each product by different rematistas. Figures 4.2 and 4.3, which give prices for manioc, plantains, corn, tomatoes, papayas, and chickens in the Iquitos market between 1982 and 1987, are based on data from the Voz de la Selva. These figures show the enormous price variability of the open market.

The wholesale prices of products in the Iquitos marketplace reflect supply and demand to an extent usually found only in introductory economics textbooks. During the 1980s, variations in supply were the major cause of changes in the price of most products. Increases in demand brought about by the growing population of Iquitos were largely counterbalanced by the worsening economic situation of most consumers.

The market prices of many products are responses to variable supply associated with the agricultural cycle and the seasonal ripening of fruits. The prices of plantains and manioc often drop in March and April when farmers harvest these crops in restingas as the rivers rise. Corn and tomatoes, which are planted in restingas after the rivers fall, tend to have low prices when they are harvested in September, October, and November. The price of chickens, which are available in approximately equal numbers year-round, does not fluctuate seasonally.

Farmers in the Iquitos area cannot guess market prices solely by looking at harvest conditions in their own and neighboring villages. Boats come into the Iquitos market from three major river systems—the Amazon-Marañon, the Ucayali, and the Napo—and flood levels differ in the three systems. Farmers in communities on the Amazon are sometimes unhappy when manioc prices drop in January when the river is still low, but the cause is likely to be unusually early floods along the Ucayali or Napo, not manipulation of the market.

Not all supply-related price variations are seasonal. Unusual river conditions that affect the entire department of Loreto, for example, can have a tremendous effect on the availability of certain crops for an entire year. In 1982, for example, floods ruined many fields in restingas, and prices for manioc and plantains were exceptionally high. Similarly, prices of

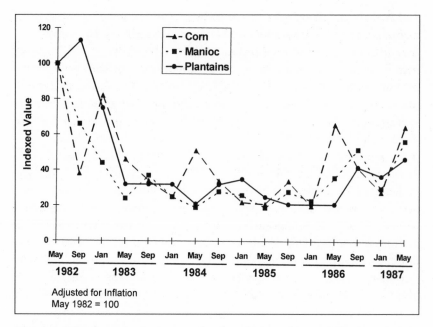

Figure 4.2. Prices in the Iquitos market for corn, manioc, and plantains

some commodities, especially tree crops and fish, sometimes drop quickly when boats carrying large amounts of a particular product arrive in port at Iquitos.

Campesinos sometimes say that the municipal government of Iquitos should provide a farmers' market where producers could sell directly to consumers. They claim that farmers would get better prices if rematistas and vendors were eliminated from the marketing chain. In particular, campesinos point out that the retail prices vendors charge their custom-ers are usually much higher than the wholesale prices farmers get from rematistas. Determining the difference between wholesale and retail prices for manioc and plantains (the most important food staples sold in the open market) is a difficult task. Ordinarily, manioc is brought to the marketplace in sacks and sold to rematistas in smaller units called *paneros* (literally, baker's baskets). Vendors buy manioc from rematistas in paneros and sell it to consumers by the piece. A sack of manioc weighs about 65 kilograms, and there are about three paneros per sack. In March 1986 farmers were selling manioc to rematistas at about 10 intis per panero. This is equivalent to about 0.45 intis per kilogram. By weighing several pieces of manioc sold by vendors, I estimated that vendors were charging their customers about 2 intis per kilogram. Making similar calculations for plantains is almost impossible. Farmers sell plantains to rematistas by the *racimo,* or bunch, and each bunch includes anywhere from 40 to 150 plantains. Vendors sell plantains to consumers in smaller bunches that also vary greatly in size. Bunches of different sizes often sell for the same price. The markup from rematista to vendor for plantains appears to be high but somewhat less than that of manioc.

Sizable differences between wholesale and retail prices do not necessarily indicate that intermediaries are exploiting the farmers. The largest markups in the marketing chain are between what vendors pay for products and what they charge their customers. Yet most vendors are poor women with small stocks of goods who clearly make very little money, partly because they must pay rematistas or cargo handlers to transport the goods from the port to their stalls and partly because their goods sell very slowly and much of their produce is perishable. Every other intermediary in the Iquitos marketing chain makes smaller profits per unit but

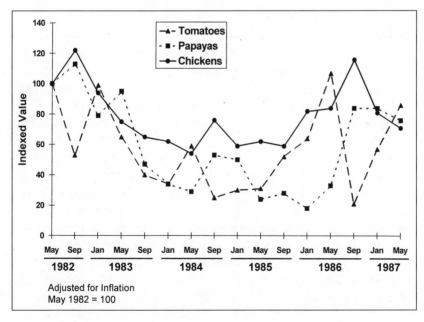

Figure 4.3. Prices in the Iquitos market for tomatoes, papayas, and chickens

turns over goods much more quickly. A farmers' market would doubtless allow producers to get more money for their crops but would entail a loss of time few could afford.

Inflation

The Peruvian government calculates an index of consumer prices for the largest cities in the country. Starting from a baseline figure of 100 for Iquitos in 1979 (see Table 4.4), this index had reached 22,984 by 1987. During this time, average prices approximately doubled each year. In the late 1980s, however, Peru experienced an appalling hyperinflation. After Alberto Fujimori came to power in the early 1990s, the annual inflation rate dropped to the level of the early and mid-1980s.

Because this index may not always reflect the cost of items most needed by poor people, the government compiles another index of essential goods bought by urban residents. This family market basket includes many food items and is largely irrelevant to rural families, who grow most of what they eat. The state does not compile an index of essential goods for the rural poor. The publications of campesino organizations based in Iquitos sometimes compare the prices farmers receive for their crops in various years with the cost of soap, which is purchased by all rural families. Increases in the prices of soap and matches (another consumer good all ribereños buy) between 1982 and 1987 closely paralleled changes in the government's index of average consumer prices.

Campesinos suffer less from inflation than do urban Loretanos. They are largely self-sufficient in food and buy few consumer goods. Nonetheless, they often complain that the prices they receive for their products do not keep up with inflation. To examine this claim, I divided monthly market prices for several products between 1982 and 1987 by the general inflation index compiled by the Regional Office of Statistics (see Figures 4.2 and 4.3). These data only partly support the campesinos' complaints. For all products examined, inflation-adjusted prices in 1982 were considerably higher than in ensuing years. Prices dropped sharply in 1983 but remained about the same between 1984 and 1987. Changes in the urban cost of living, moreover, may have had relatively little effect on farmers' total sales of food staples such as manioc and plantains. The demand for food in Iquitos, as elsewhere, is fairly inelastic with respect to price.

Table 4.4. Average Yearly Consumer Price Index in Iquitos, 1975–1989
(1979 = 100)

Year	Average Consumer Price Index	Year	Average Consumer Price Index
1975	22	1983	1,098
1976	29	1984	2,454
1977	38	1985	6,452
1978	56	1986	11,249
1979	100	1987	22,984
1980	160	1988	193,191
1981	295	1989	7,032,948
1982	506		

SOURCE: Webb and Fernández Baca 1990:619–20.

Inflation did have some important effects on the economy of rural Peruvian Amazonia during the 1980s, however. The amount of credit given by the Agrarian Bank to farmers growing cash crops such as rice and jute was often insufficient to cover their transportation and labor expenses. Increases in the price of gasoline forced colectivo owners to raise shipping rates. The wages paid agricultural laborers rose, though they were still remarkably low by the standards of industrial countries.

5. Ribereño Villages

Most ribereños live in small communities along major rivers or their tributaries. These hot and muddy villages can seem much alike to casual visitors. Wooden houses raised on stilts are connected to one another by winding dirt paths hacked out of the jungle. The only cement structure is a school, which may also serve as a community center. Residents fish in rivers and oxbow lakes, raise chickens and ducks, and cultivate fields of rice, corn, manioc, and plantains. At twilight the hum of an astonishing number of insects can be heard. The only immediately noticeable costly consumer goods are radios, outboard motors, and sewing machines. There is no electricity or running water, and there are few outhouses.

Despite their superficial similarity, ribereño communities display considerable socioeconomic variability. Some villages sell large amounts of rice grown in barreales; others rely on tree crops and fruits as major sources of income. Some ostensibly independent villages have close ties with nearby commercial estates; others have few inhabitants who borrow from or work for patrones. Some villages mobilize agricultural labor with festive work parties; others use formally organized groups in which farmers take turns working in one another's fields.

Settlement Patterns

The concentration of ribereño settlements along the major rivers of Loreto is a consequence of the cultural ecology and economic conditions of the Peruvian Amazon. Farming and fishing are better in floodplains than in interfluvial areas, and ribereños who live along the Amazon, Marañon, Ucayali, and Huallaga rivers can transport their crops to market more easily than those living elsewhere.

Near Iquitos and the major towns of Loreto, the floodplains are almost continuously occupied. Settlements farther away from urban areas tend to be concentrated in places where there are good barreales and extensive restingas. In some areas, one side of a river is much better suited for agriculture than the other and has more settlements. In the more remote parts of the major rivers and along tributaries, villages may be separated by many kilometers. Population densities are very low in interfluvial areas and on parts of tributaries far from the larger rivers.

With few exceptions, residents of villages along major rivers are ribereños. Amerindian and ribereño communities are scattered along tributaries. Interfluvial zones are inhabited by Amerindians. The closer a community is to an urban center, the more likely the residents are to be ribereños.

Settlement patterns vary according to the land types used by farmers. A community with agricultural land only in floodplains is likely to be strung out along one side of a river. This spatial arrangement allows farmers to be near their fields. Such floodplain villages usually do not have centers; the port and the school may be several kilometers apart.

When a community has fields in alturas, houses are almost always located in upland areas and are often bunched together near the school and other community buildings. Agricultural methods make it impractical for farmers to construct houses near their fields, because shifting cultivation and agroforestry cycles require them to change their upland sites frequently. Villagers often have several dispersed plots in alturas. Farmers in some upland communities are also able to use restingas and barreales.

The houses in ribereño villages do not vary much. Roofs are thatched, and walls are made from wood or other forest materials. Ordinarily, tin roofs and concrete walls are found only on public buildings. Houses are raised above the ground on stilts for protection from mud, animals, and flooding, and the space under the house is used for storage. Most houses have one big room, two or three smaller rooms, and a separate kitchen. Many rooms are partially open on one side. Furniture consists of a few wooden chairs and tables. There is usually a hammock or two, but these are used for resting during the day rather than sleeping. Most people sleep on mats on the floor under large mosquito nets; some houses also have a bed used by an adult couple. Although there are many people per room, houses do not seem very crowded. Rooms are relatively large, and people spend most of their time outside or in the kitchen.

Despite the low population density of the rural Peruvian Amazon, riverine villages are not especially quiet during the day. Adults walk back and forth between their houses and fields and go to the river to fish, wash clothes, get water, and bathe. Children walk to school, visit their relatives, play with their friends, and work with their parents around the house and in the fields. The sounds of growling dogs and squawking chickens, turkeys, and ducks can be heard throughout a village. Because most houses are partially open, people inside can easily hear what is happening outside, and noise from within residences travels long distances.

A few statistics from the 1981 census serve to indicate the general standard of living in ribereño communities. No rural household contacted in the province of Maynas had running water, and only 1.9 percent had electric light. In the department of Loreto, 33 percent of rural households had a radio, compared with 66 percent of urban households and 55 percent of all Peruvian households.

Land Tenure

The complex land tenure system of the Peruvian Amazon can be confusing to both local people and outsiders. Certain ethnic groups in Peru, including Andean "campesinos" and Amazonian "Indians," are legally permitted to own land communally, but this right, granted by the military government that ruled from 1968 to 1980, has not been extended to ribereño villages. A few Amazonian communities once officially classified as mestizo have successfully sought recognition as Indian and have obtained land rights as a group, but most ribereño communities are unwilling or unable to adopt this strategy, because their residents do not consider themselves Indians and often feel superior to members of officially recognized indigenous groups.

The Ministry of Agriculture has the responsibility for assigning land rights to individuals in ribereño communities. There are two general types of land use permits in the Peruvian Amazon: titles and certificates. Titles give the possessor permanent rights to land and aboveground resources. The ministry ordinarily gives individual titles only to owners of commercial estates and group titles only to officially recognized native communities. Disputes frequently arise when the ministry gives an estate owner title to land used by the inhabitants of a ribereño village. The other type of permit, the certificate, gives campesinos temporary use rights to land.

Certificates were instituted as part of the agrarian reform program of the Velasco government of the late 1960s and early 1970s. (Ribereños previously had no officially recognized claims to land.) According to the law, holders of certificates can use their land for farming but not for collecting fruit or fishing. These restrictions are routinely ignored.

In restingas and alturas, certificates give possessors rights over land only while it is being used. This provision often leads to confusion and conflict in alturas, where farmers' agroforestry cycles rely on land that appears to outsiders to be fallow and unused. In barreales, certificates for up to ten hectares are given for one year, beginning in September and ending in August. Land tenure in these low-lying regions is complicated by the annual formation and disappearance of mud and sand bars because holders of a certificate for a barreal ordinarily maintain use rights only if their land does not change from one year to the next. Disputes often occur, however, within and between communities concerning rights to newly formed barreales. Individual farmers and communities that lose barreales often think that they should be given priority when allocations of new barreales are made.

To obtain a land use permit, a ribereño must go to the regional office of the Ministry of Agriculture with a *certificado de domicilio*. This document, which shows that a ribereño is a resident of a particular community, is signed by the *teniente gobernador*, the village political leader. The villager must also present a rough map of the land in question that has been signed by the teniente gobernador.

Some campesino organizations have challenged the right of the Ministry of Agriculture to assign land rights via titles and certificates. They cite a broadly phrased 1980 article of the Peruvian Constitution that gives Amazonian communities the right to the "democratic use of natural resources" (Pinedo-Vásquez 1986:6). Despite the campesinos' efforts, the ministry has retained complete control over the assignment of land titles and use rights.

The Ministry of Agriculture rarely interferes in villages' internal land allocation decisions. Disputes within communities over rights to restingas and alturas are unusual because these land types are not ordinarily scarce. Barreales—which are scarce, impermanent, and valuable—present special problems for community decision making. During the mid-1980s, many communities allocated barreales in two separate meetings. The first meeting took place before the rivers fell and barreales appeared. A preliminary division of barreales was made for the specific purpose of enabling certificates to be given to farmers applying for rice credit from the Agrarian Bank. Once the rivers fell and villagers knew where the barreales were, a second meeting was held to make a binding division. Documents outlining the two divisions were signed by all heads of household and sent to the Agrarian Bank and the Ministry of Agriculture (Pinedo-Vásquez 1986).

The allocation of barreales in the Santa Sofía area in November 1985 shows how ecology and local politics influence decision making about land tenure in the lowland Peruvian tropics. When the Amazon River receded in June, new barreales formed on an island near Santa Sofía. Although parts of the island were claimed by Santa Sofía and the nearby communities of Manatí and Capironal, the land was not legally divided among the villages. Furthermore, customary use patterns did not provide clear guidelines for the distribution of the newly formed barreales. The island was farmed in 1985 by campesinos from the three villages and employees of a commercial estate near Manatí. The campesinos freely admitted that they needed the Ministry of Agriculture's help in allocating the new land among the three communities. Residents of Santa Sofía, Manatí, and Capironal all wanted the commercial estate owner to be prohibited from using the new barreales but worried that this might not happen because of social ties between the estate owner and government bureaucrats.

Farmers in Santa Sofía hoped to gain access to about 20 hectares of new land. Prior to the formation of the barreales on the island, they had been using about 10 hectares of a mud bar in a different location. No one farmed more than two hectares of mud bars, and many people lacked access to any barreales at all. The older barreal, which was on higher land than the island, was unlikely to disappear. Nonetheless, it was regarded as agriculturally less desirable than the newly formed mud bars on the island. The older land was more likely to become sandy as the river changed course.

The official of the Ministry of Agriculture assigned to allocate the land on the island was well respected by the villagers. After consulting with the teniente gobernadores of Santa Sofía, Capironal, and Manatí, he quickly devised a land allocation plan satisfactory to all three communities. Village leaders were especially pleased that the estate owner was not given access to the new barreales. Santa Sofía's farmers received the 20 hectares on the island that they had requested, and the 30 hectares of barreales the community now had was sufficient for its agricultural needs.

I attended the meeting in which the community allocated the land. The process was not altogether straightforward. For one thing, people disagreed about whether farmers currently using land in the old barreal should be given rights in the new barreal. These decisions were eventually made on a case-by-case basis. Perhaps a more difficult problem concerned the allocation of plots among households. The suggestion was made that the new barreal be divided into 20 one-hectare plots, but more than 20 requests were made for land because in some households several people asked for plots. The problem was resolved by placing limits on the number of plots given out to certain households.

Village Economies

Ribereño household economies resemble those of many other peasant groups around the world. Villagers produce primarily for home consumption, but also sell some of what they grow and make at markets. Although agriculture is the most important source of food and income, ribereños also fish, work for wages, and hunt. The most important economic units are the household and the cooperative work group. Villagers sometimes hire a few wage laborers to help with agricultural tasks, but few can afford capital-intensive economic ventures.

There is a marked division of labor by gender within ribereño households. Producing and marketing agricultural products are the only major economic activities in which both men and women routinely participate. Women take part in all types of agricultural work except for the felling of large trees. Because women have the primary responsibility for cooking and caring for children, they spend less total time in the fields than men. Both men and women take crops to Iquitos for sale. Fishing is mostly men's work, and hunting is an exclusively male activity. Except for rice harvesting, women rarely do wage labor in rural areas, though they sometimes leave their villages for extended periods to work in Iquitos as domestic servants or market vendors.

Ribereño villages have little occupational specialization. With the exception of schoolteachers and their families, every household participates in agriculture and fishing. Some communities include a transportista, who earns money carrying passengers and cargo between villages and urban centers. This man ordinarily is also a farmer who uses some of his income from transport to hire laborers to work in his fields. Very few ribereños earn much money from storekeeping; most shops consist of a few basic provisions kept in the back room of a house.

Despite the absence of much occupational specialization, there is substantial household economic variability within ribereño communities. Households differ in crop mixes and in the use of family, cooperative, and hired agricultural labor. Some ribereños sell fish and fruit in Iquitos, some sell these products only locally, and some do not sell them at all. Some men work as wage laborers on commercial estates, others work as hired agricultural laborers for their village neighbors, and some never do wage work. Some rural Loretanos take out loans from the Agrarian Bank, some borrow from habilitadores, and some try not to borrow money from anybody.

These differences do not usually result in significant socioeconomic stratification. Some residents of ribereño villages have bigger houses and more material possessions than most of their neighbors and can afford to send their children to secondary school. They are more likely than poorer villagers to hire agricultural labor and to host cooperative work parties. But except for schoolteachers and some transportistas, the most prosperous residents of independent ribereño communities are usually considerably poorer than rural habilitadores, minor civil servants, and owners of tiny shops in Iquitos. Domestic servants, common among the upper and middle classes of Peru, are rarely found in ribereño villages. Hiraoka (1985a:214) conducted a detailed inventory of possessions in San Jorge, a ribereño village not far from Tamshiyacu and Tapirillo. The involvement of San Jorge in the market economy is typical of rural communities between 30 and 70 kilometers from Iquitos. In 1984, San Jorge had 249 inhabitants living in 34 households. Village residents owned 24 cast nets, 29 dugout canoes, 21 beds, 19 radios, 2 kerosene refrigerators, 10 sewing machines, 10 shotguns, 8 gill nets, 4 outboard motors, 3 kerosene lamps, 3 kerosene stoves, 18 mortars and pestles, 1 electric generator (an unusual item to find in a ribereño village) and 1 chain saw (also unusual). Although campesinos often own a set of dress clothes, they spend most of their days in very well worn garb. Men and boys wear shorts or trousers and T-shirts, and women and girls invariably wear dresses. Clothing quickly becomes dirty and sweat-soaked as people work in the hot and humid climate. Adults usually wear some sort of footwear, but children are ordinarily barefoot.

Most ribereño households spend little money on food over the course of a year. The staple foods of rural Loreto are manioc, plantains, and fish. These are eaten at two meals, one at mid-morning and the other late in the afternoon. Ribereños usually either grow manioc and plantains themselves or are given these foods by close relatives. Villagers frequently purchase small quantities of fish from their neighbors. A household that buys fish one day, however, may sell fish the next. The most common beverages are river water, *masato* (a mildly fermented pulpy drink made from manioc), and *refrescos,* sweet waters flavored with local fruits. Some men spend considerable amounts of money on aguardiente. Beer and soft drinks are too expensive to be consumed except on special occasions and are often unavailable in villages.

Rice and chickens are raised primarily for sale. Villagers are reluctant to eat much rice because of its good market price. Chickens are regarded as insurance, to be sold to cover unexpected or extraordinary expenses. They are eaten only at cooperative work parties, fiestas, and other festive or ceremonial occasions. Ribereños are less reluctant to eat eggs, but they are rarely part of ordinary meals.

Village Economic Differences

The relative importance of particular economic activities varies considerably among ribereño communities. The two most important influences on village economic patterns are the availability of types of land and the accessibility of markets. Communities with fields in floodplains are likely to devote large amounts of land to rice production. Forest products and hunting are usually of little economic importance in such communities, as residents must spend much of their time working their rice fields and may lack access to alturas. Villages without fields in restingas and barreales, however, often derive a significant part of their income from fruits and other forest products. Altura villages tend to have lower household incomes and to be poorer than those with land in floodplains. There are, however, some important exceptions. Some altura communities earn sizable incomes from fruits; others use their backwater lagoons to become commercial fishing centers.

The closer a community is to Iquitos (or, to a lesser extent, other urban centers), the more likely residents are to sell products at a market. Ribereños living near Iquitos have access to cheaper and more frequent transport and can sell perishable items more quickly than those living in more isolated areas. Villages on the Amazon within approximately a 100-kilometer radius of Iquitos are served by colectivos. Residents of more distant villages on the main rivers either take their products to market on more expensive and less convenient lanchas or sell to intermediaries. Farmers living on tributaries, who usually must sell to habilitadores and regatones, find cash cropping less profitable than their counterparts who live on major rivers.

Three other factors can influence the relative importance of the various economic activities in villages. First, access to good fishing spots, game, and particular forest resources varies from community to community. Second, some villages have had more success than others obtaining credit for rice and jute farming from the Agrarian Bank. Third, residents of certain communities can obtain seasonal wage work on commercial estates or timber operations.

A few ribereño communities are organized semifeudally in ways little different from those of the 1920s. In these, fundos are owned by a patrón who raises cattle, makes aguardiente from sugarcane, or extracts a forest product. Community residents must work as paid laborers for the patrón. In return, they are permitted to use some of the patrón's land for their own subsistence crops. Workers on a fundo may include temporary migrants from other villages. The patrón provides loans to both community residents and temporary workers in return for future labor. Such loans were formerly goods; nowadays they are almost always cash.

Owners of these commercial estates are not fundamentally different from the patrones of earlier times, but today the term *patrón* is often applied to other rural entrepreneurs as well. The current meaning encompasses any relatively wealthy rural or urban person who lends money to rural residents in return for future labor or crops. Many contemporary patrones live in rural towns or on estates adjoining independent ribereño villages. They may be involved in several enterprises. One noted patrón, Noé Ferry, operates a lancha that runs between Iquitos and Requena, and he also owns cattle and buffalo. Others manufacture aguardiente or contract for the delivery of forest products.

Much of this book is about the struggle between campesinos and patrones over access to natural resources. The rhetoric of the campesino unions and much of my analysis emphasizes the wealth, political power, and social connections of the patrones. It must be emphasized, however, that these comparisons are with the campesinos of Loreto. The standard of living of Noé Ferry, one of the more prosperous patrones, would not impress a member of even the middle class of Lima.

Geographical Mobility

Ribereños are not firmly rooted in their villages. They move around the Peruvian Amazon as they marry and pursue economic opportunities. Of 81 adult men interviewed in Porvenir, Santa Sofía, and Tapirillo in 1985–86, only 15 had always regarded one village as their home. (Some of the 15 had spent a year or two in the military.) Table 5.1 shows where the men interviewed had previously lived. Almost half of the 81 men had spent time in Iquitos, and a third had lived in villages near their current home. A smaller but still sizable number had lived in other parts of the Peruvian Amazon. While I do not have comparable data for women, they seem to have been equally mobile.

A significant number of ribereño households (10 of 82 surveyed) have homes in both a village and Iquitos. The city houses are usually in the poorest parts of Iquitos and may not differ much in construction from those in the villages. Some families with urban and rural residences regularly move back and forth. More often, some family members spend most of their time in the city, and others spend most of their time in the village.

Even villagers who have never lived in Iquitos know the city well. Iquitos is where they market crops, obtain bank loans, and buy consumer goods. Every ribereño has relatives in Iquitos. Although villagers make the typical complaints of rural people about the crime, noise, and crowds of the city, most enjoy the excitement and adventure of their visits. Adults in Porvenir, Santa Sofía, and Tapirillo ordinarily travel to Iquitos once or twice a month. The great majority (51 of 69 interviewed) stay with relatives; most of the rest spend nights in houses of their own or on a boat.

Although many ribereños find their spouses in nearby villages, ties between neighboring rural communities are weaker than rural-urban connections. Most ribereños have no economic reason to visit or trade with residents of other villages. Furthermore, people emigrating from a rural community are as likely to move to Iquitos as they are to go to another village. Residents of rural communities therefore know many people in Iquitos but only a few in most nearby villages.

Ribereños often encounter friends, relatives, and acquaintances from other rural communities on colectivos and in the markets and ports of Iquitos. Because Iquitos is the hub of the transport system, meetings of rural organizations and family gatherings involving people who live in

Table 5.1. Previous Residences of Adult Men in Porvenir, Santa Sofía, and Tapirillo[a]

	Porvenir (N = 28)		Santa Sofía (N = 23)		Tapirillo (N = 30)	
Previous Residence	Number	%	Number	%	Number	%
None	3	11	5	22	7	23
Iquitos	10	36	11	48	18	60
A nearby village	11	39	6	26	8	27
A nearby town	2	7	1	4	2	7
Department of San Martín	2	7	0	0	2	7
Along the Ucayali River	2	7	2	9	2	7
Along the Marañon River	1	4	1	4	5	17
On a tributary in Loreto	2	7	4	17	1	3
In another place	6	21	2	9	6	20

SOURCE: Survey in three villages in 1985–86 (see Appendix 1).
[a]Some men had more than one previous residence.

different places are most conveniently held in the city. Rural Loretanos from different communities also see one another in the countryside. Residents of communities with land only in alturas migrate temporarily to floodplain villages to work as paid laborers during rice harvests. Men from several villages may work together on commercial estates. Members of neighboring communities meet socially at fiestas and soccer games.

Quasi-ethnic Boundaries

The quasi-ethnic boundaries between locally born non-Amerindians and other groups are important social features of the tropical lowlands of Peru and other Amazonian countries. The self-identity of the residents of riverine villages near Iquitos involves a complicated mixture of descent, cultural features, class distinctions, occupational categories, and regionality. Nevertheless, anthropological theory concerning ethnicity is useful in understanding the ways in which ribereños distinguish themselves from other Peruvians.

Anthropologists disagree among themselves concerning the most appropriate definition of *ethnic group* (Barth 1969; Cohen 1978; Hawkins 1984; van den Berghe and Primov 1977). There is, however, general agreement that ethnic groups have members who identify themselves and are identified by others, as constituting a category distinguishable from other categories of the same order (Barth 1969:10–11). Ronald Cohen observes that these identities always have about them an "aura of descent" (1978: 387). Members of ethnic groups regard themselves as alike by virtue of their common ancestry, whether real or fictitious, and are so regarded by others (Shibutani and Kwan 1965:47). Cohen notes (1978:387) that once ethnic identities are acquired, by whatever process, they are passed down the generations for as long as the grouping has some viable significance to members and nonmembers. Although the criteria used to establish ethnic identity vary from place to place, they frequently involve language, religion, historical origin, and physical appearance. Ethnic identity can also be situational, with the same person categorized by others according to different criteria in different situations (Handelman 1977:192). Moreover, individuals may choose to invoke different ethnic identities in different circumstances. Ethnic identity is often "nested," whereby the terms individuals use to contrast themselves with outsiders vary in their specificity.

Ethnic groups are not immutable. Many anthropologists have described the formation, merging, and disappearance of particular groups (see Cohen 1978:397–98 for examples). Furthermore, the characteristics used by both insiders and outsiders to place people in a particular area into ethnic groups can change over time. Because ethnic definitions change, Fredrik Barth has influentially argued, the "critical focus" for those examining ethnicity in particular places should be the "ethnic *boundary* that defines the group, not the cultural stuff it encloses" (1969:15). This implies a careful investigation of the features local residents examine when classifying individuals into ethnic groups. Members of a particular ethnic group may not define themselves in the same ways as outsiders do. If there is substantial disagreement by both insiders and outsiders about the ethnic classification of many individuals, group boundaries are blurred.

One of the trickiest problems in delineating ethnic boundaries in large, complex societies is distinguishing ethnicity from class. Van den Berghe and Primov note that social scientists are especially likely "to subsume ethnicity under class or vice versa . . . when membership in one group overlaps greatly with membership in another, such as when the ruling class is overwhelmingly of one group and the peasantry of another" (1977:2–3). This, they claim, has sometimes led sociologists and anthropologists astray. For example, analysts of highland Peru have sometimes regarded the Indian/non-Indian distinction as primarily a class distinction. Van den Berghe and Primov assert, however, that in highland Peru and elsewhere class and ethnicity are "often antithetical modes of social organization" and that "unless the overlap in group membership is nearly complete, class identification tends to undermine ethnic loyalties, and vice versa" (1977:3).

Ribereños have some of the characteristics of ethnic groups. Members identify themselves, and are identified by others, as a distinct category of people. Group identity is passed on from generation to generation, and many members believe that they share common origins. Some of the defining features of ribereños, however, are either loosely related or totally unrelated to conventional notions of ethnicity. The term *ribereño* has strong class and occupational connotations, for example: even though some ribereños are middle-class rural entrepreneurs, the great majority are campesino farmers and fishers.

The anthropologist Anthony Stocks has argued that ethnic categories are important in the Peruvian Amazon. According to Stocks, lowland Amazonians cannot be simply divided into two groups, ribereños and Amerindians. He says that, instead, classifications of ethnic and quasi-ethnic groups in the Peruvian Amazon should include *cholos,* "detribalized, acculturated, but unassimilated Indians who have made a wide range of adjustments to Peruvian society" (1978:v). Stocks estimates that about 7 percent of the people of contemporary Loreto are cholos.

Stocks believes that linguistic features are not crucial to cholo identity, as many cholos are monolingual in Spanish or bilingual in Spanish and an Indian language. Ethnic boundaries result from a scarcity of marriages between cholos and other Peruvians. (The term *marriage* is used here to describe a long-term sexual and economic union between a man and a woman. Only a small proportion of such unions in the Peruvian Amazon are formal marriages recognized by the state.) This low proportion of outmarriage is caused by both prejudice among white-mestizos (a term Stocks often uses instead of *ribereños*) and the desire of cholos to maintain their ethnic integrity.

Stocks's research focused on Cocamilla living around the town of Lagunas on the lower Huallaga River. The customs of the Cocamilla differ in important ways from their ribereño neighbors. Cocamilla, unlike ribereños, participate in the Catholic fiesta cycle and prohibit marriage with persons bearing one's paternal surname. The Cocamilla's self-identity is neither Indian nor white-mestizo. Because the word *cholo* can be derogatory, many Cocamilla do not use it when talking about themselves. Instead, Cocamilla often say they are members of a particular community. This enables them to "bypass terminological distinctions based on class, ethnic group, and race" (Stocks 1978:287).

In the past, Cocamilla and ribereños occupied different economic niches. Many ribereños were estate owners or traders during the rubber boom, with Cocamilla being in a debt relationship to them as laborers. These occupational and status differences persisted for some years after the rubber boom. Because ribereños have been downwardly mobile during the past half-century, the economic activities of the two groups are becoming less distinct. Furthermore, many Cocamilla have attended school and have absorbed many elements of the larger national culture. The increasing economic and cultural similarity of the Cocamilla and their ribereño neighbors does not necessarily mean that ethnic boundaries will disappear. There is still little intermarriage between the groups. Cocamilla, moreover, can now gain legal advantages by distinguishing themselves from ribereños. Cocamilla communities that are able to gain official recognition as "native" can obtain certain land rights (such as communal title) unavailable to ribereños.

There is no distinct group of self-identified cholos in communities along rivers within 100 kilometers of Iquitos. The term *cholo* is occasionally used in the Iquitos area to describe rural and urban people with indigenous surnames, but it is considered extremely derogatory and is almost never used for self-description. Furthermore, *ribereño* is not the most frequent identifying term used. Occupational/class terms (e.g., *campesino, patrón*) and regional/local terms (e.g., Loretano, Santa Rosino) are much more common. Most rural residents self-identify occupationally as campesinos and regionally as Loretanos.

Superficially, Stocks's term *cholo* appears to describe many of the "quasi-ribereños" who lived on fundos and spoke both Spanish and Amerindian languages in the years immediately after the rubber boom. However, there is no evidence that such people formed an endogamous group similar to the cholos around Lagunas. Furthermore, accounts of the period do not mention a self-identified group differing from both Indians and ribereños.

Gow (1991) has conducted the most detailed examination of terms describing "kinds of people" in a mixed Peruvian Amazonian population, and the picture he presents is quite different from that of Stocks. Gow reports that the central distinction on the lower Urubamba is between "native people" and "white people." Native people can be further defined as Piro, Machiguenga, Amahuaca, and so forth. Some are "wild Indians" of the forest; others are members of officially recognized "native communities" that have schools and own land communally. There are in addition *moza gente,* who are from downriver places in Amazonia, such as the Lower Ucayali, the Amazon, and the Napo. These people (who presumably include most of the ribereños near Iquitos) are said to be mestizo and are not considered the same as "white people" (*gente blanca*). Gow writes:

> There is thus a continuum of kinds of people on the Bajo Urubamba, running from the "wild Indians" in the forest, through "native people," the *moza gente,* the "white people," to the "white foreigners." This continuum follows the spatial continuum from the center of the forest out of the forest and down-river towards the cities and outside of Amazonia. The continuum is also one of civilization, going from the source of civilization on the outside to its antithesis among the "wild Indians" of the forest. (1991:87–88)

Although Gow says that this continuum is of "immense importance" to the inhabitants of the lower Urubamba, he notes that it is extremely difficult to place specific individuals at a single point in it (1991:88). Individuals differ in their classification of particular people, and a person's identification changes from context to context.

A brief examination of the ancestry of two villagers in the Iquitos area shows some of the variability in the background of people classified as ribereños. César Flores Bardales of Tapirillo was in his mid-forties during the period of my research. His father came from Brazil to the Iquitos area as an infant in the 1920s, and his mother was born and raised in Iquitos. Her parents had migrated to the Amazon from the high jungle of eastern Peru. César therefore is descended from Spanish- and Portuguese-speaking settlers, and his self-identity is ribereño.

Amalia Gil Olemar was born in 1963 and has lived her entire life in Santa Sofía. The Gil surname is very common in Santa Sofía; about 30 percent of the current residents of the village have the paternal surname Gil, and another 5 percent have Gil as their maternal surname. (In the

Peruvian Amazon, as in other Spanish-speaking regions, people have two surnames. The paternal surname is the same as that of one's father; the maternal surname is the paternal surname of one's mother.) The first Gils came to Santa Sofía from Caballococha (near the Peru-Brazil-Colombia border) around the end of the rubber boom. Some of the Gil men had children with Yagua women. The offspring of Gil-Yagua unions ordinarily knew only a few Yagua words. They did not self-identify as Indians, and many came to regard Yaguas as backward and primitive. These men and women mostly married ribereños from outside the community. Amalia, a third-generation Santa Sofía Gil, is monolingual in Spanish. Despite a recent Amerindian background, Amalia is unequivocally identified by herself and others as a ribereño. She and César belong to the same quasi-ethnic group.

Community Sociopolitical Organization

Every village in Loreto has a teniente gobernador, who is responsible for internal land allocation and law enforcement and who represents the community in many of its dealings with the outside world. Teniente gobernadores are almost all middle-aged men, and they are usually somewhat more prosperous economically than most of their neighbors.

To choose a new teniente gobernador, a village selects three nominees for the position. A regional political official (*gobernador* or *subprefecto*) has the ultimate responsibility for choosing the teniente gobernador. The regional official almost always picks one of the village's nominees but does have the option of choosing someone else. The political affiliation of the nominees can influence this decision. The person who selects teniente gobernadores is always a member of the political party that runs the national government, though this party may not be the most popular one in Loreto. Once a teniente gobernador is selected, communities annually decide whether to keep the incumbent or select a new group of nominees. Some teniente gobernadores have served many years through various changes in regional and national governments.

Teniente gobernadores represent their villages in land disputes with patrones, commercial enterprises, and other communities. The diversity of these resource struggles is illustrated by some conflicts that occurred in 1985 and 1986. In one dispute, teniente gobernadores from Porvenir and neighboring communities were pursuing claims against a foreign-run "nature tourism" enterprise that forbade campesinos from hunting and fishing on its land. In another, the teniente gobernador of Porvenir was attempting to prohibit commercial fishing boats from entering the village's backwater lagoons. Finally, the teniente gobernador in Santa Sofía met several times with representatives of the Ministry of Agriculture to discuss land disputes with a nearby patrón.

The law enforcement duties of teniente gobernadores are usually not very onerous. Their most common tasks are breaking up fights after drinking parties and catching and punishing thieves from other communities. Drunken disputes and thefts most often occur when people from several different villages gather at events such as soccer games, dances, and meetings of campesino organizations. Several villagers serve as police to help the teniente gobernador resolve disputes. A few communities have small, rarely occupied jails.

Teniente gobernadores also supervise periodic communal work days. Some communities have a communal work day every week; others have one a month. Each household in a village must either send a representative or pay a small fine. Typical tasks are cleaning paths, clearing the schoolyard and soccer fields, constructing a community center, building a house for a teacher, and working a small plot of collectively farmed land. In many villages, communal work parties maintain the local cemetery. The land is too low for cemeteries in some floodplain communities, and the dead must be buried elsewhere.

Education

Today, almost all ribereño children finish primary school and learn how to read and write, but this has not always been the case. According to the Peruvian census of 1981, 27 percent of rural Loretanos 15 and older were illiterate. This figure compares to an illiteracy rate of 35 percent in 1972 and 46 percent in 1961 (Censo 1961, 1972, 1981). Men have been more likely to receive formal education than women. Only 18 percent of adult rural men could neither read nor write in 1981, whereas 39 percent of adult women were illiterate. Illiteracy is more common in the countryside than in Iquitos and the towns of Loreto. The 1981 census reported that in the adult urban population of Loreto only 3 percent of adult men and 10 percent of adult women are illiterate, though I suspect that these figures are either underestimates or else employ a very loose definition of literacy.

Every ribereño village has a primary school and one or more teachers. Two parents' groups are associated with the schools: the *padres de familia* for students' fathers, and the *madres de familia* for mothers. The Peruvian government has provided the money to construct concrete schoolhouses in most rural communities. Villages provide furniture and pay for some instructional materials, but parents must buy uniforms for their school-age children.

Primary school lasts five years. Because of the young age structure of ribereño communities, a large proportion of the residents of most villages are enrolled in school. In October 1985, 37 of the approximately 180 residents of Santa Sofía were attending the one-teacher primary school. At the same time, about 50 of the 200 or so inhabitants of Tapirillo were enrolled in that community's two-teacher school.

Rural teachers are rarely from the community in which they work. Some are from other rural areas, and many are from Iquitos. Most attended secondary school in Iquitos; the rest received their higher education in one of the towns of Loreto. Many teachers are men and women in their twenties who do not plan to spend the rest of their lives in the countryside. They may have second houses or families in Iquitos and may return to their city residences during their vacation (December, January, and February) and as often as possible at other times of the year. Teachers are the wealthiest residents of most ribereño communities. Young single teachers use some of their salary to hire people to prepare their food. Some older teachers with families are small-scale patrones, hiring others to work for them as paid agricultural laborers.

The expense of primary school is insignificant in comparison to the cost of secondary school. There are no secondary schools in ribereño villages. A rural student seeking higher education usually must move to Iquitos or a town. Although most such students live with relatives, their parents may be expected to help out with living expenses. The tuition at secondary schools, while not high by middle-class standards, is more than many campesinos can afford. Except for teachers, very few graduates of secondary schools return to rural areas. Of the 81 male heads of household interviewed in Porvenir, Santa Sofía, and Tapirillo, only 2 had attended secondary school.

Ribereño families sometimes move to urban areas to allow their children to attend secondary school. Families who do not make such moves may not be able to afford the cost of higher education. Although the overall wealth of a community influences how many of its children are able to go to secondary school, the proximity of a village to a secondary school is more important. In communities where students can commute daily to Iquitos, Requena, Indiana, or Tamshiyacu, a relatively high proportion of teenagers attend secondary school. But Porvenir, Santa Sofía, and Tapirillo are neither especially prosperous nor within commuting distance of a secondary school. Very few people from Porvenir and Santa Sofía go on to secondary school. In Tapirillo, where incomes are somewhat higher, perhaps 10 percent of primary school graduates continue their studies.

Religion

According to the 1981 census, 93 percent (72,364 of 77,935) of the rural residents of the province of Maynas were Catholic. Baptisms and celebrations of saint's days are eagerly awaited rituals. Ties of compadrazgo between the parents and godparents of a child establish long-lasting mutual obligations, and most villages have an *animador cristiano*, a lay Catholic leader.

Nevertheless, the influence of the Catholic church in rural communities is not as overwhelming as the census figures indicate. The Catholicism of many ribereños is quite nominal. Few villages have a separate building used as a church. Priests (mostly French-Canadian and Spanish) visit communities only occasionally, and masses are infrequent. Church-sanctioned marriages are expensive and not very common. Some marriages take place after a man and a woman have lived together for decades and have raised children to adulthood.

Most adherents of other religions, in contrast, are intensely committed to their faiths. Evangelical Protestants exert a greater influence on local life than their numbers would suggest. They shun alcohol, are usually hardworking, and can often be found among the leaders of campesino organizations. In some places an indigenous messianic Amazonian Christian religion called the Hermanos de la Cruz (Brothers of the Cross) has gained converts. Members of this group, which stresses the value of rural life, do not drink alcoholic beverages and condemn sex outside of marriage. The Hermanos de la Cruz have incorrectly predicted the end of the world on several occasions in recent years (Aguero 1985; Regan 1988). Finally, some rural and urban Loretanos have incorporated certain indigenous Amazonian religious beliefs into their medical practices (Dobkin de Rios 1972, 1984:173–89; Lamb 1985; Luna 1984a, 1984b). Many of these involve shamans (*curanderos*) guiding people through visions while using the hallucinogen *ayuahuasca* (*Banisteriopsis caapi*).

Medical Care

Every ribereño village has a community medical supply. The money for first-aid equipment and pills usually comes from sales from a communal field or donations from nongovernmental development organizations. Villages select a resident to be in charge of the communal medical supply, but the extent to which this person dispenses medical care varies. Pedro Tamani Moncada, who held this position in Porvenir in 1985–86, gave more advice than most. He had a copy of a well-known book for paramedics (Werner 1977) and was attempting to obtain some medical texts.

There are no doctors or nurses in rural communities. The only health facilities with professionally trained staff are in Iquitos or in mission complexes in towns such as Indiana and Tamshiyacu. Many campesinos think that medical personnel in these hospitals (especially in Iquitos) do not treat them as well as they do urban patients.

Unexpected hospital costs are the single biggest financial worry of many ribereño households. Most villagers cannot afford the cost of adequate medical treatment when they fall ill or have an accident. The economic effects of the inadequate health care that results became quite clear to me when I interviewed people in March and April 1986 about their use of credit from the Agrarian Bank. Farmer after farmer told me that they had to use this money for medical expenses and were unable to repay their loans. Other ribereños were unwilling to take out loans because they worried that health problems would prevent them from raising crops.

The credit histories of two households in Porvenir illustrate how health affects economic strategies. Pedro Tamani was a longtime borrower from the Agrarian Bank. In November 1985 his wife, Olinda Ahuanari, became very ill with a disease that may have been meningitis. Despite Pedro's interest in Western medicine, the family was unable to afford the cost of long-term treatment in a hospital in Iquitos. Olinda went instead to a curandero who lived in a village near Tamshiyacu. Pedro, unable to maintain the household alone, sent the family's four children to live with relatives and sought work in Iquitos. Although Olinda's physical health improved in January, she remained mentally disoriented and could not even recognize Pedro. She did not recover completely until late March 1986. Her illness was economically disastrous for the family. Pedro used much of his credit from the Agrarian Bank to pay for Olinda's medical care and his family's living expenses. Because Pedro left Porvenir for several months, his agricultural income dropped in 1985. He was unable to repay his loan and was prohibited from borrowing from the bank in 1986.

A similar case was that of Alfonso Amuño Bardales, who was the first campesino in Porvenir to obtain a government agricultural loan. When I talked to him about credit in April 1986, he did not know if he would ever again borrow money from the Bank. Alfonso had suffered some agricultural setbacks in previous years and was indebted to the bank. To get more government credit, he would have to pay his outstanding debts. In early March 1986 he fell out of a tree while collecting fruit, and even though Alfonso's injuries were not life threatening, they prevented him from farming. He spent much of his time lying desolately in a hammock. Alfonso thought that he would not be able to farm much in the next year and was not sure when he would be able to repay the bank.

Except for the poorly stocked community medicine chests, public health facilities in ribereño communities are virtually nonexistent. The scarcity of latrines in most villages is noteworthy. Santa Sofía and Tapirillo have no latrines; Porvenir—with a more concentrated settlement pattern—has a few, but they are not used much. Some ribereños died during the Peruvian cholera epidemic of the early 1990s.

The charts of global health organizations indicate that malaria occurs in Loreto. Nevertheless, medical personnel in Iquitos say that the disease rarely occurs in nearby villages, and I heard of no cases of malaria during my stay in the area. Malaria is prevalent in parts of the Brazilian Amazon, however, and may well recur in the Iquitos region.

Excessive drinking is a serious sociomedical problem in some villages. Although few women consume much alcohol, every village has a group of men who get together in one another's houses to drink aguardiente on Sundays and holidays. Many men also drink on their trips to Iquitos. Women complain that men spend too much of their income from crops in city bars. Although most men restrict their drinking to nonworking days, every village has a few men whose use of alcohol affects their farming and fishing. These are the only people recognized by most ribereños as having a drinking problem.

Soccer Clubs

Soccer is very popular in the Peruvian Amazon. In some communities, a daily game is held near dusk. Besides periodic informal games within communities, village teams play one another. Although women and girls sometimes play informally, team competition is ordinarily restricted to males. Villages often have several teams, representing boys, young men, and "veterans." The several teams within a village may be part of a soccer club that raises money to buy uniforms and balls.

Intervillage soccer matches can be elaborate events involving three or four communities. Because of the small size of riverine villages, a scaled-down form of soccer called *fulbito* is often played. Fulbito teams have six players per side and play on a smaller field than is used for soccer. Wagering may accompany games, and festive meals and dances take place after the games end. Battery-operated record or cassette players provide music (*cumbias* are very popular), and beer is brought into the host village from Iquitos.

Cooperative Work Parties

Ribereño households differ in their recruitment of agricultural labor. Some households rely exclusively on family laborers and occasional hired workers. Others frequently use extrafamily labor, which is paid for with food and drink. These agricultural work groups (*mingas*) usually consist of 10 to 20 laborers who spend a day or less on a task such as clearing land, weeding, or harvesting. The frequency and types of cooperative work parties found in a village profoundly affect community socioeconomic organization. Chapter 8 closely examines how ribereños recruit extrafamily labor, the social relations associated with different types of cooperative work parties, and the effects of changing economic conditions on the prevalence of mingas.

Campesino Unions

Local chapters of campesino unions play an important role in many ribereño villages. There are two types of unions: producer and multipurpose. The producer unions are legally recognized national organizations whose members grow particular crops. The most active and influential of these organizations in the Peruvian Amazon is the rice growers' group. Several multipurpose unions have operated around Iquitos since 1970. The unions engage in political action aimed at improving the general welfare of campesinos and disseminate information about health, agriculture, and education. The producer and multipurpose campesino organizations are described in detail in Chapter 11.

6. Porvenir, Santa Sofía, and Tapirillo

Miguel Pinedo and I closely examined the economic activities of residents of Porvenir, Santa Sofía, and Tapirillo. Our research in these small places was not intended to be a controlled comparison of several villages differing along a few key dimensions. The variability among ribereño communities is much too great to make that a reasonable objective. Our less ambitious goal was to investigate some of the ways in which ribereño communities differ, and in doing so we found that although Porvenir, Santa Sofía, and Tapirillo have a lot in common, they differ in thousands of details.

Three criteria influenced our choice of villages. Since agricultural credit was the major large-scale, state-sponsored development effort in the region, Miguel and I wanted to look at communities where a significant number of farmers took out loans for rice, jute, or other cash crops. I thought it would be interesting to compare cash cropping in villages that varied in their access to the marketplaces, banks, and buying centers of Iquitos. In addition, Miguel urged me to compare communities with different relationships to neighboring patrones.

We traveled to six potential research sites where Miguel knew people. Our first exploratory trip upriver from Iquitos included visits to Porvenir and Tapirillo. Miguel had stayed for extended periods in Porvenir on several occasions when the community was involved in land conflicts with patrones, and one of the residents of Tapirillo, an active union leader, was a good friend of his. Porvenir and Tapirillo contrasted well in several respects. Porvenir had only recently become an independent village, and a number of its residents borrowed money from and worked for owners of commercial estates. Tapirillo had been an independent community for a longer time, and its residents had fewer ties to patrones. Porvenir's farmers used alturas; Tapirillo's did not. Farmers in Tapirillo had access to much more land in barreales and restingas than did those in Porvenir. Tapirillo is closer to the markets of Iquitos than Porvenir.

After discussing and visiting several other villages, Miguel and I selected the community of Santa Sofía as a third research site. Santa Sofía is about 50 kilometers downriver from Iquitos. Miguel had known the long-time teniente gobernador of Santa Sofía for many years but had visited the village only once or twice. Santa Sofía, like Tapirillo, is a floodplain village whose residents lack access to alturas. Although Santa Sofía is about the same distance from Iquitos as Tapirillo, colectivo service is less frequent. Residents of Santa Sofía have much less contact with patrones than residents of Porvenir and Tapirillo. Santa Sofía is the only one of the three communities where farmers have borrowed money from the Agrarian Bank to raise jute.

Table 6.1 summarizes some of the ways in which Porvenir, Santa Sofía, and Tapirillo differ. While the villages exhibit some of the economic variability found in ribereño communities, they also resemble one another in important ways. All three villages have worked closely with the regional campesino organizations. Farmers in each of the villages have access to barreales and restingas. Finally, all are nearer Iquitos than the majority of rural communities in Loreto. Their residents market their products more easily and rely less on intermediaries than inhabitants of communities farther from the city.

The three villages' involvement in the cash economy in the mid-1980s was fairly typical for communities near Iquitos. The incidence of borrowing from the Agrarian Bank and of ownership of consumer items such as radios and boat motors was about average for the area. Approximately half of the households in Porvenir, Santa Sofía, and Tapirillo raised rice, the region's most important cash crop. In Porvenir and Tapirillo, between a third and half of the households included someone who did wage labor outside of the community in 1985, while in Santa Sofía almost no one did this kind of work.

Village Histories

There are few written materials concerning the history of most ribereño villages. The published histories of the Peruvian Amazon (d'Ans 1982; Regan 1983; San Román 1975) rarely refer to particular ribereño communities. The names of villages given in occasional references in these

Table 6.1. Characteristics of Porvenir, Santa Sofía, and Tapirillo

	Porvenir	Santa Sofía	Tapirillo
Location on the Amazon[a]	70 km upriver from Iquitos	50 km downriver from Iquitos	50 km upriver from Iquitos
Establishment as independent community	1981	1972	about 1955
Population in 1985–86[b]	260	180	200
Number of households in 1985–86	37	25	34
Agricultural land types	altura restinga barreal playa	restinga barreal playa	restinga barreal playa
Most important cash crops[c]	rice plantains	plantains rice corn	rice manioc plantains corn
Other important income sources[c]	pigs fowl fishing wage labor	fowl fishing	fowl fishing wage labor

[a]Distances are straight-line distances.
[b]The figures given for populations are close approximations (see Appendix 1).
[c]Listed in approximate order of importance in mid-1980s.

books, moreover, can be confusing because communities have moved, fissioned, and consolidated in response to the breakup of commercial estates and changes in the paths and levels of rivers. Travelers' accounts (e.g., Herndon 1952 [1854]; Marcoy 1875; Raimondi 1929 [ca. 1874], 1942 [1862]) sometimes provide interesting details about particular places, but are usually based on very short visits and are not altogether reliable.

Although the village histories presented here make use of available written materials, they are primarily based on interviews, which present only a partial view of the past. Since no one interviewed was older than 70 in 1985–86, villagers' direct knowledge of previous events started around 1925. Their statements about earlier times, usually given quite hesitantly, relied on hazy memories of stories told by their parents and grandparents. People often disagreed about exactly when particular events occurred and the precise relationships among the various owners and operators of commercial estates. The histories that follow are therefore sketchier than I would like at certain points.

Porvenir

The present-day community of Porvenir is located near the final site of San Joaquín de Omaguas, the principal mission and commercial center of the Jesuits in the region. The mission was located near Porvenir between 1726 and 1767, and several indigenous groups lived at the mission site during and after the Jesuit period. Even though the population of Omaguas was only about 250 in the early nineteenth century, the village was one of the largest in the Peruvian Amazon. The ethnic self-identity of the people of Omaguas at this time is difficult to ascertain. They were Christianized Indians, but whether most considered themselves Cocamas, Omaguas, or members of other groups is not clear. During the second half of the nineteenth century, Omaguas was eclipsed in importance first by Nauta and later by Iquitos. Most residents probably identified themselves as Cocamas.

During the rubber boom, the riverine area around Omaguas was divided into commercial estates. Rubber was brought into the fundos and then transported down the Amazon to Iquitos. There was a fundo along the Amazon in 1904 called Porvenir (Fuentes 1908:81), but I have been unable to determine whether this was on the site of the present community. Contemporary residents' accounts of Porvenir begin around 1910, when Pablo Solsol, a colonist from the Peruvian highlands who was involved in the rubber trade, married the daughter of the owner of the local estate. After the rubber boom ended, the fundo began producing aguardiente, raising cattle, and cutting timber. Solsol maintained control of the estate until his death around 1930.

Various sawmills, stills, and sugar mills have opened, moved, and closed in Porvenir over the years. The ownership of mills and stills has not always coincided with the ownership of land and cattle. When patrones died or left the area, their property was divided among their children and in-laws or was sold or rented to outsiders. The current inhabitants of Porvenir have not kept track of all the owners and renters and their exact period of residence in the community. They agree, however, that the most important patrones have been members of the interrelated Solsol, del Cuadro, and Montoya families.

During the period of Pablo Solsol's ownership, the fundo ceased to operate for about a decade. The peons on the estate became angry at Solsol when he tried to prohibit them from farming independently and allowed his cattle to destroy their fields. They moved to Miraflores, an island in the Amazon River, but when their fields there were destroyed by floods, they were forced to abandon the island and move back to Porvenir. Solsol, who had left Porvenir, returned to the fundo.

In the early 1930s, Juan del Cuadro bought the estate's land from Solsol's widow. One current resident says that del Cuadro was married to a daughter of Solsol, but others are unsure about this. Some of del Cuadro's land was eventually sold to a man named López. This land, which had been the site of the Omaguas mission, is now the community of San Salvador de Omaguas. The remainder of del Cuadro's land is now divided between two different communities. Porvenir has two parts: the Primera Zona and the Segunda Zona. The village called Porvenir in this book is legally Porvenir Segunda Zona. The neighboring community of Esperanza is officially Porvenir Primera Zona.

The management of the Segunda Zona came into the hands of Nestor Montoya around 1940. He ran this part of the estate until his death around 1970. Nestor Montoya was one of the people who had migrated to Miraflores and later returned to Porvenir. He married a daughter of Juan del Cuadro and gained control of the estate's still. Montoya later managed other parts of the fundo as well.

When Juan del Cuadro died around 1960, the portion of land now called Primera Zona or Esperanza was inherited by a relative (perhaps a nephew or grandson) named Orlando del Cuadro. In 1985–86 he was operating the 360 hectares of Esperanza as a commercial estate that raised cattle and water buffalo and made aguardiente. He was the teniente gobernador of the community. Every adult male resident of Esperanza worked for Orlando some of the time. A fence, which prevented cattle and buffalo from leaving the fundo, separated Esperanza and Porvenir.

For about a decade after Nestor Montoya died, the various enterprises of Porvenir Segunda Zona were managed by a series of renters. Fernando Montoya, one of Nestor's sons, took over the operation of the fundo in 1978, but land use conflicts soon arose with the residents of Porvenir. These disputes can be attributed partly to Fernando's prickly personality, as most people in the area agree that he is more difficult to work with than Orlando. The struggles over land in Porvenir during this period were also related to the Peruvian Agrarian Reform of the 1970s. Campesinos in the Peruvian highlands had been given land that had been part of commercial estates (called haciendas in the sierra). Even though similar land redistributions were not compulsory in the selva, ribereños involved in disputes with owners of commercial estates hoped that the state would be on their side. Porvenir's residents disliked their poorly paid compulsory labor on Fernando Montoya's fundo and wanted to establish their own independent community.

The most important conflict at Porvenir occurred after some pigs owned by local residents destroyed a pasture used by Fernando Montoya's cattle. When men hired by Fernando killed some of the pigs and burned four residents' houses, the people of Porvenir sought help from the campesino unions. After numerous confrontations and negotiations, residents of Porvenir Segunda Zona obtained 150 hectares from Fernando in 1981. Fernando retained 450 hectares for his various enterprises.

Porvenir Segunda Zona consists of both Fernando's property and the land ceded to the campesinos. Only three families lived on Fernando's land in 1985–86 and worked more or less full-time for him. A number of people living on the land given to the campesinos, however, worked part-time in Fernando's still.

Santa Sofía

In the late nineteenth century, the territory around present-day Santa Sofía was occupied mostly by Yaguas, but mestizo families from various parts of Peru began entering the area around 1900. The largest single group of migrants was from Caballococha, though other families emigrated from Contamana along the Ucayali River and Cajamarca in the department of San Martín.

The fundos that were established at Santa Sofía were not very involved in the rubber boom. The Fernández, Braga, and Vela families controlled the area in the early 1900s. These minor patrones recruited workers to extract timber (especially mahogany), hunt, and fish. Buenaventura Guerrero bought the fundo from the Velas in 1922, and the Guerrero family maintained legal title to the area for almost fifty years. The family's holdings included the present-day adjoining communities of Santa Sofía and Puerto Rico and the nearby island of Manatí.

Many of the mestizos who migrated to Santa Sofía originally planned to work at extracting gums such as leche caspi and balata. Some may have done this for short periods, but most ended up doing independent agriculture and working on the fundo's enterprises. The fundo employed both Yaguas and mestizos. During the first part of the century the two groups performed different types of work on the estate. The Yaguas hunted in nearby alturas and made fishing nets from *chambira* (*Astrocaryum chambira*). The mestizos specialized in extracting the vegetable ivory called tagua. Both the Yaguas and the mestizos engaged in subsistence agriculture and fishing.

The mestizos and the Yaguas intermixed, and over time ribereñoization occurred. Santa Sofía became more mestizo in 1954, when representatives of tourist enterprises made contact with some of the remaining self-identified Yaguas in the area. These enterprises take tourists to jungle camps where they can see Amazonian flora and fauna under comfortable conditions. Many camps have shows in which "natives" wearing allegedly local costumes sing and dance. Some Yaguas from the Santa Sofía area were persuaded to perform in these spectacles and ended up leaving their communities.

Probably because their fundo was not very profitable, the Guerrero family exercised less and less control over the inhabitants of the area as the years passed. By the 1960s, nobody paid rent and few if any local people worked on the owner's enterprises. In 1970, residents of the moribund fundo asked the Ministry of Agriculture for help in gaining ownership of the land. The Guerrero family offered little resistance. When the community of Santa Sofía was created in 1972, 22 campesinos were given the equivalent of current temporary-use certificates.

The Guerrero family was left with two parcels of land, which were quickly sold to individuals. Not long afterward, however, the Ministry of Agriculture gave both parcels to the campesinos living on them. These parcels became the communities of Puerto Rico and Manatí. People from Puerto Rico are more likely to acknowledge Yagua ancestry than their counterparts in Santa Sofía and Manatí. The residents of Puerto Rico also have closer ties with people living in Catalán, a nearby government-recognized Yagua community.

Tapirillo

Many mestizos from Caballococha and the department of San Martín settled in the vicinity of present-day Tapirillo around 1900. The settlers were part of the rubber boom and mixed with Christianized Indians (mostly Cocamas), creating a ribereño population. After the rubber industry collapsed, the inhabitants of the area worked on three fundos. These commercial estates extracted tagua and timber, raised cattle, and cultivated fruit orchards.

Present-day Tapirillo was part of the community of Tapira Chica between 1912 and 1942. The owners of the various fundos at Tapira Chica controlled access to land and could demand rent and labor from local inhabitants, though the poorer inhabitants of the area were apparently not forced to work as much on the estates as their upriver neighbors in Porvenir. Older residents of Tapirillo recall spending several days a month working on a fundo in the 1940s.

The fundo owners in Tapira Chica had frequent disputes among themselves concerning rights to land, other property, and labor. Each patrón attempted to marshal support from the public officials and merchants of Iquitos. After one dispute was resolved in 1942, the political entity of Tapirillo was established with its own school. Tapira Chica continued to exist as a separate community.

During the 1930s and 1940s, local ribereños sold many of their products to warehouses owned by the Morey family, who operated one of the fundos at Tapira Chica. These warehouses handled almost all the tagua extracted in the area and also sold firewood to the steamboats that plied the river. There were no severe floods during these years, and the various fundos were able to raise native fruits, oranges, and cattle. However, after a severe flood destroyed pastures and fruit orchards in 1952 and the price of tagua dropped, the commercial estates closed. The last fundo shut down around 1960.

The movements of the Amazon River have influenced settlement patterns and political demarcations around Tapirillo. First, the 1952 flood destroyed much of the nearby community of Libertad, and many of its residents moved to Tapirillo. Next, gradual changes in the course of the Amazon during the next decade forced many families in Tapirillo to relocate their houses, which left some of them inconveniently located with respect to the community school. As a result, a section of Tapirillo far from the school joined part of Tapira Chica to form the new community of Mangua. Tapirillo lost still more people when an upriver section seceded in 1980. Finally, changes in the course of the river once again caused some residents to move their houses far away from Tapirillo's school, and the new village of Ocho de Mayo was established with its own school.

Residents of Tapirillo have been able to take their crops to market in Iquitos for many years. During the 1930s and 1940s several people row-ing a boat could make the downriver trip to the city in about eight hours, though villagers returning upriver had to obtain passage on a steamship or other motorized boat. Selling crops in Iquitos became much easier with the introduction of regular motorized colectivo service in the 1950s and 1960s.

Many residents of Tapirillo raised cattle and fruit between 1952 and 1970. During this period villagers also increased their sales of plantains and fariña. Severe floods along the Amazon have become more common since the 1970s. Some ecologists (e.g., Gentry and López-Parodi 1980) attribute these floods to increasing deforestation in the high jungle. Whatever their cause, floods in Tapirillo have destroyed the village's pastures and have led to decreasing sales of plantains and fruit. Rice grown in barreales has become a more important source of income in the past several decades, and villagers continue to sell substantial amounts of fariña.

Demography

Figure 6.1 shows the age-sex composition of households surveyed in Porvenir, Santa Sofía, and Tapirillo in early 1986 (see Appendix 1 for a discussion of the sample). The low median age in the villages (about 14) is the result of high birth rates and extensive outmigration to towns and cities by teenagers and young adults. The rate of outmigration appears to be about the same for males and females. Both young men and young women move to Iquitos to seek work and attend secondary school.

Household Size and Composition

In many parts of the world, households cannot be clearly delineated, because units of production and consumption may not coincide with one another (Netting et al. 1984; Wilk 1989). Some resources may be shared among people in two or more dwellings, while other resources may not be shared within a dwelling. In the ribereño communities of the Peruvian Amazon, a researcher who assumes that residents of a particular dwelling constitute one and only one independent household can sometimes get a misleading impression of economic relations. Such an assumption is especially problematic for dwellings inhabited by more than two adults. Nonetheless, the residents of most dwellings in riverine villages can be regarded as members of more-or-less discrete households, which are usu-

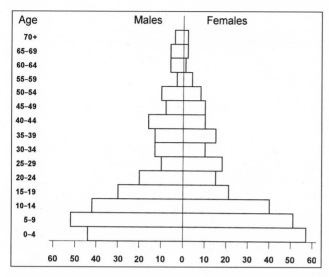

Figure 6.1. The number of males and females of various ages in Porvenir, Santa Sofía, and Tapirillo, March 1986

ally units of both production and consumption. Residents eat together, share possessions, and pool the results of their labor. Most dwelling units are economically self-sufficient. They include an adult male and an adult female, produce most of what is consumed, and receive only occasional monetary infusions from relatives living elsewhere. In the discussion that follows, I assume that the residents of a dwelling constitute a household.

The mean household size in 20 riverine communities that were part of a careful census in the early 1970s ranged from 5.6 to 10.8. Most communities had a mean household size between 6 and 8 (San Román et al. n.d.:120). The mean household size among those included in our 1986 census was 7.1 in Porvenir, 7.3 in Santa Sofía, and 5.6 in Tapirillo.

In the following discussion of household composition and domestic cycles in the three villages, adults are defined as anyone over 18. A "couple" is a man and a woman living in the same dwelling with a sexual and economic relationship. Members of a couple may be under 18. I refer to members of couples as husbands and wives married to one another.

Table 6.2 provides information about the relationships among people living in 82 households surveyed in Porvenir, Santa Sofía, and Tapirillo.

Table 6.2. Number of Households of Various Types in Porvenir,
Santa Sofía, and Tapirillo

Household Type[a]	Porvenir (N = 28)		Santa Sofía (N = 23)		Tapirillo (N = 31)	
	Number	%[b]	Number	%	Number	%
I	14	50	12	52	20	65
IIa	4	14	4	17	3	10
IIb	1	4	0	0	4	13
IIc	3	11	2	9	1	3
III	5	18	5	22	1	3
IV	1	4	0	0	2	6

[a]With men and women 18 and older defined as adults, households are classified as follows:

Type I: Households with a couple but no other adults.

Type II: Households with three or more adults, including one couple.

Type IIa: Type II households in which the only adults are a husband and wife and sons and daughters of one or both members of the couple.

Type IIb: Type II households in which the only adults are a couple and a parent of either the husband or wife.

Type IIc: Type II households other than those included in Types IIa and IIb.

Type III: Households that include two or more couples.

Type IV: Households with no couple.

[b]Percentages may not add up to 100 because of rounding.

These households, which included 541 people, can be divided into four general types:

Type I: Households with one couple but no other adults. There were 46 such "nuclear" households, all but 3 of which included children under 18. The children were almost always the sons or daughters of one or both members of the couple. Type I households included 256 people; their mean size was 5.6.

Type II: Households with three or more adults, including one couple. The 22 households of this type included 166 people. Eleven were not very different from Type I households. In Type IIa households the only adults were a husband and wife and sons or daughters of one or both members of the couple, though the children in such households sometimes included the offspring of nonresident adult sons and daughters. These households included 85 people, and their mean size was 7.7. In five households (Type IIb), the only adults were a couple and a parent of either the husband or the wife. Children lived in four of these households. The mean size of such households was 5.4, and they included 27 people. Although the other six Type II households varied in composition, they all included children. Two included a sibling of the husband, two an adult friend of the couple, and one a daughter-in-law of the couple. The remaining unusual household consisted of a man, his two wives (sisters), and eight children. There were 54 people living in the Type IIc households, and their mean size was 9.0.

Type III: Households that included two or more couples. The 11 households of this type all included children. Ten of these households had two couples, and the eleventh had three. Two households included additional adults not part of a couple. Children from more than one couple lived in a number of these households. Four Type III households included children who were not the offspring of any of the adult residents. There were 108 people living in Type III households, and their mean size was 9.8.

The couples in these households were related to each other in diverse ways:

1. An older couple, their son, and his wife (four cases).

2. An older couple, the wife's son, and his wife (one case).

3. An older couple, the husband's son, and his wife (one case).

4. An older couple, the wife's daughter, and her husband (one case).

5. An older couple, their son and his wife, and their daughter and her husband (one case).

6. A half-brother and sister and their spouses (one case).

7. Two sisters and their husbands (one case).

8. A couple, the wife's uncle, and his wife (one case). The older couple moved out and established a separate household soon after the census was completed.

Type IV: Households with no couple. There were only three households of this type. One was a recent widower, his two adult sons (aged 19 and 23), and four younger children. Another was a 50-year-old woman and two grandsons (aged 6 and 11). The remaining Type IV household was a 75-year-old man living alone. These three households had 11 people, and their mean size was 3.7.

Table 6.2 suggests that the low average household size in Tapirillo in 1986 reflects the distribution of household types in that village. The three household types with the lowest mean size are I, IIb, and IV. Tapirillo had a higher proportion of Type I households than Porvenir and Santa Sofía. Four of the five Type IIb households and two of the three Type IV households were in Tapirillo.

Domestic Cycles

By the time a woman is 18 or 19, she is usually part of a couple, whereas most men delay marriage until they are in their twenties. Thus, men are usually older than their wives. Of 82 couples surveyed (most but not all first marriages), the husband was older in 65 cases, the wife was older in 12 cases, and the spouses were the same age in the remaining 5 cases. The mean age of husbands was 5.7 years older than the mean age of their wives. Many spouses meet while visiting relatives and friends; others meet in dances and fiestas. Couples often meet while a young man is serving in the military.

Women begin having children soon after they are married and often continue to give birth throughout their twenties and thirties (Censo 1972:511–12). Newly established couples sometimes live with the parents of one of the spouses. By the time their first child is born, most have established a separate household. Some, however, remain in two-couple households for many years.

Newly established households grow quickly as children are born. Over the years, various adult relatives without spouses (single, widowed, or "divorced") may move in with a couple. These relatives, who include parents, siblings, and half-siblings, may bring some or all of their children with them. Most households stop growing about twenty or twenty-five years after being established as children begin leaving for work in Iquitos, secondary education, marriage, or military service. Parents die, and adult siblings marry and move out. Households gradually become smaller and may eventually consist of only the original couple. When one member of the couple dies, the survivor is likely to move in with an adult son or daughter. The survivor's dwelling may be occupied by other relatives or abandoned.

Marriage Patterns

Because I did not collect information on where members of couples were living when they married, I do not know the exact rate of village endogamy in Porvenir, Santa Sofía, and Tapirillo. Information collected about the birthplace of spouses in 66 marriages suggests that between a fifth and a third of villagers marry within their community. In 13 of these marriages, both spouses were born in the village where they lived. In another 31 marriages, one spouse was living in his or her natal village, and the other spouse was born elsewhere. In some of these cases, the spouse born elsewhere had moved to the community prior to marriage. These figures show that in most marriages, one or both members of a couple have strong ties to the village in which they live.

Husbands and wives are equally likely to move away from their community after marriage. There were 16 couples in which the husband was living in his birthplace and the wife was from elsewhere, and 15 in which the wife was living in her birthplace and the husband was from elsewhere. Furthermore, husbands and wives were about equally likely to have been born in the immediate area. Of the 66 couples, 47 husbands and 44 wives were born either in the community where they lived or a nearby village.

Ribereños usually deny that significant social status or economic differences exist within their group. Nonetheless, people in the three villages with European surnames tended to marry others with European surnames (mostly Spanish) and people with Amerindian surnames (mostly Cocama, Quichua, and Lamista) tend to marry others with Amerindian surnames. Cabrera, Lozano, Paredes, and Perez are examples of European surnames, and Ahuanari, Capinoa, Manuyama, Tapullima, and Tangoa are examples of Amerindian surnames.

Amerindian surnames have been adopted, of course, since the European conquest. These surnames have varied origins (Gow 1991:65–66, 255–56). Some are names of indigenous groups; others were arbitrarily given by patrones to people living on their fundos. In addition, unions between rubber-boom workers and local women brought Amerindian names from other parts of Peru into the Iquitos region.

I examined the maternal and paternal surnames of adults in the three villages. Tables 6.3, 6.4, and 6.5 demonstrate the considerable surname endogamy in the area. People in the three villages tended to have either two European surnames or two Amerindian surnames (Table 6.3). The "ethnic types" (European or Amerindian) of men's paternal surnames

Table 6.3. Ethnic Origins of Surnames of Men and Women 21 and Older in the Three Villages

	Maternal Surname		
Paternal Surname	European	Amerindian	
			Total
European	41	28	69
Amerindian	11	34	45
Total	52	62	114

Yule's Q (gamma) = +.64
Chi-square = 13.4, significant at .001 level

Table 6.4. Ethnic Origins of Paternal Surnames of Husbands and Wives in the Three Villages

	Wife's Surname		
Husband's Surname	European	Amerindian	
			Total
European	28	9	37
Amerindian	4	17	21
Total	32	26	58

Yule's Q (gamma) = +.86
Chi-square = 17.4, significant at .001 level

Table 6.5. Ethnic Origins of Maternal Surnames of Husbands and Wives in the Three Villages

Husband's Surname	Wife's Surname		
	European	Amerindian	
			Total
European	15	10	25
Amerindian	8	14	22
Total	23	24	47

Yule's Q (gamma) = +.45
Chi-square = 2.7, not significant at .05 level

tended to match those of their wives (Table 6.4). There is also a weak association between the ethnic type of men's maternal surnames and those of their wives (Table 6.5).

Surname endogamy cannot be attributed primarily to ethnic social stratification, because in the Iquitos area there are geographical concentrations of surnames of particular ethnic types. European names predominate in some areas, and Amerindian surnames in others. For example, only 22 percent of the paternal surnames examined in Porvenir are European, compared to 79 percent in Santa Sofía and 75 percent in Tapirillo. Since most people in the three villages marry neighbors, their offspring tend to have two European or two Amerindian surnames (see Chibnik 1991 for details). Ribereños' surnames, moreover, do not always reflect their ethnic background. Although Amerindian surnames indicate at least some indigenous ancestry, Spanish surnames may not indicate a European background. In the area around Santa Sofía, many people of Yagua descent have adopted Spanish surnames over the past century, and in Tapirillo, a small number of people born with Amerindian surnames have changed them to Spanish surnames.

In order to examine whether surname endogamy was disappearing, I compared the paternal and maternal surnames of people aged 40 and older with those of people under 40. The degree of surname endogamy was about 70 percent in both groups, suggesting that the tendency for people to marry others with surnames of the same ethnic type persists.

The husband is European-surnamed in the majority of "mixed-surname marriages" examined (that is, those in which the parents of interviewees had surnames of different ethnic types). Table 6.3 provides information about paternal surnames of spouses in past mixed-surname marriages. There were 28 adults with a European paternal surname and an Amerindian maternal surname, while only 11 adults had an Amerindian paternal surname and a European maternal surname. Tables 6.4 and 6.5 provide information about contemporary mixed-surname marriages. Table 6.4 shows that in 13 cases husbands' and wives' paternal surnames are of different ethnic types. The husband has a European paternal surname in 9 cases. Table 6.5 shows that there are 18 cases where husbands' and wives' maternal surnames are of different ethnic types. The husband has a European paternal surname in 10 cases.

Even though surnames do not always indicate ethnic origin, the existence of some surname endogamy in Porvenir and Tapirillo may indicate minor stratification according to ethnic background in the area. The relatively high proportion of people with European paternal surnames and Amerindian maternal surnames (Table 6.3) may be a remnant of rubber-boom days, in which European-surnamed males often entered into sexual unions with several different Amerindian-surnamed local women. Such sexual unions continued for several decades after the rubber trade ended, when European-surnamed men owned fundos in the region. The children of these unions have European paternal surnames and Amerindian maternal surnames. It is not clear why men in the three villages are more likely than women to have European surnames in contemporary mixed-surname marriages. Perhaps men have been more likely than women to change their Amerindian surname to a Spanish surname.

7. Food and Income Sources

The residents of Porvenir, Santa Sofía, and Tapirillo obtain most of their food and income from agriculture. Farmers have fields in alturas, restingas, barreales, and playas, and agricultural practices and crop choices differ greatly among these diverse land types. Fallow periods are long in alturas, short in high restingas, rare in low restingas, and inconceivable in barreales and playas. Planting and harvesting are carried out year-round in alturas, but the timing of these tasks in barreales and to a lesser extent restingas depends on the seasonal rise and fall of the water level. Crops with long growing seasons can be raised only in alturas and high restingas, while crops requiring fertile soils are best raised in low restingas, barreales, and playas.

Alturas

In alturas, ribereños use slash-and-burn agricultural methods that resemble those of many other farmers in the humid tropics (for detailed discussions of ribereño agricultural practices, see de Jong 1992; Denevan and Padoch 1988; Hiraoka 1985a, 1986, 1989, 1992; and Padoch and de Jong 1987, 1989, 1990). Because there is ample rainfall in every month, upland farming in the Peruvian Amazon is not necessarily seasonal. However, many farmers prefer not to clear land in March, April, and May, when rains can be especially heavy. After an upland field is cleared and burned, annual crops such as rice, corn, manioc (*yuca*), and plantains are planted. Rice and corn are usually grown only once after a field is cleared, but plantains and manioc may be planted and harvested two or three times in succession. In many ribereño communities, perennial crops are planted in alturas. Agroforestry cycles have been carefully described for the town of Tamshiyacu (Hiraoka 1986; Padoch and de Jong 1987; Padoch et al. 1985). Fields there are dominated by pineapples and *uvilla* (*Pouruma cecropiifolia*) in the second through fourth years after clearing. In subsequent years, land is principally devoted to tree crops such as peach palm (*pijuayo, Bactris gasipaes*), *umarí* (*Poraqueiba sericea*), and Brazil nuts. Commercial agroforestry was the largest single source of income in Tamshiyacu in the mid-1980s (Padoch and de Jong 1987:186).

Most Amazonian communities with access to alturas place considerably less emphasis on commercial agroforestry than Tamshiyacu. The situation in Santa Rosa is more typical. In many swiddens, cropping and maintenance cease after two or three years of intensive annual crop production. These fields are then fallowed, often for five to six years, and used again. However, most farmers choose to turn at least one or two of their swidden fields into agroforestry plots (Padoch and de Jong 1987:188). In Porvenir, agroforestry is less important than in Santa Rosa. Alturas are used primarily for growing rice, corn, manioc, and plantains.

Restingas

In many years, only the very lowest parts of restingas are covered with water when the river is at its highest point. In other years, all but the highest parts are flooded. Thus the possibility of floods strongly influences ribereño agricultural practices. Farmers try to plant as long before the river is expected to rise as possible. Crops with long growing seasons, such as plantains, tend to be planted on the higher parts of restingas. In order to prevent floods from destroying all of their manioc fields, farmers sometimes have plots in higher, less fertile, parts of a restinga as well as in lower, more fertile areas.

The high soil fertility of low restingas induces many farmers to plant crops with short growing seasons there. Crops that mature in three or four months, such as rice and most vegetables, can be grown in low restingas with little risk of flood damage. Agriculture can be quite intensive in low restingas. Many farmers allow the fields to lie fallow for only a year or two after five or six years of continuous planting. Even in less fertile high restingas, fallow periods rarely last for more than three years and ordinarily follow extended periods of land use, perhaps five or six years. Plantains are sometimes grown continuously in high restingas for more than a decade. Because of differences in fallow periods, labor requirements for some agricultural tasks are not the same in restingas and alturas. Although restingas must be weeded more carefully, they require less land clearing prior to planting.

Much intercropping occurs in restingas. Corn, manioc, and plantains are an especially common combination. Nevertheless, many plots in restingas are monocropped. Ribereños refer to monocropped fields in restingas and alturas by appending the suffix *-al* to the name of the crop being grown. Thus farmers speak of *yucales, platanales, maizales,* and so forth.

Barreales and Playas

Only crops with short growing seasons can be grown in barreales and playas. Rice predominates in barreales, while cowpeas and peanuts are the principal crops grown in playas. Changes in water levels determine the scheduling of agricultural tasks in barreales and playas. Planting begins in late May or early June immediately after floods recede, and harvesting must take place before the rivers rise. Fields in barreales are sometimes covered with water in November, and those in playas may be inundated even earlier.

The types of agricultural tasks carried out in barreales and playas differ from those done in restingas and alturas. Farmers planting in barreales and playas do not have to clear land but simply remove debris and weeds after the harvest before the river rises. This cleaning is labor-intensive and may require the use of hired workers or mingas. When cleaning is done immediately before the annual flooding, not much weeding must be done prior to planting. However, farmers often guess incorrectly when the river will rise. If a flood comes before cleaning is completed, considerable weeding must be done after the river recedes, and if the cleaning is done too early, the task must be repeated because weeds regrow prior to the flood. Sometimes a field in a barreal is not inundated after rice is harvested. Weed problems ordinarily make such fields unusable in the subsequent year, so any labor farmers may have spent on cleaning such a field is wasted.

Crops

Ribereños raise an enormous number of crops for home consumption and sale. I discuss only those which are significant sources of food and income in Porvenir, Santa Sofía, and Tapirillo. The largest-scale farmers have about five hectares of non-tree crops such as manioc, plantains, rice, corn, cowpeas, tomatoes, and watermelons under cultivation. The smallest-scale agriculturalists grow these crops on about half a hectare. The great majority of households cultivate between one and two and one-half hectares of these crops. Most crops omitted from my discussion are raised in small quantities in house gardens; a few (such as umarí and aguaje) are important sources of income in some ribereño communities.

Primary Food Crops

The most important food crops by far are plantains and manioc. Ribereños obtain the bulk of the calories in their diet from these two crops, with one or both eaten at virtually every meal. Plantains and manioc are also cash crops sold in large quantities in the Iquitos market.

Plantains. All of the numerous varieties of plantains in Amazonia bear a cluster of fruit between nine and twelve months after they are planted. Because of this long period of maturation, ribereños suffer greatly when floods destroy fields of plantains, sometimes being left without an assured supply of a food staple for a year or more. To reduce the possibility of flooding, plantains are usually grown in high restingas and alturas. They can be planted at any time of the year.

After a stalk of plantains bears fruit, it dies and is replaced by new sprouts. Soil characteristics influence how long a field of plantains continues to produce. Plots in alturas produce sizable harvests only twice, but production in restingas usually lasts between five and seven years. Manioc and corn may be interplanted with plantains in both alturas and restingas.

In a careful study of a Shipibo (Amerindian) village along the Ucayali River, Bergman (1980:127) reported that the average labor inputs required by a one-hectare platanal in a restinga were 91 hours for clearing, 75 hours for planting, and 106 hours for weeding (weeding is a more time-consuming task in a corn-manioc-plantain field).

Researchers have encountered formidable difficulties in their attempts to estimate plantain yields because harvesting is done piecemeal as bunches ripen over time. Yields differ according to variety, land type, and the length of time plantains have been grown in a particular field. Finally, plantains are sold in bunches rather than by weight. Perhaps because of these complications, the two estimates that have been made of plantain yields in restingas in the Peruvian Amazon differ greatly. Bergman (1980:133) reported 5,880 kilograms per hectare in a Shipibo village in 1971–72, but Hiraoka (1985c:243) estimated 12,000 kilograms per hectare in the ribereño village of San Jorge in the early 1980s.

Most ribereños think that plantains are a good cash crop. They appreciate the crop's multi-year production and relatively low labor demands. Also, because plantains store fairly well, they do not have to be taken to market until two weeks after harvesting. Farmers do, however, worry about the unpredictable prices of plantains on the open market and the possibility that floods will destroy their fields in restingas.

Manioc. Many varieties of sweet manioc are grown near Iquitos. Although some can be harvested within four months after planting, most take about six months to mature. Because of its shorter growing season, manioc can be planted on lower ground than plantains. It requires more weeding than plantains but otherwise has similar labor requirements for various tasks.

Since manioc is a root crop, it is easily damaged by water. Many ribereños attempt to reduce the risk of flooding in low restingas by planting manioc soon after the river recedes. In high restingas and alturas, farmers are unconcerned about seasonality and plant manioc any time they find convenient. When floods threaten restingas, farmers harvest as much manioc as they can. Most is made into fariña, but some is buried in higher ground.

Two researchers who carefully examined manioc yields in ribereño communities (de Jong 1992; Hiraoka 1986:359–60) found that they average 9 or 10 metric tons per hectare. The shade from plantains, however, often lowers yields of second plantings of manioc in intercropped fields. Farmers I interviewed were reluctant to estimate manioc yields. When pressed to make a guess, their estimates ranged from 5 to 20 metric tons per hectare. They agreed that manioc yielded more kilograms per hectare than plantains.

Because ribereños raise manioc mostly for home consumption, they rarely compare its profitability with cash crops such as rice, corn, and cowpeas. They are occasionally willing to compare the profitability of manioc with that of plantains. Plantains are said to be more profitable per unit of labor input. However, manioc provides quicker returns to labor investments and is slightly less susceptible to diseases and pests.

Primary Cash Crops

Rice and corn are the most important crops grown principally for sale by residents of Porvenir, Santa Sofía, and Tapirillo. In the mid-1980s, rice and corn were easier to sell than manioc and plantains. Farmers who sold rice and corn usually knew that they could receive a guaranteed price at a government buying center, but farmers who sold plantains and manioc had to cope with fluctuating prices at the open market in Iquitos. Rice and corn, moreover, were not particularly good subsistence crops. Plantains and manioc provide much greater caloric returns per unit of labor. The larger amount of protein available in rice and corn is irrelevant; ribereños easily satisfy their protein requirements by eating fish at most meals.

Rice. Rice is the largest single source of income in ribereño villages near Iquitos. Nevertheless, it is an important crop for only a minority of households and does not dominate the local economy. Many farmers do not raise rice at all, and others plant less than a hectare. Some communities derive more income from jute, fruits, vegetables, or fish than from rice.

There are two principal reasons why rice, despite its potential profitability, is unimportant economically in many ribereño households. First, the crop is grown best in barreales, which are not available in some communities and are in short supply in others. Second, growing more than a hectare or two of rice requires credit, and many farmers are either unable to obtain loans or are unwilling to become indebted.

Farmers begin planting rice in barreales soon after the annual flood recedes in late May or early June. During the approximately four months between planting and harvesting, labor demands and cash outlays are modest (see Tables 7.1 and 7.2). Although weeding can require as much as 20 labor-days per hectare, this task is primarily carried out by family members and cooperative work groups. Money is spent in purchasing pesticides and weedkillers, constructing a roofed structure to store the harvest, and sometimes in hiring a few workers to help with weeding.

Harvesting and transport account for about a third of the labor inputs and half the cash outlays associated with growing rice in barreales. Harvesting is labor-intensive and must be done as rapidly as possible to avoid damage from flooding, so households can rarely carry out this task using only family labor. Furthermore, campesinos have trouble assembling mingas for harvesting because many potential work group members are busy with their own rice fields. Therefore, much of the harvesting is done

Table 7.1. Rice Production in Barreales, 1985: Cash Outlays and Labor Demands for 4 Hectares Yielding 8 Metric Tons[a]

	Cost (Intis)	Paid Labor-Days	Unpaid Labor-Days
Cleaning	1,420	80	20
Weeding and pest control	2,681	60	50
Harvesting and transport	5,296	60	20
Interest	494		
Miscellaneous	934		
Total	10,825	200	90
Gross income	14,592 intis		
Profit	3,767 intis		

[a]Because of revised assumptions, the figures presented in this table differ somewhat from those published in Chibnik 1990:289.

by hired workers (*jornaleros*). Some hired laborers are local people who do not grow rice; others are imported from villages that do not have barreales. Farmers also spend large sums of money transporting rice to Iquitos for sale. All rice producers must pay loading, shipping, and unloading charges, and those selling rice to ECASA in the 1980s also had to pay for transporting their crop from the Iquitos port to the buying center.

Because they sell most of their rice on one or two trips to Iquitos, farmers in Porvenir, Santa Sofía, and Tapirillo are able to give accurate estimates of the yields from this crop. Rice yields are quite variable. In 1984, farmers surveyed in these villages planted 65 hectares of rice (56 in barreales, 8.5 in restingas, and 0.5 in alturas) and obtained a mean yield of 2.4 metric tons per hectare. Rice production was much lower in 1985, when many barreales were not inundated after the river rose, leaving much of the land weed-covered and practically useless for rice farming. In 1985, farmers planted 34 hectares of rice (22 in barreales, 11.5 in restingas, and 0.5 in alturas) and obtained a mean yield of only 1.9 metric tons per hectare. In other years, farmers may be unable to complete harvesting before the river rises. Some barreales are less productive than

Table 7.2. Rice Production in Barreales, 1985: Cash Outlays and Labor Demands for 2 Hectares Yielding 4 Metric Tons

	Cost (Intis)	Paid Labor-Days	Unpaid Labor-Days
Cleaning	560	30	20
Weeding and pest control	1,258	20	44
Harvesting and transport	2,248	20	20
Interest	247		
Miscellaneous	435		
Total	4,748	70	84
Gross income	7,296 intis		
Profit	2,548 intis		

others because of sand deposits or the presence of ravines, and pests and diseases can destroy parts of some fields and leave others untouched. About one-quarter of the farmers in both 1984 and 1985 reported yields of one metric ton per hectare or less. Farmers with high yields in one year often had low yields in the other. The correlation (Pearson's r) between yields per hectare in 1984 and 1985 for the 18 farmers growing rice in both years was actually slightly negative (−.15).

The large amount of labor required at harvest time has two important effects on the economics of rice production. Because they do not have to pay as much for hired labor, households with many members ordinarily earn more money from a rice field of a given size than households with fewer members. Since households that plant three or more hectares in rice must spend relatively large sums of money on jornaleros, rice production entails some diseconomy of scale. Farmers with several hectares of rice hire a higher proportion of their labor than their neighbors with smaller plots. They therefore earn less per land unit. (Farmers with larger fields may, however, earn more per day of unpaid family labor.)

Rice growers often must pay for seeds, pesticides, herbicides, fumigator rental, shipping, drying, and interest on loans. Tables 7.1 and 7.2 present cost-benefit analyses for rice production in barreales in 1985 by an average-sized household with two different fields. One field is four hectares and yields eight metric tons; the other is two hectares and yields four metric tons. (Appendix 2 discusses the many complicated assumptions used in constructing these tables.) The larger field provides a profit per hectare of 942 intis (about $65) and a profit per day of unpaid family labor of 42 intis (about $3). The smaller field provides a profit per hectare of 1,274 intis (about $90) and a profit per day of unpaid labor of 30 intis (about $2.15).

Ribereños recognize that rice growing has several distinct advantages and several equally salient disadvantages. The potential for high profits is the main attraction of rice as a cash crop. A farmer planting 5 hectares of rice that yields 15 metric tons could earn as much as 9,500 intis (about $600) in 1985. Farmers in the 1980s also appreciated the guaranteed prices offered for rice at buying centers and the availability of credit from the Agrarian Bank. The drawbacks of large-scale rice production are all risk-related. Farmers who raise several hectares of rice must borrow money to pay for hired laborers and other production costs. When returns from the crop are poor, they become indebted. Floods, diseases, and pests can all lead to rice yields that are sufficiently low to prevent farmers from repaying their loans.

Corn. Corn matures within three months after planting. This short growing season allows farmers to have maizales on lower restingas than is possible for most platanales and yucales. Corn grown in low restingas is usually planted soon after the flood recedes. On higher ground, the crop is planted year-round. Yields in restingas average one metric ton per hectare. They are somewhat lower in alturas.

Corn is sold in a variety of units. The government buying center in Iquitos purchases shelled corn by the kilogram. Farmers sell corn to rematistas in sacks averaging about 25 kilograms. Vendors in the Iquitos market sell corn by the ear. Residents of the three villages sold little corn to the government buying center in Iquitos in 1985–86. When the center reopened in the beginning of 1986 after having been closed for over a year, the price offered for corn was 3.3 intis per kilogram, compared to 2.2 intis per kilogram on the open market. Farmers selling to the government, however, had to pay for transporting their crop from the port to the buying center. Many, wishing to avoid the bureaucratic complications associated with sales to the state, continued to sell on the open market.

Ribereños say that corn is easier to raise than rice. Growing corn entails no more cash investment than raising plantains or manioc, whereas growing rice ordinarily entails a much greater cash investment. Corn is also more easily interplanted with other crops than is rice and is less prone to insect depredations. Nonetheless, farmers agree that rice provides greater returns per hectare. In March 1986 the price per kilogram of corn and rice at the government buying centers was the same. The average yield in kilograms per hectare of rice, however, was about twice that of corn. Because rice requires a greater cash investment, a hectare of rice was not twice as profitable as a hectare of corn. Exactly how much more profitable rice was as a crop depended on several factors, including the amount of family labor available to the household planting the crops, the cost of wage labor, and interest rates on government credit.

Farmers' decision making with respect to cash crops seldom involves direct comparisons of rice and corn. The two crops occupy rather different ecological niches, with most rice being grown in barreales and most corn in restingas. In addition, the crops are grown for somewhat different purposes: rice is primarily a cash crop; corn has multiple uses. Although most corn raised by ribereños is sold, significant amounts are eaten at home or fed to chickens and pigs.

Secondary Crops

The farmers of the Peruvian Amazon are noted for their diversity of plant use. Hiraoka (1986:362) found 52 "plants associated with swidden agroforestry" in alturas in Tamshiyacu. Bergman (1980:223–25) lists 45 "cultivated crops," 14 plant "wild foods," and 17 "commonly used trees and miscellaneous plants" in a Shipibo community.

Although jute is an important source of income in some ribereño communities, nobody in Porvenir and Tapirillo planted this crop in 1985–86. Jute has been grown in Santa Sofía for several decades. About a dozen farmers in that community have at some time taken out loans for jute production from the Agrarian Bank. When the guaranteed price at buying centers did not increase in the mid-1980s, most farmers in Santa Sofía stopped raising jute. In early 1986, jute prices at buying centers rose sharply, and many farmers in Santa Sofía began growing the crop again.

Jute is usually grown on the higher parts of restingas and can be an attractive cash crop under the right circumstances. The crop can be planted at any time of the year, and farmers who grow jute ordinarily have fewer problems with diseases and pests than those raising rice or corn. But jute production also has its disadvantages. The crop provides slow returns to investments of time and money because of the long growing season (six or seven months); jute, unlike rice and corn, cannot be eaten by people or domestic animals. Also, jute growers often must hire jornaleros to help with harvesting. Finally, even farmers who cheerfully work long hours on sweltering days and pay little attention to swarming insects at night complain about the unpleasantness of jute harvesting. After jute is cut, it must be soaked in water for two to three weeks. Farmers next must perform the difficult task of separating the fiber from the rest of the plant. The fiber is then hung and dried for several days. Ants, chiggers, and mosquitoes are especially prevalent in the places where jute is harvested.

Jute and rice fields are about the same size. In Portugal (a community near Santa Sofía where jute has continued to be an important crop) the largest field in 1985 was 4 hectares. The average jute yield is about 3 metric tons per hectare. The state has traditionally provided credit and a guaranteed market, but prices in the mid-1980s were so low that farmers agreed that the monetary returns per labor-day from jute production were much lower than those from rice and corn.

Some households in Porvenir, Santa Sofía, and Tapirillo earn a substantial income from crops other than plantains, manioc, rice, corn, and jute, and all villagers supplement their manioc-plantains-fish meals with a variety of fruits and vegetables. The most important secondary crops in the three villages are cowpeas, papayas, watermelons, and tomatoes. Cowpeas are raised in long, narrow strips in playas and low barreales. Farmers rarely plant more than one hectare of cowpeas, and most fields are much smaller. The crop matures in about three and a half months and is relatively free of diseases and pests. Yields average 600 to 900 kilograms per hectare (Hiraoka 1985b:255). Cowpeas sold for about 4 intis per kilogram on the open market in early 1986.

Fruits sold by residents of the three villages include papayas, watermelons, star apples (*caimito, Pouteria caimito*), *guaba* (*Inga edulis*), breadfruit, peach palm, pineapple, *shimbillo* (*Inga perizifera*), and *taperiba* (*Spondias dulcis*). Papayas are seldom deliberately planted. They grow well in high restingas in Santa Sofía but are sometimes lost in floods. Residents of Santa Sofía occasionally sell large quantities of papayas in the Iquitos market. Watermelons are grown in high barreales and low restingas. They do not require much labor and are regarded as having a good market price. Watermelons are difficult to raise, however, as many crops fail after being damaged by pests or animals.

Tomatoes, sweet peppers, *caihua* (*Cyclanthera pedata*), coriander, and onions are raised in small quantities for sale in Iquitos. Tomatoes are sold by the *cajita* (little box), which contains 7 to 10 tomatoes. A farmer in Tapirillo sold 1,500 cajitas in 1985, and one in Santa Sofía sold 1,350, though no other resident of the three villages sold more than 500. The price of tomatoes in the Iquitos market in late 1985 was about 2 intis per cajita. The most money any household in the three villages made from tomatoes was therefore about 3,000 intis ($200).

The Relative Importance of the Various Crops

Assessing the relative importance of crops in Porvenir, Santa Sofía, and Tapirillo is not a straightforward task. Some crops, such as rice, are especially important as income sources; others, like manioc, are especially important for home consumption. Comparisons of cash income derived from raising the various crops therefore give a misleading picture of their relative importance. Similarly, comparisons of the areas devoted to various crops, while less misleading, are also imperfect measures of their significance in local economies. Crops vary in their labor inputs, yields, and monetary returns per unit of land.

Table 7.3 gives the percentage of households in the three villages that planted eight crops in 1984 and 1985, and Table 7.4 gives the areas devoted to these crops. Rice, corn, manioc, and plantains are clearly the most important crops in ribereño communities near Iquitos. Jute is very important in some communities and not at all important in others. Cowpeas, tomatoes, and watermelons may be no more important regionally than other minor crops such as peanuts and sweet peppers.

The most commonly grown crops in Porvenir, Santa Sofía, and Tapirillo are the two staples, manioc and plantains. Although manioc was raised by almost every household in 1984–85, plantains were less omnipresent. Corn was an important crop in Tapirillo and Santa Sofía. Other crops were grown by only a minority of farmers. Cowpeas were somewhat more common than tomatoes and watermelon, while jute was planted by only a few farmers in Santa Sofía.

The three villages differ considerably in the amount of land devoted to corn, watermelons, and tomatoes (Table 7.4). These differences can be attributed to geographic and economic conditions. Residents of Porvenir have access to only a limited amount of land in restingas. Corn, water-

Table 7.3. Percentage of Households That Planted Various Crops in
Porvenir, Santa Sofía, and Tapirillo, 1984 and 1985

	Porvenir (N = 28)		Santa Sofía (N = 23)		Tapirillo (N = 31)	
	1984	1985	1984	1985	1984	1985
Manioc	96%	92%	100%	100%	96%	100%
Plantains	69	81	75	95	57	79
Rice	46	27	55	57	46	38
Corn	31	35	90	86	82	86
Cowpeas	54	42	45	24	14	21
Jute	0	0	16	19	0	0
Tomatoes	4	8	10	19	25	45
Watermelons	4	15	33	19	34	31

melons, and tomatoes, which are best grown in restingas, are therefore
less popular in Porvenir than in the other two villages. Tomatoes, moreover, are perishable and are grown mostly in ribereño communities with
good transportation to the Iquitos market. Residents of Santa Sofía and
Tapirillo can find colectivos going to the city more easily than can inhabitants of Porvenir.

The number of households that raised each of the eight crops did not
change much between 1984 and 1985. There was, however, a substantial
increase in the land area in plantains and a substantial decrease in the
land area in rice. Ribereño communities can change their crop patterns
dramatically as prices, credit terms, and land conditions vary. A recent
striking change was observed by Wil de Jong, who conducted economic
surveys in the village of Yanallpa in 1986 and 1989. A tenth of the farmers in Yanallpa raised plantains in 1986, but more than nine-tenths raised
them in 1989 (de Jong 1992).

Table 7.4 does not fully indicate the economic importance of rice growing in some households. Many farmers had rice fields of two or more
hectares. Furthermore, rice is usually monocropped, while manioc, plantains, and corn are often interplanted with one another. A farmer who
raises a hectare of rice, a hectare of manioc, a hectare of plantains, and a

Table 7.4. Mean Area in Hectares of Various Crops Planted by Households in Porvenir, Santa Sofía, and Tapirillo, 1984 and 1985[a]

	Porvenir (N = 28)		Santa Sofía (N = 23)		Tapirillo (N = 31)	
	1984	1985	1984	1985	1984	1985
Manioc	0.7	0.6	0.7	0.6	0.7	1.2
Plantains	0.5	0.6	0.8	1.0	0.5	0.8
Rice	0.6	0.4	0.8	0.4	1.0	0.5
Corn	0.2	0.2	0.7	0.8	0.7	0.9
Cowpeas	0.2	0.2	0.1	0.1	0.2	0.2
Jute	0.0	0.0	0.1	0.1	0.0	0.0
Tomatoes	0.01	0.01	0.02	0.02	0.1	0.2
Watermelons	0.01	0.03	0.1	0.02	0.2	0.2

[a]Means are calculated by dividing the total area devoted to a crop by the number of households surveyed (including those not growing the crop).

hectare of corn may have only two hectares in fields, with one hectare as a rice field and the other interplanted with the other three crops.

Villagers planted only small amounts of cowpeas, tomatoes, and watermelons in 1984 and 1985. Cowpeas are the most widely raised of these crops. In 1984 the 82 households surveyed raised 13 hectares of cowpeas, but they also grew 65 hectares of rice, 40 hectares of corn, 54 hectares of manioc, and 46 hectares of plantains. In 1985 these households raised 12 hectares of cowpeas, 34 hectares of rice, 49 hectares of corn, 66 hectares of manioc, and 61 hectares of plantains.

The low floods of 1985 affected agricultural strategies in Tapirillo. Rice growing had accounted for a large proportion of the cash income in that village in 1984. Farmers reacted to the loss of potential rice income in 1985 because of low flood levels by increasing the amount of land planted with manioc, plantains, and corn. The low floods had less effect on agricultural strategies in Porvenir and Santa Sofía, where rice is usually a less important crop.

Table 7.5 shows the proportion of manioc, plantains, rice, and corn grown on various land types in the three villages in 1984 and 1985. Land

Table 7.5. Percentage of Major Crops Grown on Various Land Types in Porvenir, Santa Sofía, and Tapirillo, 1984 and 1985[a]

	Porvenir			Santa Sofía		Tapirillo	
	Altura	Restinga	Barreal	Restinga	Barreal	Restinga	Barreal
Manioc							
1984	75	25	0	100	0	100	0
1985	69	31	0	100	0	100	0
Plantains							
1984	98	2	0	100	0	100	0
1985	77	23	0	100	0	100	0
Rice							
1984	9	0	91	16	84	48	52
1985	4	7	89	5	95	61	39
Corn							
1984	100	0	0	100	0	100	0
1985	32	68	0	100	0	100	0

[a]Percentages refer to the areas planted in different land types for the various crops.

use in Santa Sofía and Tapirillo can be summarized easily. Manioc, plantains, and corn are grown in restingas, and rice is raised mostly in barreales and low restingas (mainly ceticales). Porvenir's farmers grow most of their rice in barreales, and because of the shortage of restingas in their community, raise most of their plantains and manioc in alturas.

Domestic Animals

Some residents of Porvenir, Santa Sofía, and Tapirillo earned significant amounts of money in 1985–86 from the sale of fowl and pigs. Chickens provided some income in most households in all three villages, whereas pigs, which are most easily raised in alturas, were common only in Porvenir.

Fowl

Small-scale chicken raising is an attractive economic option in ribereño communities. The price of chickens in the Iquitos market varies less than most other products that farmers sell. When cash is needed quickly, households that sell their chickens can acquire fairly large sums of money. In addition, chickens and eggs are prestige foods needed by hosts of cooperative work parties.

Because chickens are usually fed with staple food crops, most ribereños are reluctant to raise more than several dozen at one time. Keeping large numbers of chickens requires an expansion of subsistence production that many farmers think is not worth the effort. Further, chicken raising entails some risks. Although chickens sell for a decent price, some die before they are old enough to be sold. Also, chickens are often lost during floods in communities that lack access to alturas.

Almost every household in the three villages had some chickens in 1985–86. The mean number per household was 11 in Porvenir, 27 in Santa Sofía, and 25 in Tapirillo. The largest number of chickens owned by any household was 120, and no household sold more than one hundred chickens in either 1984 or 1985. About a fifth of the households sold no chickens in 1984, and about a quarter sold no chickens in 1985. The mean number of chickens sold per household in 1984 and 1985 was about 15. Hens sold for 60 intis apiece in the Iquitos market in February 1986; thus a household selling 15 hens would earn 900 intis (about $50).

A third of the households in Porvenir, Santa Sofía, and Tapirillo sold eggs to their neighbors, and about one-tenth sold eggs outside of their community. Few households made much money selling eggs. Indeed, many families bought as many eggs as they sold. About a third of the households in the three villages kept ducks, but they were rarely an important source of income.

Pigs

Pigs are potentially more profitable than chickens. Fernando Chávez, a ribereño living in the town of Yanashi, provided me with some figures on the economics of pig raising. Fernando sold ten pigs in 1984 for about 300,000 soles ($40) apiece. (The monetary unit of Peru was changed from the sol to the inti at the end of 1985, with the value of the inti set at 1,000 soles.) Fernando estimated that he had spent about 1.5 million soles tending pigs that year. His net income from pigs in 1984 was therefore about 1.5 million soles ($200) or about 150,000 soles ($20) per pig.

Like chickens, many pigs contract illnesses and die before they are ready for the market. The relatively large amounts of money that can be earned through the sale of pigs nonetheless makes them attractive as a source of funds in an emergency. The mean number of pigs owned by 28 households in Porvenir was 2.9, and nineteen had at least one pig. Eighteen households sold pigs in 1984, and fourteen in 1985. The mean number sold was 2.8 in 1984 and 1.9 in 1985. The sale of even two or three pigs can be important in local household economies. The gross income from the sale of one pig is equivalent to what can be earned by 20 days of wage labor, and the net income is equivalent to that earned in 10 days.

Most ribereños who raise pigs live in communities with access to alturas. Pigs in these communities can forage in secondary growth on land left fallow or in the later stages of an agroforestry cycle. In communities lacking access to alturas, a much larger proportion of land is used for food crops. Pigs in such communities are likely to destroy fields and cause intravillage disputes. Only one household in Tapirillo kept a pig in 1985–86, and there were no pigs in Santa Sofía during these years.

Fishing and Hunting

Mário Hiraoka has estimated (1985b:286) that in the early 1980s fish comprised 75 to 85 percent of the animal protein consumed by residents of San Jorge. The diet of the inhabitants of San Jorge is similar to that of people living in most other ribereño communities near major rivers. Manioc and plantains, the most important plant foods eaten in these communities, are low in protein. Even though few residents of Porvenir, Santa Sofía, and Tapirillo know about protein requirements, they all think that their diet is inadequate when fish are scarce.

Many ribereño men fish several times a week. Women fish only occasionally. About a quarter of the time that men in San Jorge spend obtaining food is devoted to fishing (Hiraoka 1985b:262). I did not attempt to collect such precise data in Porvenir, Santa Sofía, and Tapirillo, but I included some questions about fishing in household socioeconomic surveys conducted between November 1985 and April 1986. Interviews took place during periods of both good and bad fishing. Miguel Pinedo and I asked 81 adult men how many days they had fished in the week prior to being interviewed. About 85 percent of the men interviewed said that they had fished in the week prior to the interview, and most had gone fishing two or three times. A typical fishing session lasts several hours.

Ribereños use several different fishing methods, none requiring complex technology. Fishers use gill and cast nets in the river and spears, trotlines, and bows and arrows in oxbow lakes and flooded forests. Although fishing is done at all hours, it is perhaps most common in the late night and early morning. Men like to fish before they go to work in the fields.

Most meals include small fish of various species. Some fish commonly eaten are *bagre* (*Pimelodus* sp.), *boquichico* (*Prochilodus vulginum*), *lisa* (*Leporinus fasciatus*), *palometa* (*Mylosoma duriventris*), *sábalo* (*Brycon melanopterum*), piranha (*Serrasalmus* sp.), *yahuarachi* (*Curimata leucisca*), and *carachama* (*Ptergoplichtys multiradiatus*). Ribereños also sometimes eat larger fish such as dorado (*Ilisha deauratus*), *saltón* (*Brachiplatystoma* spp.), and *tigre zungaro* (*Zungaro zungaro*). *Gamitana* (*Colossoma bidens*) and *corvina* (*Plagioscion auratus*) are eagerly sought because of their size, taste, and relative lack of bones but are caught only occasionally.

Many ribereños note that they have been forced to eat smaller and bonier fish in recent years. They say that commercial fishers plying the rivers and oxbow lakes have depleted stocks of larger, more palatable species. The famous *paiche* (*Arapaima gigas*) is rarely caught nowadays by either ribereños or commercial fishers.

Several attempts have been made to measure how many kilograms of food can be obtained per hour through fishing. Hiraoka (1985b:263) reported that fishing in San Jorge yielded 1.2 kilograms per hour, and Bergman (1980:235) gives a similar figure for a Shipibo village. In the town of Jenaro Herrera, the ichthyologist Kate Clark (personal communication) observed catch rates of 8 kilograms per hour during a migration of fish.

Almost half (46 percent) of the adult men surveyed in the three villages had sold fish in the week prior to their interview. Most of these sales were within their communities. Perhaps the most interesting aspect of these small-scale transactions is their existence. Although ribereños often give surplus fish to relatives, unrelated neighbors are ordinarily expected to pay for any fish they receive.

Ribereños can earn substantial sums of money by selling fish in Iquitos. Many villagers take fish to market in colectivos; a few take their own boats. Fish are sometimes sold to intermediaries along the river. Some intermediaries are the owners of colectivos, and most specialize in trading fish. Only 10 percent of the adult men surveyed had sold fish in Iquitos the previous week, though almost half (44 percent) said that they occasionally sold fish in the city.

Since my research focused on the economics of agriculture, I did not conduct the detailed studies necessary to estimate yearly income from the sale of fish. Villagers sold fish sporadically and could not provide even rough estimates of yearly sales. Nonetheless, fishing clearly was not a major source of income for anyone in the three villages. Many residents said that they earned about as much money from fishing as they did from selling chickens.

Ribereño men hunt nonarboreal animals such as armadillos, agoutis, and pacas, as well as shore and water dwellers such as capybaras and caymans. Hunting is more common in villages with alturas than in those lacking access to uplands. There is less habitat for game species in floodplain villages because a higher proportion of the land is devoted to crops. Nevertheless, hunting is an important source of income for some ribereños. Fernando Chávez of Yanashi goes on three to five long hunting trips a year. Such trips can last a week or two. Fernando and two friends returned from one very successful 15-day hunting trip in 1985 with 200 kilograms of meat. Game sold in Iquitos at that time for about 20 intis per kilogram. The money was split evenly, and each hunter grossed about 1,300 intis ($100). The hunters spent about 170 intis apiece on shells on this trip. Fernando is prosperous by local standards and can afford to take lengthy, expensive trips in which catches are not guaranteed, but the cost of shotguns and shells deters most ribereños from hunting on such a large scale.

In fact, few residents of Porvenir, Santa Sofía, and Tapirillo hunt much. Of 81 adult men surveyed, only 4 (3 in Porvenir and 1 in Santa Sofía) said that they ever sold game meat. Game meat is rarely eaten at ordinary meals but is sometimes eaten at mingas and fiestas. Ribereños also sell meat in Iquitos. Although such sales are prohibited by Peru's conservation laws, government bureaucrats do not prevent rural people from selling small quantities of meat in the market. There is also a lively illicit trade in the skins of animals such as ocelots, jaguars, and caymans.

Wage Labor and Remittances

Ribereños sometimes hire one another as agricultural laborers. The pay for such work is established at community meetings. Some workers are paid by the day; others are paid for particular tasks. Laborers hired by the day are expected to work about six hours. The pay for a day of work in Porvenir, Santa Sofía, and Tapirillo in 1985–86 averaged about 25 intis (about $1.50) plus food. Jornaleros hired by the task could usually earn somewhat more per day.

Rice harvesting is the agricultural task that requires the most hired labor. Jornaleros were paid 400 soles (about 2.5 cents) in 1985 for each kilogram of rice harvested. Good workers could earn 40,000 soles ($2.50) per day by harvesting 100 kilograms of husked rice. There are several reasons why the pay for rice harvesting was higher than that for most other agricultural tasks. First, labor is scarcer during the rice harvest than at other times of the year. Second, most rice harvesters work 10 to 12 hours per day. Third, in 1985 at least, farmers could receive government credit to hire laborers to help with the rice harvest, while they could not get loans that year from the Agrarian Bank to hire workers for subsistence crops such as plantains and manioc.

Jornaleros hired to help with rice harvesting include men and women of all ages. Most jornaleros who work on other agricultural tasks are men between 16 and 35. Many spend 20 to 30 days per year doing wage work for their neighbors, most of it lasting for only a few days.

Ribereño communities differ in the extent to which villagers use hired labor. Villages where many residents take out loans from the Agrarian Bank have more money to spend on jornaleros than villages where few residents have agricultural credit. In contrast, villages where cooperative work parties are common do not need as many hired laborers as villages where mingas are held less frequently. In Santa Sofía, where large mingas take place most weeks, agricultural laborers were hired to help with the rice harvest but were otherwise rarely employed.

Ribereños also work for wages on commercial estates. Such work is most common in villages adjoining fundos. In these communities, laborers can return to their homes at night. Wage workers on commercial estates raise crops, tend animals, make aguardiente, and collect forest products. The availability of other kinds of wage work in the Peruvian Amazon varies from year to year. Rural people occasionally go to Iquitos when the river is high and not much farming is being done. They stay with urban relatives and work in the informal economy as vendors, rematistas, and cargo handlers. The money they earn is used to pay for living expenses and to support relatives who remain at home. Very little is invested in village-based enterprises.

Few residents of Porvenir, Santa Sofía, and Tapirillo earn much money from work away from their villages. No adult man surveyed in Santa Sofía had any income from this source in 1985. In Porvenir, which adjoins two commercial estates, 43 percent of the adult men interviewed earned income from extravillage wage labor that year, and in Tapirillo 34 percent of adult men reported such income. Among those men who engage in wage labor, the mean amount of time spent was about a month and a half. Women and children sometimes spent short periods in Iquitos helping out relatives who work in the marketplace, but they earned hardly anything doing this.

About a quarter of the households in the three villages report incomes from sources other than agriculture, fishing, wage labor, and hunting. Most such income is received from relatives living in Iquitos and other towns and cities (no one interviewed received money from family members living in other countries). The recipients of remittances are mostly older people with adult children living elsewhere. Couples establishing a new household sometimes receive small amounts of financial assistance from older relatives.

The Relative Importance of Various Sources of Income

My estimates of income from various sources in Porvenir, Santa Sofía, and Tapirillo in 1985, presented in Table 7.6, are based on interviews about wage work and the sale of crops and animals in the previous year. Villagers were able to give precise figures for income from some sources (e.g., rice sales) and could provide estimates for others (e.g., wage work outside of the community and the sale of plantains and manioc). But because they often had no idea what their yearly income had been from intermittent income sources such as intravillage wage work, remittances, and sales of fish and fruit, I was unable to include such sources of income in Table 7.6.

The figures in Table 7.6 are very rough approximations. Ribereños can remember quantities of products sold better than the income they received from the sales. Estimates of household income from particular sources were often derived by multiplying the reported amount of a product sold in a year by its average price in 1985. Table 7.6 does not consider the cost of transportation to market, hired labor, and capital investments. A table presenting net incomes would give a somewhat different picture of the relative importance of the various income sources.

Table 7.6. Estimated Gross Household Income in Intis from Various Sources in Porvenir, Santa Sofía, and Tapirillo, 1985[a]

	Porvenir (N = 28)		Santa Sofía (N = 23)		Tapirillo (N = 31)	
	Mean Income[b]	%	Mean Income	%[c]	Mean Income	%
Plantains	1,690	29	2,015	32	2,000	22
Rice	1,760	30	1,240	20	1,635	18
Corn	0	0	1,220	19	1,130	13
Manioc	80	1	310	5	2,305	26
Cowpeas	330	6	270	4	140	2
Tomatoes	0	0	405	6	610	7
Watermelons	0	0	175	3	120	1
Jute	0	0	135	2	0	0
Chickens	500	9	500	8	770	9
Pigs	1,200	20	0	0	0	0
Wage labor[a]	320	5	0	0	200	2
Total	5,880		6,270		8,910	

[a]This table does not include income from intravillage wage work, remittances, and the sale of fruit and fish.
[b]The average exchange rate in 1985 was about 14 intis per U.S. dollar.
[c]Percentages may not add up to 100 because of rounding.

The most striking feature of Table 7.6 is the small average household income in the three villages. Clearly, Porvenir, Santa Sofía, and Tapirillo are still very subsistence-oriented communities. Another noteworthy feature of Table 7.6 is the variety of ways in which households made money. No single source of income dominated village economies in 1985. Plantains and rice were the only crops sold in large quantities in all three villages. Corn was sold by many households in Santa Sofía and Tapirillo but was not a cash crop in Porvenir. Manioc was an important income source in Tapirillo but was grown almost exclusively for home consumption in the other two villages.

When adjustments are made for inflation, the mean household income from rice in Tapirillo in 1985 was only a fourth of what it had been in

1984; in Santa Sofía it was about half. Rice may have accounted for about half of the cash income in Tapirillo and a third of the cash income in Santa Sofía in 1984. The sharp decline in rice sales from 1984 to 1985 probably decreased intervillage income differences. Santa Sofía and Porvenir had similar mean household incomes in 1985, while mean household incomes in Santa Sofía almost certainly were higher in 1984. Income differences between Tapirillo and the other two villages were undoubtedly considerably greater in 1984 than in 1985.

Because money earned from remittances and sales of fruit and fish are not included, the estimates of mean gross household income in Table 7.6 are perhaps 20 to 30 percent too low. The omission of intravillage labor from Table 7.6 has less effect on these estimates. Every inti that a villager earned from this source came from the pocket of a neighbor.

8. Agricultural Labor Organization

Many ethnographers (e.g., Guillet 1980; Provinse 1937; Saul 1983) have described cooperative agricultural work parties in which a host farm family provides unpaid guest laborers with food and drink. Although such work parties vary in size, amount and type of refreshments served, and reciprocity expected of guests, they take two general forms (Erasmus 1955; Moore 1975). In exchange labor groups, farmers work on each other's fields on a rotating basis. The food and drink served to guests are not much better than ordinary, and the amount of work that each group member provides for others is reciprocated almost exactly. In festive work parties, farmers issue an invitation to their neighbors to work on a particular task. The host family is expected to provide extraordinary food and drink but has little or no obligation to attend future work parties called by guests.

Cooperative work parties are common in Porvenir, Santa Sofía, Tapirillo, and many other ribereño communities. The most important reason why ribereño farmers participate in cooperative work groups rather than hiring laborers is to save money. Such groups, however, entail more inconveniences than hired labor. The members of exchange labor groups worry about organizational complexities and reciprocal obligations, and the organizers of festive work parties spend considerable time obtaining food and drink.

Anthropologists and rural sociologists disagree about how the increasing immersion of tribal and peasant agriculturalists in the cash economy has affected the incidence of exchange labor groups and festive work parties. Some writers (Brown 1987; Erasmus 1955; Moore 1975) claim that this increased monetization is leading farmers to rely more on hired labor and less on cooperative work groups. They contend that when rural residents make decisions about the recruitment of extrafamily workers, they are influenced more than previously by the convenience of hired labor and less by its cost.

Guillet (1980), on the other hand, presents evidence that, in the Central Andes of Peru and elsewhere, cooperative labor persists despite extensive involvement by rural residents in the cash economy. He argues that large capitalist enterprises and urban elites drain wealth from rural areas on the periphery of the world economy, and for this to take place, wages and crop prices must be kept low. Most rural residents are therefore poor, and the cost-saving aspect of cooperative labor remains important to them.

Guillet's ideas apply only partially to ribereño communities. As in the Central Andes, work groups are flourishing despite increased direct involvement by rural residents in the cash economy. Nonetheless, it is far from obvious that the persistence of cooperative labor can be attributed to the Peruvian Amazon's peripheral position in the world economy. Although large-scale capitalist enterprises have extracted much wealth from the region in the past, they have employed few ribereños in recent years. The increased monetization of the rural economy in the past several decades is principally the result of greater independent cash cropping among ribereños. This agricultural expansion has led to an increased need for extrafamily labor by farm households and the continued use of festive work parties and exchange groups.

This chapter begins with a general discussion of the use of extrafamily agricultural labor in peasant communities. I then examine the recruitment of such labor in the town of Tamshiyacu and the villages of Porvenir, Santa Sofía, Tapirillo, Santa Rosa, and Yanallpa. My descriptions of Tamshiyacu, Santa Rosa, and Yanallpa (Table 8.1) are based on research carried out in the mid-1980s by Wil de Jong (Chibnik and de Jong 1989; de Jong 1987).

Yanallpa is the only village that was never part of a fundo, though its residents used to engage in many economic transactions with the owners of nearby commercial estates. The history of Tamshiyacu (Hernández 1946) is somewhat different from that of the villages. The first settlers of Tamshiyacu were mestizo migrants who came from the neighboring department of San Martín in the 1860s. The community grew and became the district capital. The town itself was never part of a commercial estate. Although some habilitadores now live in Tamshiyacu, the majority of residents are small-scale farmers (Padoch et al. 1985).

Table 8.1. Characteristics of Santa Rosa, Tamshiyacu, and Yanallpa

	Santa Rosa	Tamshiyacu	Yanallpa
Location[a]	Ucayali River 145 km upriver from Iquitos, 10 km downriver from Requena	Amazon River 30 km upriver from Iquitos	Ucayali River 145 km upriver from Iquitos, 10 km downriver from Requena
Population, 1985–86	335	2,000	350
Agricultural land types	altura restinga barreal playa	altura	restinga barreal playa
Markets	Iquitos Requena	Iquitos	Iquitos Requena

[a]Distances are straight-line distances.

The Causes and Consequences of Extrafamily Agricultural Labor Recruitment

Farm households in peasant communities most often need extrafamily labor for tasks that are labor-intensive and that must be completed quickly. The number of agricultural tasks in a particular community which are labor-intensive depends on local land use patterns, crops, soils, tools, machinery, and plot sizes. The speed with which particular tasks must be completed is affected by the local ecology. Shifting cultivators in areas with marked rainy and dry seasons, for example, must clear forest more quickly than those living in places where rainfall and temperature do not vary much over the course of a year. Similarly, farmers who plant in areas that are periodically flooded may need to harvest their crops more rapidly than those who plant in uplands.

Scheduling considerations sometimes lead rural households to use extrafamily labor even when they have sufficient family members to complete a task. For example, weeding one-hectare fields in alturas and restingas in the Peruvian Amazon can take as long as two weeks if only family labor is used. When extrafamily labor is recruited, the task can be done in a day or two. The time saved by hiring laborers or hosting festive work parties can be used for other agricultural activities, fishing, or marketing. Farmers who use exchange groups for weeding may not save time, because they thus incur reciprocal labor obligations. They can, however, perform activities other than weeding, as exchange groups usually operate only two or three days a week.

The form that extrafamily agricultural labor takes in a particular community can affect the local social structure (Moore 1975). Where hired labor is common, social classes of employers and employees may develop. Exchange labor groups establish clearly defined rights and obligations among participants and create intracommunity distinctions between members of different work groups. Reciprocal obligations usually result in egalitarian social relations among members. Festive work parties, in contrast, entail few long-standing rights and obligations between hosts and guests and are seldom associated with permanently distinct groups. The hosts of festive work parties may be of higher social status than many of their guests.

The choices between different forms of extrafamily labor in a community are influenced by the characteristics of the agricultural tasks. The organizational complexities and reciprocal obligations associated with exchange labor groups make them less suitable than festive work parties for tasks that occur unpredictably, require a very large workforce, or are carried out by only a few community members. Exchange labor groups, however, are better suited than festive work parties for agricultural tasks that must be performed carefully. Work quality is often low at festive parties because of the quantities of alcohol consumed and the lack of reciprocal labor obligations (Moore 1975:283).

The socioeconomic status of farmers also affects preferences for different forms of extrafamily agricultural labor. Farmers with relatively large landholdings are likely to hire laborers or host work parties. They need large labor forces, can afford the cost of wages or of providing exceptional food and drink, and find it difficult to arrange equal work exchanges with poorer neighbors. Small-scale farmers, in contrast, may prefer exchange groups because of the expense of festive work parties and hired labor.

Off-farm activities are another determinant of labor recruitment preferences. Rural residents who spend large amounts of time working for others or running small businesses (e.g., stores or transportation services) ordinarily either hire laborers or host festive work parties because they cannot fulfill the reciprocal labor obligations associated with exchange groups.

Agricultural Labor Organization in Ribereño Communities

Household Labor

Ribereño households use family labor to accomplish many agricultural tasks. Although adult men and women do much of this work, they receive significant amounts of help from younger household members. Since only some ribereños attend secondary school, many teenagers can and do spend considerable time farming. Children under twelve are in school most of the year, but they too help out with labor-intensive tasks such as harvesting rice and weeding. Exactly how much labor may be mobilized for a particular agricultural task depends on the nature of the work and the age-sex composition of the household. Households with many young children usually have few workers able to perform difficult tasks. As the children grow older, however, substantial amounts of household labor become available (see Chayanov 1966 [1920s]).

Paid Labor

When a family is too small or is otherwise unable to perform an agricultural task, additional labor can be obtained by hiring workers. Farm households needing only a few jornaleros ordinarily hire members of their own community, but when a large labor force is required, they may hire workers from nearby villages. Extravillage labor is used most often when farmers with rice in barreales need large workforces in order to harvest the crop before the river rises.

In some ribereño communities, a few wealthier residents regularly hire their poorer neighbors. Because wealth differences are small in most ribereño communities, however, hired workers are usually of about the same socioeconomic status as their employers. Differences in wealth between employers and employees may be related more to a person's place in the life cycle than to village social stratification. Many hired workers are young men whose own plots are small, while their employers are usually older men who need labor because over the years they have expanded and diversified their agricultural activities.

Informal Labor Exchange

Ribereños often use extrafamily labor paid for with only food and drink. Most informal labor exchange consists of groups of five to thirty workers who spend a day or less on a task such as clearing land, weeding, or harvesting. (In highland areas of Peru and other Andean countries, direct exchanges of labor between two individuals or households are common, but such labor exchanges, called *ayni,* are rare in ribereño communities.)

Festive work parties are common in four of the six communities examined here and occur occasionally in the other two. These work parties are called *mingas* throughout the Peruvian Amazon. They usually last most of the day and are noted for the good food and large quantities of alcoholic beverages provided. The main food is usually chicken or high-quality fish, but hosts sometimes serve local game to their guests. Masato always accompanies mingas, and aguardiente is sometimes also served.

Even though the hosts of festive work parties incur no explicit labor obligations to their guests, neighbors often expect one another to attend them. They are usually open to anyone who wishes to attend and include people from only one community. In some villages (e.g., Santa Sofía), the teniente gobernador keeps a list of mingas for each week and attempts to ensure that two are not scheduled for the same day. Between ten and twenty people usually attend a minga, but there may be as few as five guests or as many as thirty. While both men and women participate, usually most of the guests are male. All mingas include at least one woman who is responsible for preparing food and masato.

The frequency of festive work parties varies considerably from community to community and over the course of a year. One important factor influencing intercommunity variation is the incidence of alternative forms of extrafamily labor. For example, festive work parties are less frequent in Tapirillo, where exchange groups are important, than they are in Santa Sofía, where there are no exchange groups. Seasonal variability in the use of festive work parties can result from changes over the year in the number of tasks requiring large work groups. For example, excessive rains in some years limit the amount of land clearing that is done in alturas between March and May. When this happens, upland communities have few festive work parties. Mingas are also uncommon when potential hosts cannot obtain extraordinary food and drink. This occurs during times of the year when fish are scarce or after floods destroy fields.

Wil de Jong collected data during 1987 on participation in festive work parties in Yanallpa. There were 25 all-day festive work parties between January 20 and July 23 that year. They were used for harvesting manioc and corn, clearing fields, and weeding. The average number of participants was 12 (10 men and 2 women). There were also 26 *cortemañanas,* festive work parties of three to nine males that took place in the morning and at which masato, two or three bottles of aguardiente, and one meal were usually served. These morning work parties occurred in the months of April, June, and July and were used primarily for weeding.

De Jong also collected information about 78 all-day mingas and 18 cortemañanas that took place in Santa Rosa between June 16, 1985, and September 30, 1986. These comprised more than three-quarters of the festive work parties during this period. The average attendance was 13.5 persons at all-day mingas and 12.6 at cortemañanas. Work parties (both all-day mingas and cortemañanas) were used for clearing fields (36), weeding (25), other agricultural tasks (10), and such nonagricultural activities as building houses, boats, and bridges, and repairing fishing nets (25).

Exchange labor groups operated in four of the six communities in the mid-1980s. The term that people use to refer to exchange labor groups is not the same in all ribereño communities. When members of such a group are working in a field, residents of some villages say that a minga is taking place. In other communities the term *minga* is restricted to festive work parties.

Although exchange labor groups include some women and teenagers, the great majority of their members are adult males. The groups all share certain basic characteristics. They operate three to five times per week in certain months and not at all at other times of the year. Members work in a more or less fixed rotation on each other's fields. Those members who miss a work session are required either to send a replacement (sometimes a paid neighbor, more often an unpaid family member) or to give a day's labor to the host at a later date. Members who do not comply with this regulation are expelled from the group.

The differences between exchange labor work groups are as striking as their similarities (see Table 8.2). In the mid-1980s they ranged in size from four or five in Porvenir to more than twenty in Tapirillo (which represented more than half the households in the community). In Tamshiyacu, Yanallpa, and Porvenir, the groups worked all day and were served meals and masato, while in Tapirillo the groups worked two hours

Table 8.2. Characteristics of Exchange Labor Groups in Various Communities

Community	Approximate Size	Time Tasks Performed	Seasonality	Written Rules	Insurance Programs
Porvenir	5–10	all day	seasonal	no	no
Tamshiyacu	10–20	all day	year-round[a]	yes	yes
Tapirillo	20	morning	year-round	no	yes
Yanallpa	5–10	all day	seasonal	no	no

NOTE: No exchange groups operated during the mid-1980s in Santa Rosa and Santa Sofía.
[a]"Year-round" groups operate most of the year but often cease operations for several weeks.

a day in the morning and received only masato. In Tapirillo and Tamshiyacu, groups operated most of the year; in Porvenir and Yanallpa they operated only during certain busy times of the year. The most noteworthy difference among exchange labor groups was the extent to which they had become institutionalized. The groups in Tamshiyacu had written rules and regulations; the other groups did not. In Porvenir and Yanallpa, groups often disbanded several months after they were formed; in Tamshiyacu and Tapirillo, group composition changed slowly. One work group in Tamshiyacu had operated for over 50 years. Work groups in Tamshiyacu had names, made regular monetary contributions to community fiestas, and had the support of the town government in enforcing compliance with their regulations (de Jong 1987). In both Tamshiyacu and Tapirillo, participants in exchange groups contributed money to a common fund, which was used to pay the cost of funerals and provided some aid with the medical expenses of members' families. One way in which groups in Tamshiyacu and Tapirillo raised money for their insurance programs was by working together as paid laborers for nonmembers. Only a few ribereño communities have institutionalized exchange groups with written rules, and most such groups were modeled after the ones in Tamshiyacu. The campesino unions have encouraged the formation of institutionalized exchange labor groups, however, because such groups require farmers to work together to solve problems in an egalitarian setting.

Advantages and Disadvantages of Various Types of Labor

Most ribereño households prefer to do as many agricultural tasks as possible with family labor. Farmers who do so spend less money than those who host festive work parties or hire jornaleros, and they do not have the reciprocal obligations to other households required of participants in exchange labor groups. Moreover, because the rewards to workers are obvious, the quality of family labor is usually high. The only ribereños who prefer festive work parties and jornaleros to family labor are those who can spend the time saved on alternative, more profitable tasks. In most rural areas of the Peruvian Amazon today, these are schoolteachers, owners of small transport boats, operators of the remaining fundos, and moneylenders who live in towns or on estates adjacent to villages.

When farmers cannot or do not wish to complete a particular task using only family labor, they must consider the advantages and disadvantages of the various ways of recruiting extrafamily labor. These are discussed below and summarized in Table 8.3.

Hired Labor

The major reason why farmers sometimes prefer jornaleros to festive work parties or exchange labor is their convenience. Campesinos usually have little trouble finding hired laborers because jornalero work is one of the few ways ribereños can earn money quickly without leaving their community for protracted periods. Employers of hired labor spend little or no time preparing food and drink for their workers and incur no reciprocal labor obligations to their employees.

The principal disadvantage of paid labor is its cost. Unless they have government credit, few ribereños can afford to hire large workforces. Most farmers who use hired labor therefore employ only a few workers for a limited time. Even those campesinos with government credit for raising specific crops often try to save as much money as possible by using family labor and cooperative work parties instead of jornaleros.

Festive Work Parties

The principal advantage that festive work parties have over hired laborers is that the direct costs are lower. Masato is made from home-grown manioc, and the fish, chicken, or game served to guests rarely needs to be purchased. The major advantage of festive labor over exchange groups is that hosts of festive work parties do not incur future obligations to provide labor to their guests. Moreover, unlike both employers of hired la-

Table 8.3. Characteristics of Various Forms of Extrafamily Labor

	Hired Labor	Festive Work Parties	Exchange Groups
Direct cash expenses	high	low	low
Indirect cash expenses	low	high	medium
Work quality	high	low-medium	high
Time requirements for preparation of food and drink	low	high	medium
Organizational complexity	low	medium	high
Reciprocal labor obligations for host	none	minimal, implicit	extensive, explicit

bor and participants in exchange groups, hosts of the enjoyable and lavish festive work parties accrue considerable prestige in their community.

Festive work parties also have several significant disadvantages in comparison with other forms of extrafamily labor. Host families must spend large amounts of time preparing masato and catching fish or game. Even though direct costs are low, indirect costs can be high because food served to guests is not sold at the market. In addition, the quality of work done may be poor because of guests' joking, talking, and drinking. Finally, during busy times of the year, hosts cannot be sure how many workers will turn up.

Exchange Labor Groups

The most important advantage of exchange labor groups is their low cost: participants in such groups spend much less money than those hiring jornaleros. Because the food and drink served is only slightly better than ordinary fare, exchange groups entail lower indirect costs than festive work parties. Exchange labor groups have other advantages as well. First, hosts spend less time obtaining and preparing food than do the organizers of festive work parties. Second, insurance programs associated with some exchange groups provide members with needed aid during periods of illness or injury. Finally, reciprocal labor obligations ensure high-quality work and enable farmers to schedule their activities.

The major drawback of exchange groups is the time that participants must spend working on other members' fields. If for some reason members need or wish to spend time on their own economic activities for several days or weeks in a row, they are faced with several unpalatable alternatives. When replacements are hired, the cost-saving advantage of membership in exchange groups disappears. When relatives are sent as replacements, members may lose some household labor and create tension at home. When members simply refuse to attend a work session, they are either fined or expelled from the group.

Another disadvantage of exchange groups is that conflict may be engendered by their rules and regulations. Members often disagree about whether obligations are being met and accuse one another of doing sloppy work or showing up for sessions drunk. When members leave a group either voluntarily or involuntarily as a result of such disagreements, long-standing village feuds can begin.

Although Erasmus (1955:465) and Moore (1975:272) note that exchange groups do not work well when members have different-sized fields, this has not yet been a problem in most ribereño villages. Differences in landholdings and plot sizes in these communities are minor.

Labor Recruitment Choices

Farmers electing to recruit extrafamily labor are not always able to choose between festive work parties and exchange labor groups. While most ribereño communities have frequent festive work parties, many do not have permanent exchange groups. The details of a particular village's history influences whether it has exchange labor groups. Residents' labor obligations to patrones usually preclude the formation of exchange labor groups on fundos. Festive work parties, in contrast, do not interfere with the day-to-day operation of a commercial estate. Communities that have recently become independent of fundos (e.g., Porvenir in 1985–86) are therefore unlikely to have long-established, institutionalized exchange labor groups. Such groups are also rare in communities where many residents regularly work as jornaleros for owners of nearby commercial estates.

The frequency of particular agricultural tasks in a community also influences whether exchange labor groups are used. These groups are not well suited for tasks that require several consecutive weeks of intensive work in a field (e.g., harvesting rice). Exchange labor groups are also not

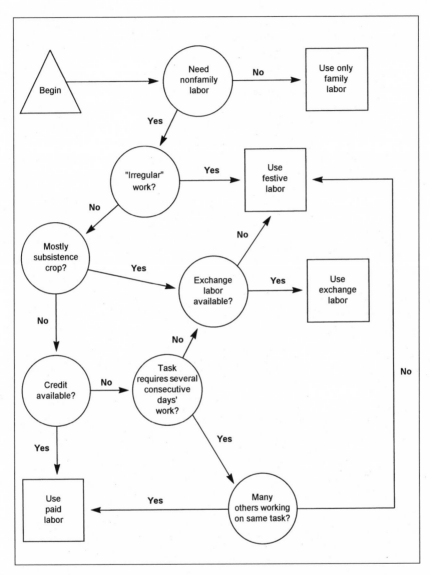

Figure 8.1. A flowchart model of extrafamily labor recruitment

as suitable as festive work parties for irregular tasks (e.g., felling trees in alturas), which can take place at any time of the year and are performed once a year or less. However, exchange groups are quite useful for regular tasks that occur at predictable intervals (e.g., weeding). They are also well suited for situations in which farmers need careful work but do not have enough money to hire jornaleros.

The flowchart in Figure 8.1 models how various factors influence ribereños' decisions about labor recruitment. It attempts to show what types of labor recruitment are most suitable for tasks with particular characteristics. Though no ribereño explained labor choice in precisely the form shown in the chart, the model does include all the variables I was told are important in the recruitment of extrafamily workers.

The flowchart model has certain limitations. It does not indicate what conditions lead a household to seek extrafamily labor and does not account for the presence or absence of exchange groups in a particular community. Although ribereños often use both cooperative work parties and jornaleros to complete a particular task, the model results in a single choice of extrafamily labor form.

The model does not predict labor recruitment choices very well in Tamshiyacu, where exchange labor groups (called *sociedades agrícolas*) have become institutionalized and are sometimes used for irregularly scheduled tasks for which they are not ideally suited, such as felling trees (de Jong 1987:15). Thus, members of the sociedades agrícolas rarely host festive work parties even in situations for which they are theoretically better suited than exchange groups. The model makes these assumptions:

1. Households use cooperative work parties and jornaleros only when family labor is insufficient to complete a task.

2. Festive work parties occur in the community of the decision maker.

3. Festive labor is used for irregular tasks.

4. Farmers do not use paid labor for crops that are grown mostly for home consumption.

5. For regular tasks on subsistence crops, farmers prefer exchange labor groups to festive work parties because of indirect and direct monetary savings.

6. If credit is available for a cash crop and a task is not irregular, farmers use hired labor because of its convenience.

7. If credit is not available for a cash crop, farmers prefer not to use hired labor because of its cost. Their choices about labor recruitment in this situation are affected by whether the task requires several consecutive days of work and whether many people in the community are simultaneously working on the task.

   a. If the task does not require several consecutive days of work, cost-saving considerations lead them to prefer exchange groups to festive work parties.

   b. If the task requires several consecutive days of work, farmers cannot use exchange groups and will, if possible, host festive work parties.

   c. If the task requires several consecutive days' work and many others in the community are working on the same task, farmers cannot recruit laborers via festive work parties and will be forced to hire jornaleros.

Table 8.4 lists the characteristics of four important ribereño agricultural tasks and indicates the type of labor organization predicted by the flowchart. De Jong's and my ethnographic observations suggest that the flowchart is generally successful in predicting the predominant form of labor organization for these tasks.

Harvesting rice grown in barreales requires extrafamily labor for plots of more than about 1.5 hectares. Harvesting takes place from October through January and must be completed quickly before the river covers the barreal. Rice is produced mostly for sale. Government credit was available for rice harvesting in the 1980s, but not all farmers were able to obtain loans. The flowchart predicts the use of hired labor for a "regular" task on a cash crop for which credit is available.

In the survey that Miguel Pinedo and I conducted in Porvenir, Santa Sofía, and Tapirillo in 1985–86, we asked 82 farmers if they had used cooperative work parties or paid laborers the last time they performed various agricultural tasks. Of the 36 farmers surveyed who had harvested rice recently, 14 (mostly with small plots and no credit) used only family labor. Of the remaining 22, who had recruited extrafamily labor, 18 used only hired labor, 1 used only festive work parties, and 3 used both.

Umarí, a native fruit that is the principal cash crop in Tamshiyacu, is weeded once or twice a year. Since weeding an average umarí field of about one hectare takes 20 to 25 labor days, a large work group can complete this task in about one day. No government agricultural credit is available for umarí or other native fruits. The flowchart predicts that exchange labor, if available, will be used for regular one-day tasks on

Table 8.4. Flowchart Predictions for Four Important Agricultural Tasks

	Harvesting Rice in Barreales	Weeding Umarí	Harvesting Plantains	Clearing Manioc Fields[a]
Requires extrafamily labor	usually	usually	no	usually
Regularity	regular	regular	irregular	irregular
Predominantly subsistence or cash crop	cash	cash	subsistence	subsistence
Credit available, 1985–1986	yes	no	no	difficult to obtain
Usual duration	several days to several weeks	a day[b]	a few hours[c]	a day
Local labor availability[d]	scarce	abundant	abundant	abundant
Flowchart prediction	hired labor	exchange groups	household labor	festive work parties

[a]Manioc is usually interplanted with plantains and also often with corn.
[b]It takes about one day for a work party of 20 to 25 people to weed a one-hectare umarí field.
[c]Plantains are harvested over a period of several months as different varieties ripen. Since the crop is planted year-round, this activity is not seasonal. "A few hours" refers to the amount of time spent in one harvesting session.
[d]Availability depends on the number of people in a community who are busy on the same task at the same time.

cash crops for which credit is not available. The exchange labor groups in Tamshiyacu spend more time weeding umarí than doing any other activity (de Jong 1987:15). Farmers in Tamshiyacu who are not members of exchange groups ordinarily weed umarí using only family labor. When such labor is insufficient, they hire jornaleros. Festive work parties are rarely used for weeding umarí.

Harvesting plantains is done piecemeal. Planting takes place during most months of the year, and varieties differ in the length of time they take to mature. Because the crop does not rot in the field unless the restinga where it is planted is flooded, there is little reason in most years to complete the task quickly. Since harvesting plantains does not ordinarily require the recruitment of extrafamily labor, the flowchart assumes that campesinos will carry out this task using only household labor, and in fact, of the 71 campesinos surveyed who had harvested plantains recently in Porvenir, Santa Sofía, and Tapirillo, 67 used only family labor.

Ribereños frequently must clear away growth before planting manioc in alturas and restingas. In alturas this usually entails clearing substantial secondary growth, but in restingas the task is somewhat less onerous. Depending on the size of the plot and the age-sex composition of a household, clearing a manioc field may or may not require extrafamily labor. Clearing can be done at any time of the year. The flowchart predicts the use of festive labor for irregular tasks on subsistence crops. Of the 82 campesinos surveyed who had recently cleared manioc fields in Porvenir, Santa Sofía, and Tapirillo, 25 used only family labor. Of the remaining 57, who recruited some form of extrafamily labor, 12 used only jornaleros, 14 only festive work parties, 15 only exchange groups, and the remaining 16 used some combination of cooperative labor and jornaleros.

Although the flowchart correctly predicted that cooperative work parties would be used more than jornaleros, the prediction that festive mingas would be used more than exchange groups was not fulfilled. This is largely a result of the fact that most campesinos were not able to choose between these two forms of labor. In Porvenir, festive mingas are rarely held, while in Santa Sofía there are no exchange groups. In Tapirillo one exchange group operated during 1985–86, and a second group was formed in 1987. Members of Tapirillo exchange groups rarely participated in festive work parties, and nonmembers did not have access to exchange group labor.

Changing Economic Conditions and Agricultural Labor Organization

The history of the Peruvian Amazon provides some support for Guillet's (1980) dependency theory argument for the survival of cooperative work groups. One of the main reasons why ribereños are poor is that various capitalist enterprises that deal in rubber, other forest products, and petroleum have extracted wealth from the region, invested most of the profits elsewhere, and paid local workers miserable wages. The continued poverty of most campesinos is an important reason why festive work parties and exchange labor groups persist in ribereño communities.

However, the amount of direct extraction of wealth from the Peruvian Amazon and the consequent peripheralization of campesinos have declined in recent years. The extractive industries of the past several decades have not approached the scale of the rubber boom. Furthermore, the demise of semifeudal commercial estates has accelerated. Although campesinos in independent villages continue to complain justifiably of mistreatment by local rural and urban elites, the exploitation that occurs is more indirect, less obvious, and undeniably less blatant than that which takes place on fundos.

Ribereños, moreover, have been selling larger amounts of cash crops in the Iquitos area. Cash cropping was spurred in the 1960s and 1970s by the spread of motorized river transport and the greater availability of credit for growing rice, jute, and corn. The breakup of many fundos also contributed to an increase in campesino cash cropping. On fundos, many campesinos spend much of their time working directly for their patrón on tasks such as growing sugarcane, making aguardiente, gathering forest products, or tending cattle. Their own agricultural activities are largely confined to cultivating small subsistence plots of manioc and plantains. Residents of independent villages, in contrast, have more time to devote to their own cash crops.

Increases in cash cropping and government credit have not led to the replacement of festive work parties and exchange groups with hired laborers in most ribereño communities. Although there are no quantitative data on the past incidence of the various types of extrafamily labor in these communities, ribereños agreed in the mid-1980s that government credit was allowing farmers to hire more jornaleros. However, residents of most communities reported that this increase in hired labor was not accompanied by a decline in the frequency of festive work parties. Furthermore, exchange groups appeared to be increasing in importance in the region. There were more such groups, they operated over longer stretches of the year, and more groups had written rules and some sort of insurance program.

One reason why festive work parties and exchange labor groups are still frequently used by ribereños is that communities have remained egalitarian and poor. The increase in cash cropping has not created an upper class to hire labor and host work parties and a lower class to work as jornaleros and form exchange labor groups. Because the increases in cash income have not been dramatic for most campesinos, even the wealthiest farmers who recruit extrafamily labor prefer festive work parties to jornaleros for some tasks. More prosperous campesinos also sometimes conclude that the cost saving of exchange groups outweighs the time saving of festive work parties.

Another reason for the persistence of cooperative labor in the region is that increases in cash cropping have led to greater demand by campesinos for extrafamily labor. Although ribereños now hire workers to help with many tasks formerly performed by family labor alone, they cannot afford the cost of extensive use of jornaleros. Farmers who need extrafamily labor therefore continue to host festive work parties and participate in exchange labor groups.

The cultural ecology of the Peruvian Amazon also encourages the use of cooperative labor. Because little machinery is used, sizable labor forces are needed for many important tasks. Clearing land and weeding can be efficiently and quickly completed by large festive work parties. Furthermore, the agricultural cycle and climate are such that many tasks can be carried out at different times of the year by the various households. The reciprocal labor obligations associated with exchange labor groups do not prevent farmers from completing such tasks.

Guillet (1980) has argued that in areas on the periphery of the world economy, cooperative labor is useful for employers who wish to keep wages down and national politicians who wish to keep urban food prices low. He points out that because cooperative work groups enable some peasants to avoid total economic disaster, they indirectly reduce the amount of rural political protest over low wages and crop prices. This argument seems of limited relevance to the Peruvian Amazon. Few contemporary ribereños are employed by large-scale capitalist enterprises, and most of the food crops they sell are staples consumed by residents of Iquitos. Although Iquiteños grumble about the cost of rice, manioc, plantains, and other locally produced foods, they complain much more about the price of goods imported into the region (e.g., sugar, kerosene, soap, and clothing). Politicians neither encourage nor discourage the use of cooperative labor.

9. Economic Strategies

Residents of Porvenir, Santa Sofía, and Tapirillo make hundreds of economic decisions every year. Most of them result in a continuation of time-tested agricultural and fishing practices and may not, in fact, involve a conscious weighing of different options. Some decisions, however, are carefully considered responses to changing economic, environmental, and sociopolitical conditions and may be part of a long-term plan to improve the material conditions of one or more members of a household.

The principal short-term goal of ribereño households is to maintain their self-sufficiency. Households allocate the land and labor at their disposal in order to ensure a steady food supply under ordinary circumstances. They also do as much as they can to acquire resources that enable them to remain economically viable when floods ruin fields, crop prices drop, and family members become ill. A distinctly secondary short-term goal is to retain sufficient flexibility to be able to take advantage of economic opportunities such as new types of agricultural credit, higher guaranteed prices for certain crops, and improvements in the marketing system.

Long-term economic strategies of ribereño households can involve several different and sometimes conflicting goals. All households attempt to maintain access to good land, and many also attempt to maintain access to off-farm work on commercial estates. Newly established households try to ensure economic self-sufficiency as the number of mouths to feed grows, while long-established households attempt to maintain self-sufficiency as their workforce ages and shrinks. Some families strive for upward mobility by making capital investments, migrating temporarily to Iquitos, and educating their children.

Risk and Decision Making

Economists and anthropologists frequently report that poor peasant farmers are reluctant to try risky agricultural techniques, crop varieties, and marketing methods. Although this reluctance was formerly attributed to a "peasant conservatism" typical of "traditional" cultures (e.g., Foster 1962; Rogers 1969), most researchers (e.g., Barlett 1982; Ortiz 1979) now agree that such behavior is economically sensible. Poor rural families cannot afford the loss of a substantial investment of land, labor, or capital.

Social scientists have defined "risk" in numerous ways. Some (e.g., Freund 1956; Lin et al. 1974) say that risk should be a measure of the consistency of returns associated with a particular economic option. Others (e.g., Boussard and Petit 1967; Kunreuther and Wright 1979) favor defining risk as the probability that returns to a particular economic option will fall below some critical threshold. Furthermore, researchers (e.g., Cancian 1979; Chibnik 1981a, 1981b) sometimes make a distinction between risk and uncertainty. These definitional issues are largely irrelevant, however, to the analysis of ribereño economic behavior that follows. I use the term *risky* loosely to encompass a variety of decisions in which the outcome is unpredictable and may be unfavorable.

Most short-term economic decision making by ribereños is entirely consistent with theories about peasant risk-aversion. One widely noted aspect of risk-avoidance behavior is participation in a diversity of economic activities. Ribereños are creative and indefatigable diversifiers. They obtain food and income from multiple sources and use a wide variety of crops, land types, and farming and fishing methods. Few ribereño households earn more than two-thirds of their annual cash income from any single source, and none obtain more than half their annual caloric intake from any one food.

Another way ribereños lessen risk is by spending most of their work time on subsistence production. Ribereños' economic strategies aim first at ensuring a reliable home-grown food supply and only secondarily at earning income via cash cropping, wage labor, and the sale of fish. This enables households to survive even when prices are low and wage work is hard to find. Plantains and manioc, the most important subsistence crops, are grown on high land that is unlikely to flood. The most important cash crops, in contrast, are grown on barreales and low restingas and are often lost to floods.

The large number of children in many ribereño households also reduces risk. A large family workforce ensures that agricultural tasks will
be completed even if one or more household members become incapacitated. In addition, larger families can engage in a wider variety of economic activities than smaller ones. Ribereños with many children hope
that one or more will later provide them with some financial assistance
or a place to live.

Ribereños do not engage in most security-enhancing activities explicitly to reduce risk. Many "choices" are so ingrained in the local culture
that their rationale is rarely explicitly considered (see Gladwin and Murtaugh 1980 for a good general discussion of such "preattentive" decisions). For example, ribereño households "choose" to raise most of their
own food. An alternative economic strategy might involve raising cash
crops such as rice, jute, melons, onions, tomatoes, and cowpeas and using the profits to purchase manioc, plantains, and fish. Ribereños were
usually puzzled when I asked why this was not done. They considered
my question a stupid one about an inconceivable possibility. When pressed
for an answer, they sometimes said that cash crops were riskier than subsistence crops, but in day-to-day life no one thinks about this. Fishing
and growing manioc and plantains are simply what ribereños do. Cash
cropping has not been sufficiently attractive to lead ribereños even to
consider abandoning subsistence agriculture and fishing.

Few ribereño women and men plan the size of their families. Although
ribereños are quite willing and able to discuss the advantages and disadvantages of large families, they make little effort to control the spacing
and number of births. Since the advantages of large families probably
outweigh the disadvantages, women and men have little reason to limit
the number of children they have. Furthermore, the state makes almost
no attempt to promote family planning in the countryside, and few rural
people have access to condoms, birth control pills, diaphragms, and intra-
uterine devices.

Much of the diversity of ribereño fishing and farming can be explained
without reference to risk aversion. During certain parts of the year, fishing
is better in rivers than in oxbow lakes, and during other parts of the year
the reverse is the case. Farmers who plant both subsistence and cash crops
inevitably use a number of different land types. Most subsistence crops
are best suited to high restingas and alturas; most cash crops are best
suited to low restingas and barreales. Farmers who want to spread their
labor out evenly over the course of a year must plant a variety of crops.

Although some crops can be grown year-round, others have to be planted and harvested at specific times.

Nonetheless, some economic activities are undertaken explicitly to reduce risk. As noted in Chapter 7, many villagers keep fowl and pigs in order to be able to raise cash quickly during emergencies. Vegetables are planted in small fields because the likelihood of crop failure is high. Slowly maturing varieties of manioc are planted in high restingas and alturas even though yields are better on lower land more prone to flooding.

Many economic decisions involve a consideration of both risk and other factors. One important and complex choice of this type has already been described. Households use family members, hired laborers, and co-operative work groups to carry out agricultural tasks. The potential profits from hiring workers are high, but the potential losses are also high. Many households prefer the safer strategy of using family labor and hosting cooperative work parties. Another risk-related choice, described in detail in the next chapter, concerns the use of loans from the Agrarian Bank. Most decisions about government credit involve weighing the pros and cons of borrowing money for rice production. When such loans are taken, farmers can raise several hectares of rice and earn substantial profits by local standards. Rice crops often fail, however, and farmers are left with large debts. Decisions about rice loans are especially complicated because ribereños sometimes regard money borrowed for agricultural production as a type of insurance that can be used for other purposes during emergencies.

Experimentation and Socioeconomic Change

Some anthropologists argue that many customary rules of behavior enable individuals and groups to cope with ecological, economic, and demographic problems. Although such functional explanations may place little emphasis on the origins of such rules, evolution-oriented analyses attempt to examine the process by which useful beliefs and behaviors become incorporated into cultural repertoires. Using analogies from natural selection in biological evolution, cultural evolutionists (e.g., Harris 1977, 1979) argue that individuals and groups try out a variety of behaviors over time and retain only those which are in some way preferable to previous cultural practices. Perhaps because people are often unaware of the ecological advantages of new beliefs and behaviors, cultural evolutionists seldom claim that individuals or groups consciously calculate efficient methods to solve environmental problems. Instead, satisfactory (although not ordinarily optimal) cultural solutions to problems are said to evolve through an undescribed process of random trial and error.

Several writers (e.g., Boehm 1978) point out that, because human responses to environmental and sociopolitical problems are frequently conscious and purposive, conventional cultural evolutionary theories provide incomplete descriptions of sociocultural change. These critics have rarely attempted to specify how human rationality and purposiveness affect cultural evolution. Some years ago, however, Allen Johnson argued cogently that small-scale experimentation is a characteristic of all domains of human behavior and is "the basic stuff of which adaptation and evolutionary change are made" (1972:156). Such experimentation allows people to try something new without incurring much risk.

When I planned my research in the Peruvian Amazon, one of my major goals was to describe the role of small-scale experimentation in socioeconomic change. I expected ribereños to make numerous innovations in response to changing economic conditions and government policies. While I was in Peru, however, I did not observe much experimentation. Households responded to changing river levels, crop prices, and government policies by altering their mix of economic activities, but such changes rarely involved innovation. They were instead different combinations of familiar activities.

I probably would have seen more economic innovation if I had stayed in Peru longer. Ribereños have shown that they are quite willing to seek out new income sources. Since 1940, rural residents of the Peruvian Amazon have adopted rice and jute as cash crops, have begun using government credit, and have established colectivo services to link their villages with Iquitos. They have been employed by petroleum explorers, smugglers of goods from Brazil, producers of aguaje-flavored ice cream, and exporters of tropical fish. All of these changes began with a few people taking advantage of a new economic opportunity.

Ribereños were making two potentially important economic experiments in 1985–86: individuals were borrowing money from the Agrarian Bank to raise plantains and manioc for the first time, and communities were experimenting with gasoline-operated threshers used in rice harvesting. Neither innovation, however, ultimately resulted in significant changes in the local economy.

The extension of credit for plantains and manioc was part of the populist program of the government led by the APRA party (the Alianza Popular

Revolucionaria Americana). The party, headed by Alán García, had won an overwhelming victory in the national elections of 1985, and the new government pledged to improve conditions for the rural and urban poor. A cornerstone of the government's plans in rural areas was to provide more credit to campesinos.

Many ribereños were reluctant to borrow money from the Agrarian Bank to increase their production of plantains and manioc, as the APRA program did not include establishing buying centers and guaranteed prices for these crops. Farmers worried about becoming indebted to the bank if prices for plantains and manioc fell on the open market, which many thought would be the case if credit spurred increased production. Some ribereños nonetheless attempted to take advantage of the new loan program. Only a few succeeded in obtaining credit for growing plantains and manioc, however, and most of these were men and women who lived along a road slowly being built between Iquitos and Nauta. The new program was largely rhetoric. Further, as Peru's economy crumbled in the late 1980s, the APRA government abandoned most of its programs for rural development. As in the past, ribereños could get credit only for growing rice, jute, and corn, and by the early 1990s, campesinos could rarely obtain bank loans even for these crops.

During 1985–86, Tapirillo and 22 other ribereño communities agreed to purchase gasoline-operated rice threshers from the Comité de Productores de Arroz de la Provincia de Maynas (COPAPMA), the rice producers' union. The machines save considerable labor during harvesting, but few individual ribereños could afford to buy them. COPAPMA had been given 25 threshers by international development organizations, and it offered to sell them to groups if they agreed to certain conditions. Machines were to be purchased and managed by communities or local chapters of the rice producers' union. If a thresher was later sold to an individual, COPAPMA had the right to repossess the machine. All members of the owning group would have equal access to the thresher. Communities would not have to make any payments for the machine until the first rice harvest; after that, user fees would be assessed. These "payments" for the machine were actually attempts by the union to raise some money for its operating costs.

The use of a thresher entails some organizational complexities. The thresher's only function is to separate rice grains from stalks; farmers still must cut the stalks from the plant before operating the machine. About 25 people are needed to operate a thresher efficiently. Three transport rice plants from fields to the machine, sixteen cut the stalks from the plant, and six operate the thresher. Before distributing the threshers, COPAPMA held meetings to discuss these labor organizational requirements.

Many communities were eager to obtain threshers. Farmers were attracted by the possibility of reducing labor costs at harvest time and the opportunity to try the machines with little risk and no initial outlay of money. Ribereños had little trouble learning to use the threshers and were often willing to pay the user fees. Despite the success of the thresher distribution program, however, the machines had little immediate effect on the local economy. COPAPMA had given away all its machines by mid-1987, and many communities did not receive threshers. (Several years later, COPAPMA received more threshers and began "selling" them again.) Moreover, some communities that received threshers could not increase rice production very much because they were already using all of their best lands in barreales. Even in places where some barreales were unused, the risks of large-scale rice production deterred most farmers from planting more than one or two hectares of the crop.

Variability in Short-Term Economic Strategies

Ribereño households differ considerably in their mix of economic activities. Much of this variation is related to household size. Small households need less cash and food than larger ones. However, even households of similar size can differ in their degree of involvement in the cash economy. Some families grow many cash crops and seek to raise money for secondary education for their children; others are more subsistence-oriented and have fewer hopes for their children's upward mobility. In addition, some variability in monetary orientation can be attributed to minor class differences in ribereño communities. Ribereño villages may include several interrelated households that are more prosperous than most of their neighbors. Often one or more members of these households are descended from former patrones.

A brief examination of the economic activities of three ribereño families in 1985–86 illustrates some of the interhousehold variability found in Porvenir, Santa Sofía, and Tapirillo. The households described differ in both their position in the domestic cycle and their degree of involvement in the cash economy.

A Subsistence-Oriented Household

Napoleón Panduro Gil and his wife, Arminda Piña Coespan, were in their early twenties in 1986. They lived in a small house in Santa Sofía with their two sons, four-year old Jacinto and the infant Leonardo. Both Napoleón and Arminda attended school for only a few years before leaving. Arminda has spent her entire life in Santa Sofía. Napoleón, who lived in the nearby village of Marupa until he was 17, moved to Santa Sofía in 1980 with his mother after she separated from his father. His mother was born and reared in Santa Sofía and still has many relatives in the community.

The agricultural activities of the Panduro-Piña family in 1984 and 1985 were small-scale and diverse (see Table 9.1). Except for a tiny garden with tomatoes and watermelons, their plots were monocropped. Napoleón and Arminda did almost all of the agricultural work on their fields, but they did hire a few laborers for a day or two to help weed plantain and manioc fields.

Napoleón and Arminda had 15 chickens at the beginning of 1986. They sold two dozen in 1984 for about 380,000 soles ($32) but did not sell any in 1985. In 1985 they sold approximately 1,000 papayas in Iquitos, earning about 600 intis ($42). Napoleón also occasionally sold a few fish in Iquitos.

The small-scale economic activities of this household are common among families in the earliest stages of the domestic cycle. Napoleón and Arminda do not have to plant much land with manioc and plantains to meet their household's subsistence needs. Nonetheless, the household is not yet entirely self-sufficient. Napoleón and Arminda receive some food and financial aid from Arminda's family, which is among the most prosperous families in the village. The household's economic activities will doubtless become more extensive as Napoleón and Arminda have more children. They were experimenting in 1985 and 1986 with various crops and may well have begun producing more rice, plantains, and manioc for sale. They were not especially entrepreneurial, however, and expressed no interest in obtaining credit from the Agrarian Bank to help finance cash cropping.

A Household with a Typical Mix of Economic Activities

Pedro Ahuanari Amani and Carmen Manuyama Macedo were in their mid-thirties in early 1986. They lived with their four children in Porvenir,

Table 9.1. Crop Mix of Panduro-Piña Household, 1984 and 1985

| | Hectares Planted | |
	1984	1985
Manioc	0.4	0.5
Plantains	0.0	0.3
Rice	0.0	0.4
Corn	0.3	0.9
Cowpeas	0.0	0.1[a]
Tomatoes	0.0	0.1
Watermelons	0.0	0.1
Total hectares cultivated	0.7	2.3

[a]Cowpeas, tomatoes, and watermelons were interplanted in 1985.

where Carmen had been born and raised. Pedro, who grew up in a small community near Nauta, moved to Porvenir after he left the Peruvian army in 1973. He is the village police officer, an unpaid job that does not require much work.

The household's crop mix changed little from 1984 to 1985 (Table 9.2). They interplanted plantains and manioc in a half-hectare field in altura in 1984 and interplanted the same crops with corn in a half-hectare field in restinga in 1985. They used most of the manioc, plantains, and corn for home consumption in both years. Although family labor was sufficient for most agricultural tasks, Pedro and Carmen had to recruit extrafamily workers for two jobs in 1985. They hosted a 20-person cooperative work party to clear the half hectare in restinga later planted with manioc, plantains, and corn, and they also hired workers for a total of five labor-days to help clear their plots in barreal prior to flooding.

Pedro and Carmen had 12 chickens and a pig when interviewed. They sold 6 chickens and a pig in 1984 but did not sell any animals in 1985. Although they made a little money by selling eggs in Porvenir, much of the household's income came from wage work and the sale of fish and fruit. Pedro spent four weeks in 1985 working as a hired laborer for other residents of Porvenir and another week cutting pasture for Orlando Montoya. His wage labor income for 1985 was about 500 intis

Table 9.2. Crop Mix of Ahuanari-Manuyama Household, 1984 and 1985

| | Hectares Planted | |
	1984	1985
Manioc	0.5[a]	0.5[b]
Plantains	0.5	0.5
Corn	0.5	0.5
Watermelons	none	0.5
Peanuts	0.1	0.1
Total hectares cultivated	1.6	2.1

[a]Manioc and plantains were interplanted in 1984.
[b]Manioc, plantains, and corn were interplanted in 1985.

($36). Pedro fished most days for both home consumption and sale. He estimated that he earned about 350 intis ($25) selling fish in Iquitos in 1985 and a smaller amount from local sales. The household also earned about 250 intis ($18) selling a variety of fruit in Iquitos in 1985.

Pedro and Carmen's mix of subsistence and cash-producing activities was fairly typical for households in the three villages. Although the family spent most of its time on subsistence production, they earned some income from cash cropping, wage work, and the sale of livestock and fish. Their total household cash income in 1985 was probably considerably less than 2,000 intis ($143).

A Cash-Cropping Household

César Flores Bardales and Norma Montes Ríos lived in Tapirillo with their nine children in 1985–86. Both César and Norma were born in Tapirillo and have spent most of their lives there. César was away from the community for several years of military service and lived for another three years as an adult in Iquitos. He was 50 and Norma was 38 in early 1986. Their children ranged in age from 1 to 18. Although their home is large by local standards, it is otherwise unexceptional. The family owns a sewing machine and a boat motor but does not have a radio.

César is a member of the socioeconomically and politically dominant family of Tapirillo. César was the teniente gobernador of the community in 1985–86, his brother Ricardo (profiled later in this chapter) is prominent in the regional rice producers' union, and his brother Demetrio is a transportista. Ricardo, Demetrio, and Norma's mother all had houses in both Iquitos and Tapirillo.

Table 9.3 shows some of the household's diverse agricultural activities in 1984 and 1985. They interplanted manioc and plantains in 1984 and manioc, plantains, tomatoes, and melons in 1985. They also sold significant amounts of manioc, rice, and tomatoes. Because their household included five teenage boys, César and Norma rarely had to recruit extrafamily agricultural labor, although they did host a festive work party in 1985 to clear a hectare in restinga and hired jornaleros for 17 labordays to help with the rice harvest. César took a loan from the Agrarian Bank in 1984 for rice cultivation but did not seek bank credit in 1985.

Norma and César had 36 chickens in early 1986. They sold a dozen chickens in 1984 but did not sell any in 1985. The family sometimes sells papayas, star apples, shimbillo, and other fruits in Iquitos. In early 1986 they were earning between 50 and 100 intis ($3 to $6) a week from fruit sales, and they expected these sales to continue for a few months. The family's fishing, in contrast, was strictly for home consumption.

Although this household is somewhat more involved in the cash economy than most, César and Norma are nonetheless quite small-scale farmers, usually devoting less than five hectares to crops. Their 1985 cash income was probably about the same as that of the household of Pedro Ahuanari and Carmen Manuyama, although they earned considerably more than Pedro and Carmen in 1984. Furthermore, the household's economic activities are not particularly diversified, with most of the cash income being generated by rice sales.

Long-Term Risk-Aversion Strategies

Most ribereño decision making involves short-term planning aimed at ensuring the survival of a household over the next year or so. Ribereños cannot make careful long-range plans because the macroeconomic trends and political conflicts that will affect their lives in future decades are largely unpredictable and beyond their control. Many ribereños do know, however, that their economic decision making in the years to come may be affected by new government agricultural policies, fluctuating crop prices, changing rates of inflation, a mounting national debt, the activities of the Sendero Luminoso, and the illicit trade in coca-based narcot-

Table 9.3. Crop Mix of Flores-Montes Household, 1984 and 1985

| | Hectares Planted | |
	1984	1985
Manioc	1.0[a]	1.5[b]
Plantains	1.5	1.0
Rice	2.0	1.0
Cowpeas	0.5	0.5
Tomatoes	none	1.0
Watermelons	none	1.0
Total hectares cultivated	4.0	2.5

[a]Manioc and plantains were interplanted in 1984.
[b]Manioc, plantains, tomatoes, and watermelons were interplanted in 1985.

ics. Such events are difficult to predict in the short run; they are virtually impossible to predict in the long run. Even when ribereños are able to guess future macroeconomic and political trends, they are usually too poor and powerless to make the investments necessary to take advantage of changing circumstances.

Ribereño households do what they can to ensure their long-term economic viability, and much of their planning involves political and social maneuvering. Some long-term risk-aversion strategies aim at retaining access to a diversity of land types and natural resources. Others are attempts to establish social ties that will provide a safety net in case of high floods, crop failure, or illness.

Farmers usually have few problems gaining access to fields, as land is not scarce in alturas and restingas. Ribereños are, however, sometimes unhappy about the allocations of barreales made in community meetings and may attempt to persuade the teniente gobernador and other influential villagers that they should receive better low-lying land the next time.

Threats to a household's access to land and other natural resources are most likely to arise from outside the community. Estate owners may claim some or all of a village's land, commercial boats may deplete the supply of desirable species of fish, and tourist enterprises may prohibit ribereños from fishing and hunting on their land. Because individual

ribereños acting alone are unable to counter such threats, many are willing to join organizations that further the political interests of poor rural
Amazonians. Indeed, the formation and persistence of the campesino
unions can be attributed largely to ribereños' long-term plans to preserve
their access to land and other natural resources.

Nevertheless, the campesino unions sometimes have difficulty persuading ribereños to confront patrones. Traditional long-range ribereño survival strategies involve maintaining social and economic relationships
with rural entrepreneurs and moneylenders. Patrones pay less for wage
labor than other employers and buy crops at prices well below those of
the open market and state-run buying centers, but they are also often
willing to lend money quickly to a ribereño during an emergency and
sometimes agree to defer repayment for long periods.

Ribereños had no alternative to entering into socioeconomic relationships with patrones in the three decades or so after the rubber boom
ended, but in more recent times many farmers have been able to raise
and sell their crops without dealing with the owners of commercial estates and moneylenders. Some contemporary ribereños who borrow
money from, work for, and deliver crops to patrones are making conscious choices to reduce long-term risk. They may further seek to en-
hance their security by persuading patrones to be the godparents of their
children. Most ribereño-patrón relationships today are not altogether
voluntary, however. Some ribereños are forced to borrow money from
patrones during financial emergencies, and others need the economic security provided by ties with patrones but hate their work on commercial
estates.

Ribereño households' most important hedge against adversity is to
maintain good relations with a wide variety of kin in different places.
Such ties assure that members of a ribereño household will be taken in
somewhere during hard times. One of the most common ribereño responses to flooding or illness is to move in temporarily or semipermanently
with relatives living elsewhere.

Planned Changes in Household Composition

Most changes in household demography are not the result of long-term
planning. Households grow as children are born and shrink as older
members die. Adults quickly decide to move in and out in response to
economic misfortune and family problems. Nonetheless, some changes

in household composition occur only after a careful consideration of alternative choices. These changes typically involve the establishment of new households and the dissolution of long-established ones.

Newly formed couples must decide whether to establish their own household or live temporarily or semipermanently with relatives. If they decide to move in with kin, they often have several places they might live. The choice involves a complex weighing of numerous factors, including economic opportunities in the various villages, personal relations with various relatives, and the demographic composition and space available in potential homes. Young couples living with relatives may eventually decide to establish their own household. The couple usually build their own house in the community where they are living. They may, however, decide at this point to move to be near relatives in another village or even to migrate to an urban area.

As couples age, their household gradually becomes less self-sufficient. Older men and women may not be able to carry out agricultural tasks as well as in the past, especially if they have a debilitating illness, and most or all of the couple's children may have established their own households elsewhere by then. Many ribereños therefore think about what they will do if they become incapacitated or widowed. Unless one member of the couple is incapable of carrying out ordinary tasks, most households remain intact while both the husband and wife are alive. When one member of the couple dies, the survivor must decide where to live. He or she may move to the house of a relative (usually a son or daughter), or relatives may move to the house of the survivor. Such decisions are straightforward when only one son or daughter is willing and able to take in a widowed parent, but they are more complex when there are several possibilities.

Upward Mobility

Ribereños cannot easily improve their material circumstances. Land in alturas is not well suited for intensive agriculture, and much fertile low-lying land is scarce and impermanent. Wages are miserable, and prices for crops and fish are low. Most ribereños who have been able to improve their economic condition in recent years have left their communities either temporarily or permanently. In the early 1970s, many young men worked for oil companies in remote areas of Loreto, and after the oil boom ended, many of them migrated temporarily or permanently to

Iquitos and other towns and cities. Others returned to their villages with sizable savings, although by the time of my research they were no better off than other villagers. They had not been able to invest their savings in income-generating capital investments.

Today, rural residents often seek economic opportunities in Iquitos. Most move to the port area called Belén or into a squatter settlement (*pueblo joven*) and work as rematistas, vendors, cargo handlers, or domestic servants. Although migrants' lives change dramatically after the move to the city, their economic condition and health may not be much different from those in the countryside. The few who earn substantial amounts of money ordinarily stay in Iquitos, while those who fare less well sometimes tire of urban life and return to their villages, usually without having saved much money.

Many campesinos, recognizing that their own economic circumstances are unlikely to change much, invest in secondary school education for their children. They hope that their sons and daughters will eventually get a middle-class job in Iquitos or a local town and—as schoolteachers, nurses, civil servants, or merchants—earn enough money to provide some support for their aging rural parents.

Although an increasing number of ribereños are attending secondary school, their increased educational opportunities have so far had scant effect on the economies of rural communities, for several reasons. First, most ribereños who go to secondary school leave their community permanently and are unlikely to invest much of their earnings in their parents' village. Second, many secondary school students from rural areas have academic or financial problems and do not graduate. Third, those who finish school often have trouble finding good jobs in the Iquitos area. Finally, secondary school graduates who succeed in moving into the middle class may be unwilling or unable to send much money to rural areas because of their own growing families.

Some rural men improve their economic circumstances during and after military service. All men must either serve in the military or pay a fee to the government that relieves them of their obligation. Since few campesinos possess the money and bureaucratic savvy needed to avoid military service, most spend some time in the army. Of 81 adult males interviewed in Porvenir, Santa Sofía, and Tapirillo, 53 (66 percent) had been in the army, and none had escaped military service by paying the necessary fee. Most who had not served had simply ignored the relevant government regulations. These men were neither jailed nor fined. However, they were unable to vote, borrow money from the Agrarian Bank, or obtain legally recognized rights to land use.

Many ribereño men willingly join the army because it gives them the opportunity to travel to new places, earn some money, and learn mechanical skills that may be useful in later life. Military service is rarely dangerous. Most ribereños are sent to lowland outposts near the Ecuadorian and Brazilian borders, where their presence is thought to be a deterrent to foreign invaders.

Many ribereños do not return to their communities after completing military service. Some marry while in the military and move to their wives' communities. Others, who have come to find rural life boring, move to Iquitos. Many of these men stay in the city for the rest of their lives, though some eventually return to rural areas.

A few ribereño men have been able to earn significant amounts of money by operating boats carrying people and produce between rural villages and Iquitos. In May 1986 one man was operating three colectivos near Iquitos, and another two transportistas were each operating two boats. The rest owned only one. Many communities do not have resident transportistas. Instead, villagers rely on colectivo owners from other places for passage up and down the river. Tapirillo was the only one of the three communities examined closely which included a transportista among its inhabitants.

Not many rural Loretanos can afford to become transportistas. Few have the wealth necessary to persuade bank officials to provide startup loans. Colectivo owners must bear the ever-increasing cost of gasoline, oil, and maintenance and replace worn-out boats and motors. In late May 1986 the cost of gasoline for a round-trip between Tapirillo and Iquitos was 700 intis ($44); a year earlier the cost had been 400 intis ($29). Gasoline and oil prices were rising even faster than the rate of inflation.

Boat ownership can be risky. If a motor unexpectedly fails, several months' profits will be lost. Furthermore, a transportistas' monthly income varies markedly over the course of a year. Because few products are sold when the river is high, colectivo owners often incur losses during March, April, and May. Substantial profits, in contrast, can be made in October and November as farmers harvest rice before the river begins to rise.

Transportistas must charge high prices for passage and shipping both because of their expenses for gasoline and oil and because of the long distances between most villages and Iquitos. In 1985–86, campesinos who lived 50 kilometers from Iquitos had to pay the equivalent of the daily wage of an agricultural laborer to make a round-trip between their village and the city. As a result, few rural Loretanos go to Iquitos as often as they would like. Because the demand for boat passage is low, the region cannot support many transportistas.

Miguel Pinedo and I interviewed five transportistas in the Iquitos port. All these men were more prosperous than most of their neighbors before they began their colectivo service. Without exception, they had obtained and paid back large crop loans from the Agrarian Bank, so the bank was willing to lend them money to purchase boats and motors. Few campesinos can afford to buy motors without such loans, as a new boat and motor cost 8,000 intis ($500) apiece in May 1986. But bank loans alone were rarely sufficient to cover the costs of starting a colectivo service. Most transportistas interviewed also used some profits from agriculture to pay for their initial investments.

The work of a transportista is difficult. Most one-way trips between rural communities served by colectivos and Iquitos take between five and twelve hours, with the duration of the trip depending on the location of the community, the size and condition of the boat, and whether one is going upriver or downriver. Further, colectivo operators must frequently maneuver their small craft from one side of the river to the other, loading and unloading people, produce, and animals.

Transportistas usually have an assistant onboard, either a relative (often a son) or a young village neighbor. The assistant (or occasionally the transportista) sleeps on the boat overnight in the city to prevent theft.

I cannot provide a good estimate of the average annual income of a transportista. Colectivo owners must replace their boats and motors every two or three years, so their gross income is obviously higher in years in which these purchases are not made. Incomes also vary according to agricultural conditions in the area. When harvests are good, transportistas earn substantial sums carrying farmers and their produce to market. When yields are low, colectivo operators suffer almost as much as the farmers.

All five boat owners interviewed said that their economic position had improved somewhat since they began running a colectivo service. Transportistas are ordinarily among the two or three wealthiest people in a village and can usually afford secondary education for their children. A few have bought kerosene refrigerators and operate small stores, but they rarely have many expensive consumer goods, and their houses and clothes differ little from those of their neighbors.

Two Life Histories

The lives of Ricardo Flores and Alejandro Gil illustrate the difficulties ribereños have in improving their economic circumstances. Both men are members of the politically and economically dominant families of their communities. They have spent significant periods away from their villages and are knowledgeable about urban life. Ricardo and Alejandro are community leaders who are more accustomed to dealing with outsiders than many of their neighbors. Despite these advantages, Ricardo and Alejandro are not particularly prosperous. Neither man has been able to earn substantial amounts of money through agriculture, fishing, and wage labor.

Ricardo Flores

Ricardo Flores Bardales is an outgoing, wiry man who has a remarkable number of friends and relatives in the Iquitos area. Ricardo was born in Tapirillo in 1942. His parents, who were still alive in the mid-1980s, had lived in Tapirillo since the 1920s. Although Ricardo's father, Jorge, was once a minor patrón who raised cattle, he did not prosper. By the 1960s the economic condition of his family was not very different from that of other Tapirillo households. Ricardo's mother, Cecilia, was born and raised in Iquitos. One of Ricardo's sisters, who died young, was an ambitious woman who graduated from the university in Iquitos. Ricardo has three brothers (including César, the teniente gobernador, and Demetrio, the transportista) and two sisters living in Tapirillo. He is related to many of Tapirillo's inhabitants.

Ricardo finished primary school in Tapirillo and continued living there until he joined the army in 1962. He was in the army for two years, working as a radio operator in various parts of the tropical lowlands. After leaving the military, Ricardo lived for about a year in the city of Pucallpa in what is now the department of Ucayali. He was employed there as a radio operator for a state-run airline. Ricardo spent the next several years working in this area in a series of short-term jobs such as bricklayer and timber cutter. He says that he took on these jobs mostly because he wanted to see something of the world away from Tapirillo.

When Ricardo was about 25, he returned to Tapirillo. He soon met and moved in with 17-year-old Josefa Pérez. Josefa had been born in Iquitos but was reared in Tapirillo. Ricardo and Josefa quickly began a family, and by 1986 they had ten children—three girls (age 19, 16, and 4) and seven boys (age 14, 12, 11, 8, 6, 3, and an infant). Two other children had died in infancy.

Ricardo, like his neighbors, is primarily a small-scale farmer and fisher. He grows more rice than most of his neighbors but has never planted more than five hectares in this crop in any year. Ricardo has been active in the rice producers' union both locally and regionally. He was also the principal organizer of a longstanding cooperative work group in Tapirillo and operated a store there for many years. The store, which was located in a room of his house, sold basic staples such as kerosene, salt, and soap. Ricardo's profits from this enterprise were small.

In 1983, Ricardo's family built a house in the Belén port area of Iquitos so that the children would have a place to live while they attended secondary school. Josefa and the children moved to Iquitos, but Ricardo continued to spend much of his time in Tapirillo. He is rarely alone in the Tapirillo house, as other family members frequently visit.

Josefa and the older daughters were working as vendors in the Iquitos market in 1991, and Ricardo still farmed in Tapirillo and remained active in community organizations. The family's fields were not as large as in previous years, because Ricardo often was away from the village and could not count on much agricultural help from Josefa and the children. Ricardo was less active in the rice producers' union in Tapirillo than previously but was participating more in activities of the campesino organizations in Iquitos.

Alejandro Gil

Alejandro Gil Andrade is a stocky, quiet, hospitable man who was born in Santa Sofía around 1932. He was the teniente gobernador of Santa Sofía for many years. Alejandro's father, Nemesio, migrated from Caballococha to Santa Sofía shortly after the rubber boom ended. Nemesio's many children were the result of several different unions. Alejandro's mother was a local woman descended from both Yaguas and mestizos. When Alejandro was growing up, Spanish was the language of the house. Alejandro does not regard himself as Amerindian in any way and thinks that contemporary Yaguas are uncivilized. He vividly remembers being scared by painted Indians during his childhood.

When Alejandro was ten, he moved with his family to Iquitos. Alejandro finished primary school in the city. He joined the army as a teenager and learned to drive a truck. Alejandro served in several different parts of the tropical lowlands. After leaving the military, he worked for several years as a truck driver in Lima and in the Peruvian highlands.

Alejandro returned to Santa Sofía around 1954 and began farming. A few years later he met his wife, María, who comes from a village some distance away. Except for one year in a nearby community. Alejandro and María have lived in Santa Sofía since the 1950s. They had ten children living in Santa Sofía in 1986—five boys between 11 and 25 and five girls under 10. They also had a 24-year-old daughter who was working as a domestic servant in Iquitos and a 17-year-old son in the army. The only children who had attended secondary school were two boys (including the one in the army).

Alejandro's household labor force farmed large fields by local standards and engaged in a diversity of economic activities. In 1984 rice was their most important income source. The family's four hectares of rice in barreal yielded 8 metric tons. Their rice production dropped to 1.5 metric tons in 1985, however, when the floods came late and the family was able to cultivate only half a hectare in barreal. In 1985 Alejandro's family planted extensively in restingas to make up for their loss of income from rice. They had a one-hectare field interplanted with corn, plantains, and manioc, a one-hectare platanal, a one-hectare field devoted exclusively to jute, a one-half hectare yucal, a one-half hectare of tomatoes, and a quarter-hectare interplanted with watermelon and peanuts. They also raised a half-hectare of cowpeas in playas. The family earned about 5,000 intis (approximately $350) in 1985 from the sale of fish and papayas. They sold six dozen chickens in 1984 and three dozen in 1985.

Despite Alejandro's prominence in Santa Sofía, he has not been particularly innovative in economic terms. He has taken out only one bank loan for rice (in 1970) and has never borrowed money for jute production. Alejandro and María's house is larger than most of their neighbors', but this is mostly because of the space requirements of a large family. The household had neither a radio nor a boat motor in 1985–86.

The experiences of Ricardo and Alejandro show why most ambitious ribereños move permanently to urban areas. Both men finished primary school at a time when most ribereños did not, and both are exceptionally intelligent and able. They are respected by other villagers and have been selected for important community positions. They have had skilled jobs and could have done well in an urban area but have preferred to spend most of their lives as farmers in small communities where they have many relatives. In some ways they have been very successful. Both have large, cohesive families and close ties with nearby relatives and friends. But their economic conditions have not improved much over the years. Two decades ago they were subsistence farmers and fishers who sold a little of what they produced, and they still are today.

Since the ablest men and women cannot improve their material circumstances in the countryside, less capable villagers realize that they will remain poor if they stay in rural areas. Many therefore try their luck in Iquitos and in the towns of the Peruvian Amazon. Even those ribereños who have lived for many years in rural areas consider urban migration. Such moves most often occur after adult children establish themselves in Iquitos. Although Alejandro will most likely spend the rest of his life in Santa Sofía, Ricardo might yet move in with his wife and children in the city.

10. Agricultural Credit

State-sponsored agricultural credit programs are a controversial and increasingly common feature of rural development programs in many countries in Latin America, Africa, and Asia. In these programs, government banks offer loans at interest rates lower than those charged by informal moneylenders. Proponents of agricultural credit (e.g., Lipton 1979; Zavaleta et al. 1984) say that state-subsidized low-interest loans allow many small-scale farmers to make production-increasing investments they otherwise could not afford. Critics (e.g., Adams et al. 1984) argue that cheap government credit undermines private lending institutions and politicizes financial markets. They contend that scarce government funds might be better spent on alternative rural development projects.

Both advocates and opponents of agricultural credit programs agree that small-scale farmers usually receive less money per unit of land than their wealthier neighbors. Some explanations of these inequities (e.g., Gonzalez-Vega 1984) focus on the availability of credit. Economic and social ties between bank officials and powerful rural elites lead to favoritism in dispensing loans. The economics of banking also results in preferential treatment for wealthy customers because the cost of processing a single large loan is less than that of processing many smaller ones. Other explanations (e.g., Lipton 1979) focus on differences between rich and poor in the demand for credit. Many small-scale farmers are reluctant to take out loans because of the risks and uncertainties of credit programs.

The state-run Agrarian Bank of Peru gave crop loans to some farmers in Porvenir, Santa Sofía, and Tapirillo during the 1980s. Many residents of these villages, however, were unable or unwilling to borrow from the bank because of institutional policies favoring large-scale borrowers. The effects of risks and uncertainties on villagers' willingness to borrow were double-edged. Some farmers refused to take out loans because they feared that bad harvests would result in long-term debts. Others borrowed explicitly to reduce their chance of being caught short of cash in a household emergency.

Risk, Uncertainty, and the Use of Agricultural Credit

There are complex problems associated with attempts to assess the effects of risk aversion on farmers' demand for agricultural credit from formal institutions. A decision to take out a loan involves multiple risks and uncertainties. Farmers differ in their uses and sources of credit.

Frank Cancian (1979) has sharply distinguished between a "risky" situation, in which decision makers know the odds for and against desirable outcomes of a given course of action, and "uncertain" situations, in which decision makers lack this information. I have argued (Chibnik 1981a, 1981b) that risk and uncertainty are not discrete phenomena and that it makes more sense to classify situations according to their degree of risk and uncertainty along a risk-uncertainty continuum. The distinction between risk and uncertainty nonetheless is useful in analyzing the reactions of farmers to agricultural credit. Poor farmers in the Peruvian Amazon and elsewhere may be reluctant to take out crop loans because of the many risks associated with expanded production. They may also be unable to obtain much information about credit. Bank representatives and extension agents pay more attention to wealthy farmers, and written materials about credit programs can be incomprehensible to poor farmers with little formal education.

Wealthy farmers ordinarily use agricultural credit for its intended purpose: the production and marketing of crops. They have enough savings and sufficient alternative sources of income to be able to feed their families and pay medical bills without going into debt. Small-scale farmers, in contrast, often use loans to even out predictable seasonable fluctuations in cash on hand and to insure against economic or medical setbacks (Lipton 1979). They may deliberately borrow money to pay for routine household maintenance or be forced by an emergency to divert credit away from production and marketing. If agricultural credit is repaid on time, state lending institutions may not carefully monitor its use. Even when a farmer uses so much credit for household expenses that loan repayment is unlikely, future indebtedness to a bank may be regarded as preferable to an immediate financial crisis.

Farmers' demand for formal credit has also affected their use of informal credit. Prosperous farmers are unlikely to use private moneylenders, because banks charge lower interest rates and are more willing to lend large sums. Small-scale farmers, however, often prefer informal credit. Obtaining loans from moneylenders involves much less red tape than borrowing from banks. Moneylenders are more flexible about loan schedules and are less likely to earmark loans for particular activities.

Agricultural Credit in the Peruvian Amazon

The Peruvian government—with financial support from international banks, the Agency for International Development, and other foreign donors—has offered credit to farmers since the 1950s. These loans are intended to increase the production of important food and export crops. The particular crops for which credit has been available have varied over time and by geographic region. Crop credit in the Amazon has been given primarily for rice and jute.

The availability of agricultural credit has depended on economic conditions in Peru and the ideology of political leaders. During the 1970s and 1980s many farmers were able to obtain loans from the Agrarian Bank. In contrast, state agricultural credit was virtually nonexistent in the early 1990s. Farmers could sometimes get small crop loans shortly before elections.

Although in the mid-1980s most borrowers from the Agrarian Bank were campesinos, most money loaned went to rural and urban entrepreneurs. Large-scale borrowers were eligible for certain types of low-interest loans rarely or never given to campesinos. The bank gave loans for raising chickens exclusively to the owners of urban hatcheries in Iquitos. Rural entrepreneurs received sizable loans for capital investments in timber, cattle, boats, and water buffalo. Many campesinos resented the preferential treatment given large borrowers and were suspicious of the close personal ties between bank officials and the rural and urban elites.

The process of getting a loan during the 1980s was time-consuming and costly. While entrepreneurs could obtain approval for an entire season's loan in one visit to the Agrarian Bank, campesinos ordinarily had to obtain separate loan approvals for specific activities such as land clearing, weeding, and harvesting. As recently as the early 1980s, campesinos had to obtain loans in six or seven portions for rice grown in barreales, though by the mid-1980s the number had been reduced to three.

Borrowers had to travel to branches of the Agrarian Bank in Iquitos or elsewhere to get an entire season's loan initially approved and to receive approvals for each loan portion. Since most villages are from five to fifteen hours away from the nearest branch of the Agrarian Bank, trips to get loan approvals usually involved a stay of at least one night away from home. Limited hours (from nine to twelve in the morning, five days a week), crowded conditions, and slow service at the bank often resulted in a delay of several days. Patrones and long-time campesino borrowers who knew the branch manager were sometimes able to avoid these delays by going through a side door to talk to the relevant official, but most farmers seeking loans had to wait in a long line.

Obtaining a loan involved considerable red tape. Ribereños could not obtain a bank loan without a voting certificate. In order to obtain this certificate, adult males under 30 had to show that they had fulfilled their military obligation. Before their loan could be initially approved, borrowers also had to demonstrate that they had land use rights over their proposed fields. In addition, inspectors from the Ministry of Agriculture were required to inspect a campesino's fields before each loan portion was given out. Campesinos often complained about the quality of inspections and said that inspectors treated long-term borrowers more favorably than those seeking their first loan.

Farmers usually did not know what the bank's credit policies would be in the forthcoming year. These policies often changed, and the bank made little effort to disseminate information about them. Campesinos received most of their information about bank policies from the rice and jute producers' organizations.

Credit Contracts

Few campesinos understood the complexities of the arcane forms they were required to fill out in order to obtain credit. A close examination of the contract signed by Félix Amias, a farmer from Porvenir, shows that the forms were riddled with confusing calculations and misleading clauses. In 1985 Félix began the process of taking out a loan to grow five hectares of rice in barreal. Because few campesinos grew this much rice, Félix's loan was unusually large for a resident of a ribereño village. Nonetheless, all campesinos taking out rice loans in 1985 had to agree to contracts similar to the one that Félix signed.

Félix's contract specified that the loan would be given out in three portions. The first loan portion of 1.4 million soles, to pay laborers to clean the barreal prior to flooding, was to be given out in October 1985. The second portion, to be given out around April 1986, would be 4.5 million soles to be used for buying pesticides and hiring jornaleros to help with weeding. The third loan portion, given out around August, would be 13.4 million soles and was intended primarily to cover the costs of harvesting rice and transporting the crop to market. The bank also agreed to lend Félix 1.6 million soles for "unforeseen expenses." The contract did not specify when this money was to be given out.

Félix's total loan was thus for 20.9 million soles. The contract stipulated that Félix was to repay the principal plus 4.2 million soles in interest by January 1, 1987. His total obligation of 25.1 million soles was the equivalent of about $1,400 (using the exchange rate of early 1987). According to the contract, the interest rate on the loan was 38.9 percent. The contract did not indicate how this rate was combined with loan portions and money for unforeseen expenses to produce the 4.2 million soles of interest that Félix was to pay.

The contract Félix signed included a curious section called the "loan guarantee," which indicated how the bank planned to recoup its loan and which consisted of an estimate of Félix's expected returns from rice growing. The bank assumed that Félix's yield would be 3,000 kilograms per hectare and that he would sell rice at 2,280 soles per kilogram. According to these calculations, he would earn 34.2 million soles, a figure considerably larger than the bank's loan.

Félix and the bank officials knew that these calculations were unrealistic. Few rice farmers obtain yields of 3,000 kilograms per hectare. The average is closer to 2,000. Furthermore, the estimated sale price of rice was much too low. The figure of 2,280 soles per kilogram was the price paid by the government buying center in mid-1985, but the price offered by the center rose regularly, if unpredictably, along with inflation. When Félix eventually sold his rice in late 1986, the buying center was paying 5.5 intis (5,500 soles) per kilogram of rice. To pay off his loan, according to the bank's calculations, Félix needed to average only 913 kilograms of rice per hectare (25.1 million soles = 913 kilograms/hectare x 5 hectares x 5,500 soles/kilogram).

One of Félix's forms included a list of obligations of the bank and the borrower. The clauses describing these obligations were typed in small, blurred letters and written in a legalistic Spanish that few campesinos could easily understand. One clause stated that the money for which the loan was given had to be used for the crop stipulated. Another said that the bank could modify interest rates at any time and that any such modification would change the amount that Félix owed. A third clause indicated that Félix would have to pay additional interest if his loan was not repaid on time and that the amount and manner of the payment of this extra interest would be determined by the bank.

Some clauses of credit contracts were rarely enforced. Bank officials knew that many campesinos used their loans for purposes other than those stipulated in the contract. They also were aware that any modifications in the interest rates could not be declared unilaterally by the bank but were instead set after intense, politically charged negotiations between the government and the campesino unions. When floods destroyed crops, such negotiations also determined what happened to campesinos who could not repay their loans on time.

Risk, Credit, and Rice Production

The most obvious risk taken by rice producers who borrowed from the Agrarian Bank was that their income from sales would be less than the cost of their loan (principal plus interest plus travel costs). When this occurred, farmers who wished to pay off their loans had two choices, which entailed either additional work or substantial monetary losses. First, they could earn the additional money by doing wage labor or selling other crops, livestock, and fish. Second, they could pay off their loan using money borrowed from an *habilitador* at high interest rates.

Farmers who were unable or unwilling to repay a bank loan found themselves in a precarious economic position. Although amnesties were sometimes given after regional disasters, indebted farmers were ordinarily forbidden to borrow from the Agrarian Bank in the future. This often forced them to take out loans from habilitadores. Furthermore, when heavily indebted farmers sold rice to the government buying center in Iquitos, they did not receive cash. Instead, their debt was reduced by the value of the rice sold. Rural habilitadores sometimes took advantage of this by buying rice from indebted farmers at a low price and reselling it to buying centers at a higher price.

Even farmers who had little trouble repaying their loan were sometimes disappointed by the low profits from rice production. Obviously,
what constituted an "unsatisfactory" profit depended at least in part on
the subjective judgment of particular farmers. A profit per labor-day of
less than half the daily wage of agricultural workers, however, might
reasonably be regarded as unsatisfactorily low. (Farmers rarely calculate
their profit per labor-day. Outsiders making such calculations can restrict their analyses of outputs to an examination of sales and expenditures. The value of subsistence production is largely irrelevant because
farmers sell almost all the rice they grow.)

Farmers were also unhappy when rice loans failed to cover the cost of
production and marketing. Loan plans for rice grown in barreales were
drawn up about a year before the crop was to be harvested. Even though
loans for the later portions were occasionally increased by the government in an effort to compensate for inflation, these increases were seldom enough to pay for higher costs of transport, shipping, and hired
labor. When loans were too small to cover production and marketing
costs, farmers had to raise the necessary additional cash by borrowing
from patrones or selling assets such as chickens or pigs. Ironically, loans
were most likely to be too small in years when rice yields were high and
producers had to spend large sums of money on labor and shipping.

The Probability of a Rice Loan Being Profitable

Miguel Pinedo and I interviewed twelve farmers in Porvenir, Santa Sofía,
and Tapirillo about their experiences with loans for rice grown in barreales.
These men comprised all but one of the farmers in the villages who had
taken out rice loans for more than two years. (Approximately a dozen
other farmers in the villages had taken out Agrarian Bank loans for jute
in the early 1980s, but no one in the three villages had a jute loan when
we conducted our interviews in early 1986.) The farmers interviewed
had taken out a total of 91 rice loans from the Agrarian Bank between
1970 and 1985. Of these loans, 16 (18 percent) were not paid back when
due, and in all but three of these cases insufficient rice production was
the reason for the loan default.

While these data do not allow more than a very tentative estimate of
the probability of a loan default because of insufficient production, they
do suggest that the chance of this occurring is sizable. Even if in most
years the probability of loan default is as low as one in ten, simple math-
ematical calculations show that a regular borrower is likely to default

eventually. The probability that a farmer who borrows in ten different years will default at least once is $1 - (9/10)^{10}$, which equals 65 percent. The actual probability of default is considerably greater than 1 in 10 in most years, and in some years it is as high as 1 in 3. Making the unrealistic assumption that it is exactly 1 in 5 every year, the probability that a farmer borrowing in 10 different years would default at least once is $1 - (4/5)^{10}$, which equals 89 percent. In reality, all but 1 of the 12 rice growers interviewed had defaulted at least once.

Eight of the twelve men interviewed in depth about rice credit were unable or unwilling to borrow from the Agrarian Bank in 1986 because of outstanding debts. In six cases the bank had prohibited future borrowing. Even though a government amnesty allowed the other two farmers to take out new loans, they were unwilling to incur additional debts. A lack of flooding of barreales in 1985 caused an unusual number of loan defaults in that year. Many farmers spent their first loan portion paying hired workers to help with the preflood clearing of the barreales. When flooding did not occur, these farmers had no land to grow rice on and were forced to default on their loans. Production problems caused by unpredictable flooding are common. There had also been insufficient flooding in 1983, and in 1982 and 1986 the floods came early.

Farmers were asked about their rice yields in barreales for each of the last two years they had borrowed and whether they made a profit on the loan. It is difficult to specify a precise yield figure that enabled farmers to break even on a rice loan. The economic conditions of rice production in barreales change markedly from year to year, and diseconomies of scale result in certain yields per hectare being profitable for small holdings and unprofitable for larger fields. Furthermore, households differ in the extent to which they can substitute unpaid family labor for hired workers. Nevertheless, the interviews suggest that farmers with yields of one metric ton per hectare ordinarily break even on rice loans. This figure is consistent with the results of a cost-benefit analysis of rice loans in 1985 (see Appendix 2). However, farmers are unhappy when they break even. The cost-benefit analysis indicates that a farmer who planted three hectares of rice in barreal in 1985 required a yield of about 1.2 metric tons per hectare in order to earn a profit per household labor-day equal to half the prevailing jornalero rate. In both 1984 and 1985, about 30 percent (31 percent in 1984 and 29 percent in 1985) of the farmers who planted rice in Porvenir, Santa Sofía, and Tapirillo had yields per hectare of 1.2 metric tons or less.

All but one of the farmers interviewed in depth about rice credit said that there had been at least one year in which a loan had not been large enough to cover production costs. Most said that the size of loans was usually too small. The cost-benefit analysis indicates that a campesino who planted three hectares of rice in barreal in 1985 and obtained a total yield of six metric tons needed about 7,800 intis to cover production costs. Ricardo Flores of Tapirillo received a loan of 5,386 intis from the Agrarian Bank that year for a three-hectare rice field.

Loan Strategies

Although Agrarian Bank loans for rice assumed that all tasks would be performed with hired labor, most borrowers attempted to save money by substituting family labor (and to a lesser extent cooperative work parties) for jornaleros whenever possible. This resulted in significant savings on rice fields of two or three hectares. On large fields, in contrast, substantial sums had to be spent on jornaleros, and farmers often found that the prevailing wage labor rate was higher than that assumed by the bank.

Rice loans were sufficiently likely to lead to long-term indebtedness that many campesinos did not borrow from the Agrarian Bank. My analysis of some incomplete data provided by the Agrarian Bank indicates that in both 1983 and 1984 about 20 percent of the adult males living in rural communities in the Iquitos area took out loans for rice. In Porvenir, Santa Sofía, and Tapirillo, 18 percent took out rice loans in 1984 and 12 percent in 1985.

There was considerable intervillage variation in the proportion of residents who took out loans. For example, about two-thirds of the farmers of Santa Rosa took out rice loans in 1985 (Christine Padoch, personal communication). The proportion of borrowers in any particular village was affected by numerous factors other than individual propensities to take risks. These included the farmer's distance from bank branches and government buying centers, the availability of barreales, contact with the rice producers' union, and the willingness of the bank to make loans to members of the village. These conditions change over the years. The number of loans for rice in Tapirillo dropped in the late 1970s and early 1980s when many barreales disappeared. In 1986, loan applications increased dramatically in Santa Sofía when a new barreal appeared.

Some campesinos borrowed money from the Agrarian Bank to meet household expenses. Of fourteen campesinos interviewed in depth about credit (the twelve rice farmers and two men who had taken out loans for jute), three explicitly said that they first borrowed from the bank for this reason. Another four said that they first borrowed because the bank offered lower rates of interest than patrones. Since loans from patrones are usually for subsistence purposes, these campesinos' primary reason for initially borrowing from the bank may also have been for household maintenance.

Many campesinos thought of the bank as a source of production credit and regarded patrones as a source of money during household emergencies. Nevertheless, a farmer with a bank loan for production would usually spend it on an unexpected household emergency rather than borrow from a patrón who charged high interest rates. This could lead to defaults on bank loans and eventual borrowing from a patrón for production purposes.

Characteristics of Borrowers from the Agrarian Bank

Many campesinos were reluctant to borrow from the Agrarian Bank because of the dependency such loans entailed. They knew the disadvantages of being in debt to a patrón and feared that bank loans would involve similar unfair terms and subservient personal relations. The complexity of loan forms and the arrogance and condescension of some government bureaucrats exacerbated campesinos' worries about the trustworthiness of the bank.

Campesinos who were willing to take out rice loans from the Agrarian Bank tended to be somewhat better off economically than their neighbors. They were more likely to own motors and sewing machines, to farm on a slightly larger scale, and to engage in a wider variety of economic activities (see Table 10.1). The positive relationship between wealth and borrowing might be interpreted as a reflection of the greater ability of the more prosperous farmers to afford the risks associated with borrowing. However, intravillage wealth differences are quite small, and no one in Porvenir, Santa Sofía, or Tapirillo had enough assets to repay a sizable bank loan when a rice crop failed. It is perhaps more relevant that the more prosperous farmers were somewhat more involved in the cash economy and the outside world in general than their neighbors. As a result, they were less intimidated by the red tape and numerical complexities of loans and were more likely to have acquaintances at the bank and the Ministry of Agriculture who could help them wend their way through the bureaucracy. Rice loans were therefore less "uncertain" for more prosperous campesinos than for their poorer neighbors. The weal-

Table 10.1. Economic Characteristics of Borrowers and Nonborrowers in Porvenir, Santa Sofía, and Taparillo, 1985[a]

	Borrowers (N = 20)	Nonborrowers (N = 62)
Percent planting rice	75%	24%
Mean area in rice[b]	1.3 hectares	1.2 hectares
Percent planting corn	60%	69%
Mean area in corn[c]	1.3 hectares	0.8 hectares
Percent planting manioc	100%	90%
Mean area in manioc	1.2 hectares	0.9 hectares
Percent planting plantains	89%[d]	82%
Mean area in plantains	1.1 hectares	0.9 hectares
Percent planting cowpeas	65%	17%
Percent planting tomatoes	35%	23%
Percent selling fish in Iquitos	53%[d]	40%
Percent selling fruit in Iquitos	63%[d]	56%
Mean number of chickens sold	15	11
Percent owning radios	35%	36%
Percent owning sewing machines	47%[d]	15%
Percent owning motors	37%[d]	12%

[a]The category of borrowers includes all farmers who have ever taken out a rice loan from the Agrarian Bank.
[b]Mean areas of rice, corn, manioc, and plantains are calculated only for those farmers who planted the crop.
[c]Corn, manioc, and plantains are often interplanted.
[d]These figures are based on 19 cases.

thier farmers could assess the advantages and disadvantages of such loans more accurately and were thus less likely to avoid borrowing because of an overestimation or ignorance of the chances of being unable to repay the bank.

Borrowers' Experiences with Loans

Most of the fourteen borrowers we interviewed had obtained their first loan from the Agrarian Bank some years before. One obtained agricultural credit for the first time in the 1950s, two in the 1960s, eight in 1970s, and three in the 1980s. These men had all borrowed from the Iquitos branch of the bank in recent years. (Two farmers from Porvenir had obtained their earliest loans from a bank branch in Nauta.) Five men interviewed had borrowed money from the Agrarian Bank for both crops and boat motors.

When these long-time borrowers first decided to get credit, loans were still being given out in five or six portions. Farmers who wanted to borrow money for every task associated with rice or jute production therefore had to make many trips to the bank branch. Some decided that obtaining certain loan portions was not worth all the traveling. They decided to carry out some agricultural tasks without bank aid and applied for only two or three loan portions.

Before they took out their first loan, many of these farmers had been worried about the bureaucratic complications of borrowing. Their worries were justified. Only five men said that they had few problems taking out their first loan. The rest all experienced aggravating delays. Three had trouble getting their loan approved, five received one or more loan portions late, and one spent weeks waiting for the inspector from the Ministry of Agriculture. The borrowers complained that they had been forced to make repeated trips to Iquitos or Nauta to resolve these problems; a few said that they had gone to the bank branch more than twenty times.

Most borrowers said that bank credit had significantly affected their economic activities. Six said that credit had enabled them to produce more than previously. Although only two reported that credit had made it easier to maintain their households, ten had at some time used a considerable amount of loan money to pay for medical care or to buy food after severe floods.

Repeated use of agricultural credit did not lead to steadily increasing rice production. The borrowers averaged 3.4 hectares of rice the first year they obtained a loan for that crop and 3.7 hectares in the most recent year in which they obtained credit. There were several reasons why borrowers' rice fields remained small. The Agrarian Bank is reluctant to approve loans for more than five hectares, and in any case barreales were scarce and few communities were willing to give individual use rights for more than five hectares in them. Even when land and credit were available, ribereños were rarely willing to assume the risk and uncertainty of large loans. Finally, yields were low often enough that rice farmers could rarely accumulate the capital needed to engage in large-scale production.

The long-term borrowers were asked what worried them most with respect to loans. Eight mentioned the chance of becoming indebted, three noted the possibility of losing money, and two pointed out that interest rates were unpredictable. Only one borrower said that bank delays were the most worrisome aspect of loans. These responses represent a realistic assessment of the likelihood of poor rice production in a barreal. They also reflect some decrease over the years in the borrowers' concerns about bureaucratic complications. By 1986 they had become familiar with how to fill out the relevant forms and how to learn about new regulations. Further, bank officials treated them better than most other campesinos, so the red tape at the bank, while still quite bothersome, had become less onerous.

An examination of Félix Amias's experiences with credit shows some of the advantages and disadvantages of taking out rice loans. Félix, who was born in 1939, used money borrowed from the Agrarian Bank to raise substantial amounts of rice by local standards. He also went deeply into debt when his crop failed. Félix's economic situation in 1986 was no better than it had been in 1974, when he first obtained agricultural credit.

Even though Porvenir was still part of a fundo in 1970, Félix somehow managed to get legal use rights to some floodplain land that year. Félix spent little time farming in the early 1970s but instead worked for petroleum companies in various parts of the Peruvian Amazon. When this work was no longer available, he began to seek other ways to earn income.

Félix was the second campesino in Porvenir to borrow money from the Agrarian Bank. The first was his neighbor Alfonso Amuño. In 1986, government officials still seemed to regard Félix and Alfonso as the most serious borrowers in Porvenir. When inspectors from the Ministry of Agriculture visited the community, they sometimes looked only at the fields of these two men and relied on them for information about the condition of other farmers' fields.

In 1974 Félix used a bank loan to plant 1.5 hectares of rice in low restinga. This field yielded 2.5 metric tons, a yield good enough to encourage him to continue taking out loans. He borrowed from the Agrarian Bank every year between 1974 and 1984. Félix planted three hectares in rice most of these years. His financial situation and credit record were sufficiently good in 1979 that the bank was willing to lend him enough money (425,000 soles) to buy a 25-horsepower motor. Félix used the boat to travel to and from Iquitos.

In the early 1980s, Félix was able to gain access to some land in a barreal, and his yields improved. As a result, he earned enough money to begin an irregularly scheduled colectivo service between Porvenir and Iquitos. Félix made about two round-trips a week between the village and the city. During this time he hired jornaleros to perform many agricultural tasks.

Félix suffered financially in the mid-1980s. His three-hectare piece of barreal became sandy in 1983, and he was able to harvest only 2.5 metric tons of rice from it. The 1984 season was worse. Gullies formed in much of his barreal, and the water buffalo of Orlando del Cuadro destroyed most of the rice that Félix was able to grow. He defaulted on his rice loan and was unable to repay money he had borrowed for the boat motor. The bank refused to give Félix agricultural credit in 1985 and repossessed his motor.

At the beginning of 1985, Félix's economic situation was bleak. His barreal was unsuitable for rice farming, and his colectivo was no longer in operation. Fortunately, Félix's wife, Adela, was able to obtain use rights to part of a barreal. Félix raised four hectares of rice on this land, borrowing money from Orlando del Cuadro to cover the costs of production. Félix's income from his yield of nine metric tons enabled him to pay the bank the money owed on the motor. After reclaiming the motor, Félix sold his boat. Félix used the money he earned from selling rice and his boat to pay off his debts to the Agrarian Bank and Orlando del Cuadro. Félix's rice loan in 1986, which was examined in detail above, shows that he was once again in good standing with the bank.

Were Rice Loans Risky?

Superficially, taking out a rice loan from the Agrarian Bank during the 1980s appears to have been a risky economic strategy that most campesinos would be likely to avoid. Because yields and input costs were unpredictable and highly variable, many borrowers were unable to repay their loans, and even those borrowers who were able to do so often lost money or made very little profit.

Although many ribereños avoided borrowing from the Agrarian Bank because they feared poor harvests and indebtedness, it would be a tremendous oversimplification to characterize taking out rice loans as "a risky choice." There are two fundamental difficulties with such a facile categorization. First, a choice cannot be characterized as risky without reference to safer alternative options. Second, whether taking out a rice loan was riskier than any particular economic alternative depends on both the definition of *risk* and the circumstances of the decision maker.

Choices

The fact that only a relatively small proportion of ribereños borrow from the Agrarian Bank cannot be interpreted solely as the result of individual decisions to avoid risky investments. Many potential borrowers were forbidden to take out rice loans from the Agrarian Bank because of past defaults, failure to satisfy their military obligation, or a lack of required documents concerning land rights. Others had access only to restingas and alturas, for which the bank was sometimes reluctant to lend money for rice production.

The majority of farmers in Tapirillo and Santa Sofía and a substantial minority in Porvenir were able to obtain credit for rice from the Agrarian Bank if they so chose, but campesinos had several alternatives to this economic strategy, including taking out no loans, borrowing from an habilitador in exchange for the future delivery of rice or other crops, and obtaining credit from the Agrarian Bank for a crop other than rice. Some campesinos borrowed from both the bank and individual habilitadores.

Definitions

Ribereños have at least three economic goals that fall under the general rubric of "risk reduction." They wish to ensure a steady food supply, to avoid defaulting on debts, and to be able to pay for medical emergencies. Besides these risk-reducing goals, campesinos also try to earn money in order to pay for education, clothes, boat motors, radios, and sewing machines.

The relative riskiness of bank loans compared to alternative economic activities depends on the aspect of risk being considered. Campesinos who borrowed from the Agrarian Bank varied greatly in their annual rice incomes because of yearly fluctuations in yields, input costs, and interest rates. If risk is defined with respect to consistency of monetary returns, taking out a bank loan for rice was riskier than most conceivable alternative economic strategies. When talking about the advantages and disadvantages of the various economic options, however, ribereños place much greater emphasis on threats to survival than on consistency of returns. When compared with the option of not taking out any loans, borrowing from the Agrarian Bank increased subsistence insurance for medicine and food but also (obviously) increased the chance of long-term indebtedness. Compared to loans from habilitadores, bank loans, with their lower interest rates, were less likely to lead to long-term debt. Habilitadores and the bank offered different advantages as sources of subsistence insurance. Habilitadores were more flexible about when loans could be paid or repaid, but the Bank was more willing to lend large sums of money.

Assessments of the risk and uncertainty associated with credit for rice should also consider campesinos' knowledge of variability in monetary returns to investments of labor and cash. Because ribereños had grown rice and had borrowed from the Agrarian Bank for several decades, institutional loans for rice in the 1980s were clearly not at the "extremely uncertain" end of a risk-certainty continuum. Nevertheless, rapid inflation and ever-changing bank policies led to considerable uncertainty concerning returns to rice production in the future. Information gathering was of limited use in reducing uncertainty with respect to bank loans. Campesinos could learn only a little about forthcoming government policies, and nobody could predict the many input costs that depended on the rate of inflation in Peru and market fluctuations in world oil prices.

Circumstances of Individuals and Households

Campesinos vary in both the relative importance they attach to the various aspects of risk and uncertainty and the extent to which they desire to earn cash. Some such differences are idiosyncratic, but others are predictable consequences of interhousehold demographic and economic variation. Subsistence insurance is relatively important for households with many young or aged members. Households with large workforces, in contrast, worry relatively little about incurring debt, because of their multiple income sources and their ability to cut costs by substituting family labor for jornaleros. Campesinos wishing to finance a secondary education for a child place a higher priority on earning cash than on avoiding debt.

Recent Expansion and Contraction of Credit

During the early 1980s the campesino organizations claimed that government policies inhibited small-scale farmers' willingness to take out loans. Union leaders complained about complex forms, small loans, and unhelpful, unfriendly bank officials. Furthermore, members of the rural and urban elites were the recipients of most of the money loaned by the Agrarian Bank. These policies reflected the class structure of the Peruvian Amazon. The local elite includes politicians, government bureaucrats, and rural and urban patrones. The bureaucrats channeled the bulk of credit to other members of the middle and upper classes, such as moneylenders, owners of commercial estates, and rural entrepreneurs.

Several bank policy changes in the mid-1980s briefly made credit more attractive for small-scale farmers. Interest rates were cut, the number of loan portions was reduced, and credit was made available for new crops. Between 1984 and 1987 the campesino organizations suggested a number of other changes that would have made farmers more willing to take out loans. For example, union members who met in Iquitos in August 1985 made the following requests:

1. Allowing campesino representation in decision-making processes at the Agrarian Bank.

2. Further reducing the number of portions in which loans are given out.

3. Routinely recalculating loan sizes for each portion to take into account the rate of inflation.

4. Increasing the number of places where loans could be obtained (decentralization).

5. Allowing campesino communities to obtain credit as a group.

6. Giving loans to all campesinos who requested them.

7. Giving loans to campesinos for growing crops on as much land as they want.

8. Giving a larger proportion of credit to campesinos and a smaller proportion to patrones.

9. Not penalizing borrowers when delays in payment are caused by unreliable transport.

10. Offering speedier service for borrowers and clearer explanations of paperwork requirements and interest regulations.

11. Giving farmers copies of the reports about their fields prepared by inspectors from the Ministry of Agriculture.

The unions later asked the government to consider instituting crop insurance, giving more technical assistance to rice grown in barreales, and guaranteeing prices for manioc and plantains. The government ignored most of these suggestions. Many would have involved either increased spending on rural development programs or a politically charged redistribution of credit.

Economic chaos in Peru beginning in 1988 forced the APRA government to retract many of the incentives for obtaining credit it had offered in the mid-1980s, as well as the promised decentralization of lending. In 1990 a new government headed by Alberto Fujimori came into power in Peru. Fujimori's party, which had a free-market orientation, was not particularly interested in decentralizing services, providing agricultural subsidies to small-scale farmers, or improving rural living conditions in Amazonia.

Peru's most pressing problems in the early 1990s were its collapsing economy and the civil war between the government and revolutionary groups. These problems were especially serious in the country's population centers in the sierra and the coast. The lowland tropics around Iquitos, in contrast, were relatively peaceful despite cholera epidemics and economic stagnation, and the Fujimori government concluded that it could afford to abandon some development programs in the lowland Amazon. One result was the virtual elimination of credit for campesinos in Loreto.

Agricultural credit programs in the Peruvian Amazon had some of the drawbacks that have been noticed elsewhere. Because many of the Agrarian Bank's loans went to patrones, credit programs may have increased rural inequalities. Further, a significant proportion of government development aid in Loreto was spent on credit programs, perhaps at the expense of spending for technical assistance and rural extension. Nevertheless, the cutbacks in credit in the late 1980s and early 1990s were unfortunate. Credit programs did improve the lives of many Amazonian campesinos in the 1970s and 1980s. Some rural families increased their incomes; others suffered less during floods and medical emergencies.

11. Campesino Unions

In September 1985, almost a hundred campesinos from eight different villages traveled to the town of Yanashi for a three-day meeting and celebration. The ostensible reason for their trip was the official opening of a storage center that would make it easier for farmers to market their crops. Town officials made speeches, the local priest blessed the center, instrumental groups provided entertainment, and guests consumed large quantities of fish, masato, and beer. The Voz de la Selva taped the event for a future radio presentation.

Yanashi is almost a day's journey downriver from Iquitos on a tributary of the Amazon. Because the town lacks regular colectivo service, the men and women who attended the meeting needed to make special transportation arrangements. They also had to abandon their ordinary economic activities for almost a week. Although the visitors enjoyed the festivities, few would have made the difficult trip just to go to the opening of the center. The reason most traveled to Yanashi was to attend the two-day regional campesino union meeting that preceded the opening.

This meeting consisted of lengthy speeches by union leaders and group discussions of various economic and political issues. Representatives of various communities reported on disputes about natural resources; small working groups talked about credit, crop prices, marketing, public services, and human rights; and resolutions were adopted for presentation to the new APRA government.

The Yanashi meeting was the first of many union events that I attended. I was repeatedly impressed by the campesinos' willingness to sit through often tedious and wandering discussions about such arcane matters as the intricacies of credit systems and government bureaucracies. Although many of the campesinos were barely literate, they were keenly aware of unequal class relations in the Peruvian Amazon and hoped that the activities of their unions would help improve their material conditions.

The campesino unions of Loreto are part of an important social movement in Latin America. In recent years, grassroots development organizations have become increasingly influential in both the rural and urban areas of many countries (Annis and Hakim 1988b; Hirschman 1984). These small-scale cooperatives, collectives, and unions often receive funds and technical aid from public and private international development agencies. Some grassroots groups have narrowly defined goals; others are multipurpose organizations whose activities change from year to year.

Most studies of grassroots political movements in Amazonia (e.g., Foweraker 1981; Hecht and Cockburn 1989:161–91; Schmink and Wood 1992) have focused on frontier regions with new roads, extensive colonization, and large-scale development projects. But as Richard Pace (1992) has observed, political conflict and grassroots activism are also common in the vast region of Amazonia that has not been directly involved in widely publicized, lavishly financed state development projects. Pace examines political conflicts in Gurupá, a nonfrontier town in the Brazilian Amazon that is well known to Latin Americanists because of research carried out there by Charles Wagley (1953) and his students (e.g., Kelly 1984; Miller 1985). Pace concludes that these conflicts stem largely from such "market-based tensions" as a past depression, inflation, and an extraction boom that threatens the livelihood of many people (1992:728).

Although there have been few large-scale extractive enterprises in Loreto in recent years, grassroots organizations have been active in the region since the 1970s. As in Gurupá, macroeconomic changes are the main impetus for political activism. The campesino unions of Loreto are impoverished, rely heavily on outside financial support, and have encountered logistical difficulties in organizing dispersed populations. Nevertheless, they have sometimes been able to exert considerable influence on government policies. In this chapter I examine two closely aligned grassroots organizations that were active in the rural area near Iquitos in the 1980s. The Federación de Campesinos de Maynas (FECADEMA) was a local multipurpose organization that attempted to improve economic conditions and health in ribereño villages. The Comité de Productores de Arroz de la Provincia de Maynas (COPAPMA) is the regional branch of the national rice producers' union.

The History of the Campesino Unions

In the half century after the end of the rubber boom, Amazonian campesinos had no way to influence government policies. Ribereños isolated on fundos far from urban centers had to accept wages, credit terms, prices, and working conditions established by patrones and regatones. Even after most riverine communities gained their independence, campesinos lacked political power. They still had to contend with marketing and land tenure systems controlled by rural and urban elites.

The first important campesino organizations in Loreto were established in the early 1970s by Peru's left-of-center military government. The state set up economic cooperatives and planning groups in order to promote village participation in various development projects. The new organizations were closely affiliated with certain national political factions. When these factions fell from power during the late 1970s, the government-affiliated campesino groups lost influence and rapidly dissolved.

The campesino organizations established by the military government had little direct effect on village socioeconomic conditions. The ribereños who participated in the organizations, however, became accustomed to working together for political ends. Furthermore, the populist rhetoric—and, to a lesser extent, actions—of the military government persuaded some campesinos that continued subservience to estate owners, money-lenders, and rural entrepreneurs was neither necessary nor inevitable.

During the 1970s, ribereño villages were often involved in struggles over rights to land and other natural resources. Some communities were trying to separate themselves from fundos, while others, already independent, were attempting to gain control over land claimed by owners of commercial estates. Entrepreneurs were invading lands and lakes used by campesinos for farming and fishing. During the early and mid-1970s, several "committees" formed for the "defense" of campesino communities. These committees, which were usually organized around particular resource conflicts, were locally based and short-lived. In 1978 the Federación de Campesinos de Maynas (FECADEMA), a longer-lasting regional campesino union, was established with some logistical and financial aid from left-leaning political factions in Loreto.

FECADEMA was supported strongly by outside development agencies. During the late 1970s and early 1980s, several groups affiliated with the Catholic church were trying to aid Amazonian campesinos in their efforts to form grassroots organizations. The most important of these quasi-religious groups in the Iquitos area is the Centro Amazónico de Antropología y Aplicación Práctica (CAAAP), which is funded by the Catholic church and various European (especially Dutch) public and private development organizations. CAAAP publishes the scholarly journal *Amazonía Peruana* and maintains a research library in Lima. Both the journal and the library are principally concerned with the Amerindians of Amazonia. CAAAP also carries out small-scale development projects related to agriculture, education, and public health. Some projects during the 1970s and early 1980s were technologically oriented; others were aimed at helping the rural poor gain access to land and other natural resources.

The CAAAP office in Iquitos spent little time on overtly religious activities during the late 1970s and early 1980s. The director was the late Spanish priest and scholar Jesús San Román, who devoted most of the last years of his life to efforts to improve the material conditions of poor Amazonians. Most of his staff were university-educated men and women from Loreto and other parts of Peru, but a few were Dutch and Spanish volunteers funded by European organizations. Although the political views of the staff varied, all had a strong commitment to social change and great sympathy for the rural peoples of the Peruvian Amazon. During the late 1970s the staff reached the conclusion that development workers and scholars had not paid enough attention to the ribereño population of the area. They decided to increase the proportion of CAAAP resources devoted to campesino organizations. CAAAP began giving substantial amounts of financial and technical aid to FECADEMA.

From its inception, FECADEMA suffered from fundamental organizational problems. The union depended almost entirely on financial aid from development agencies because local political organizations could not afford to contribute much money to the union. Since the government did not officially recognize FECADEMA, the union could not participate in state decision making about prices, credit terms, and the allocation of technical aid. Furthermore, FECADEMA's goals and activities were so diffuse that campesinos saw few immediate advantages to forming union chapters. Members of the rural elite who were hostile to campesino organizations could easily discourage ribereños from joining FECADEMA.

In 1981 FECADEMA decided to establish campesino groups organized around the production of particular crops. Such producer groups existed in other parts of Peru and participated in government discussions of agrarian and credit policy. Ordinarily, these organizations were formed for crops for which the government provided guaranteed prices. Farmers who sold these crops at government buying centers were legally compelled to turn over a fixed percentage of their sales to the relevant producer organization. Producer groups were easier to organize than were general-purpose campesino organizations because potential members could easily understand the importance of having strong organizations fighting for higher prices and better credit terms for particular crops. They were also easier to administer because their income was constantly generated when farmers sold crops to buying centers.

The Comité de Productores de Arroz de la Provincia de Maynas (COPAPMA) was established in 1982, and a jute producers' organization based in Iquitos was formed in 1986. The producer organizations had few problems recruiting members. In 1983 COPAPMA claimed more than a thousand members in about a hundred communities, and by 1987 it could claim a membership of about four thousand, with a local chapter in almost every ribereño community that grew rice.

The separation between the producer organizations and FECADEMA was somewhat artificial. The producer groups (especially COPAPMA) engaged in many activities only indirectly related to the marketing of particular crops. FECADEMA and the producer organizations all received financial and technical support from the same church and development agencies and shared office space in Iquitos. The various unions, however, served somewhat different clienteles. Every member of the producers' organizations grew rice or jute; many members of FECADEMA grew neither of these crops.

In 1985 FECADEMA and COPAPMA purchased a house near the business center of Iquitos and established the Casa Campesina to serve as a meeting place and information center for the unions. The bulk of financing for the house came from development organizations and private donations, and the rest from COPAPMA's income from rice sales at government buying centers. Ribereños who came to town to market crops or visit relatives stopped by the Casa Campesina for help with diverse problems. Union leaders took turns spending a week working there. The house was filled most of the day with visiting campesinos, union representatives, and advisers. The building also provided some space where ribereños visiting the city could spend the night.

In the early 1980s some of the CAAAP staff acted as advisers to the campesino organizations, but around the end of 1984 the CAAAP office in Iquitos changed its attitude toward the unions. A Swiss priest who replaced a Jesuit from the United States as head of the Lima office urged the staff in Iquitos to engage in more directly religious activities and discouraged confrontations with the local elite. After a series of disputes, most of the CAAAP workers in Iquitos quit. The departing workers were replaced by men and women from Lima who concerned themselves with uncontroversial religious, health, and education projects. CAAAP stopped working with the campesino unions.

Nevertheless, some former members of CAAAP who were paid by private development agencies continued to advise the campesino organizations. As the years passed, most of these men and women left to take other positions. The unions' meager financial resources made it impossible to hire many replacements. As a result, the campesino organizations were forced to rely more on help from unpaid local volunteers.

At first, FECADEMA and COPAPMA did not do much work with the grassroots organizations of the Amerindians of the Peruvian Amazon. Even though advisers from CAAAP and other development organizations tried to encourage class consciousness among all poor rural residents, many ribereños disdained Amerindians. Furthermore, ribereños and Amerindians have somewhat different economic and political concerns. In the past few years, however, leaders of Amerindian and campesino grassroots organizations have become increasingly aware of their common interests as representatives of rural Amazonians. In 1987 FECADEMA merged with a similar organization that represented indigenous peoples to form the Federación Departamental de Campesinos y Nativos de Loreto (FEDECANAL), which has been seeking legal recognition from the state.

FEDECANAL severed its connections with COPAPMA in 1989 after the elected president of COPAPMA joined the center-right Acción Popular party and became active in regional politics. FEDECANAL moved out of the Casa Campesina and rented office space in a building across the street. Campesino villages seeking help in conflicts over access to natural resources then worked primarily with FEDECANAL. COPAPMA, which was receiving an increasing amount of aid from a Dutch organization associated with the Catholic church, concentrated on technical aid projects.

Ideology

The ideology of the campesino organizations during the 1980s could best be characterized as populist. FECADEMA and COPAPMA were explicitly concerned with improving the socioeconomic conditions of the rural poor. Union speeches and publications emphasized the ways in which government policies favored rural and urban elites, ways in which members of the elite mistreated campesinos, and the necessity for campesinos to work together to overcome hostile bureaucrats and patrones.

Aside from this overall populism, few generalizations could be made about the ideology of the campesino organizations. Many advisers and leaders of FECADEMA and COPAPMA were influenced by Liberation Theology, and a strong moral sense pervaded union activities. Directly religious appeals to campesinos, however, were not particularly common. Although Catholic development groups were influential in their establishment, FECADEMA and COPAPMA were profoundly secular organizations, perhaps in part because a significant minority of their members— including the heads of both FECADEMA and COPAPMA in 1985 and 1986—were fundamentalist Protestants. The unusual combination of evangelical Protestantism and populist social action originated locally. The only important international Protestant group that is currently active in the Peruvian Amazon is the Instituto Lingüistico del Verano (Summer Institute of Linguistics), which works exclusively with Amerindians and is politically conservative (Stoll 1982:98–164).

Members of the campesino organizations belonged to several political parties. While no union leader in the mid-1980s favored the parties of the center and right, some championed the ruling APRA party of Alán García, and others backed the various groups that constituted the Izquierda Unida (United Left). Campesino leaders included avowed socialists who participated in training programs in Cuba and would-be entrepreneurs who dreamt of opening stores, running colectivos, and becoming small-scale patrones. Despite the diverse political views of their members, FECADEMA and COPAPMA were consistently antigovernment. As a result, in the early 1980s the campesino unions of the Peruvian Amazon were openly opposed by many regional representatives of the Belaúnde government. When the APRA government came to power in 1985, the campesino organizations were briefly hopeful because it announced new policies explicitly aimed at improving the conditions of the rural poor. After a short time, however, the unions began to attack the government for not living up to its rhetoric. *El arrocero* (The Rice Farmer), the principal publication of COPAPMA, included the following complaint in February, 1986:

> Brothers, the government says that it is popular, nationalist, revolutionary, and even socialist, but we see that much of this is just words; we who are the most forgotten would like this government to do something. WE DON'T WANT WORDS!!! WE WANT DEEDS!!! You ought to know that in our department nothing has changed; everything is the same. The rematistas do what they want and cheat the farmer because we do not have ports where we can take our products, we do not have markets where we can sell directly to the consumer. "Our" APRA mayor [of Iquitos] has not complied with his promises. (My translation)

The unions continued to criticize the APRA government throughout 1986 even though President Alán García was enormously popular at the time. When the APRA government's popularity sharply declined in mid-1987, the unions' attacks became even sharper.

Organizational Structure

The local and regional leaders of the campesino organizations are chosen in elections. Few union leaders have any secondary education, and all support their families primarily through small-scale farming. Although some union leaders are adept at organizing and at negotiating with government officials and bureaucrats, most are not altogether comfortable in these activities. Many acknowledge their dependence on the union advisers for help with organizational structure, accounting procedures, and political strategy.

The membership of the unions is predominantly male, and almost all the regional officials are men, though women occasionally hold positions on the local level. One reason for the predominance of men is that men are more involved in the production and marketing of rice and jute than women. Also, the child care and food preparation responsibilities of most women make it difficult for them to leave their communities for the protracted periods required of regional union leaders. Nonetheless, the local gender division of labor does not entirely explain the extent of male dominance in the unions. Women participate almost as much as men in the production of plantains, manioc, and many other crops. Many rural women have worked at some time in urban areas as vendors or domestic servants and have some sophistication in dealing with the government officials who patrol the marketplace. The male dominance of the unions is part of the same cultural pattern that inhibits rural women from serving as teniente gobernadores and running political parties.

Local union chapters (*bases*) were the fundamental units of COPAPMA and FECADEMA during the 1980s. Few villages had active chapters of both a producer's organization and a general-purpose union. COPAPMA was the only union in some rice-growing communities; others also had chapters of the jute-producers' union. FECADEMA (and later FEDECANAL) operated separately from the producers' organizations only in upland communities where rice and jute were not important cash crops.

Meetings of the chapters served diverse purposes. Elections were held to select union officials. Local leaders and visiting union representatives disseminated information about government policies, farming techniques, and activities of the campesino organizations. Members raised problems they thought should be brought to the attention of the advisers and union leaders at the Casa Campesina and made decisions about village-level participation in union-sponsored programs.

Even though the unions' publications emphasized local autonomy, the most important union activities took place at the regional level. The towns and cities of Loreto were where the unions put out publications, negotiated with government officials, demonstrated, and planned future actions. Leaders of local chapters often went to provincial capitals to attend meetings where they learned about union goals and activities. The geography of Amazonia could make the organization of these regional meetings a logistical nightmare. Because the participants came from small communities spread out over a large area and meetings typically lasted for three or four days, organizers were hard-pressed to mobilize their scarce resources to help arrange transportation, housing, and food.

The most active regional campesino organizations in the department of Loreto were in the province of Maynas, which includes the city of Iquitos with its many government offices. Regional unions outside of Iquitos depended on the Casa Campesina for much information and technical aid, but the long distances and poor communications between provincial capitals and the city limited the amount of help the Casa Campesina could give these organizations.

The producers' organizations were legally part of national unions of growers of particular crops, but ties between Loreto's rice growers' unions and their national representatives were actually quite weak. COPAPMA and other regional unions could rarely afford to send their members to national meetings in distant highland or coastal cities. Moreover, many issues relevant to ribereño rice growers are Amazon-specific and can only be solved locally. Almost all rice producers in Loreto are campesinos who plant fewer than five hectares and who employ little capital, while in the most productive rice-growing areas of Peru along the coast, entrepreneurs plant large fields under irrigation. These farmers, who controlled the national union during the 1980s, make larger capital investments and obtain higher yields per hectare than ribereños, and their goals and problems are often quite different from those of the members of CO-PAPMA.

Advisers' Visits to the Countryside

The unions' advisers made periodic trips to the countryside to meet with local chapters. Because there were few advisers and many local chapters, an adviser's visit to a village was an uncommon and special event. Because of his work with me, Miguel Pinedo made an unusual number of visits to Porvenir, Santa Sofía, and Tapirillo in 1985–86, and I was able to observe many meetings in which he advised campesinos. Such meetings were atypical in certain ways. Miguel got to know the people of these villages especially well. Furthermore, advisers differed in their style of interaction with the campesinos. Miguel was one of the few advisers who had been raised in the rural Amazon, which helped him greatly in his work with the unions. He could more easily understand campesinos' lives than his colleagues reared in Peruvian, Dutch, and Spanish cities.

A meeting that Miguel held in Santa Sofía in March 1986 illustrates the variety of topics discussed by advisers and campesinos. About 40 people attended, including some people who were not members of a union. The first part of this particular meeting, which began at 7:30 at night, concerned government agricultural credit. Miguel gave a detailed account of changes in the interest rates for rice and corn, described new credit opportunities for plantains and yuca, and noted that the Agrarian Bank was not charging late fees for people who were overdue on their loans from the previous year. He suggested that people take advantage of the current low-interest credit (well below the rate of inflation), saying that the government was now placing a priority on agriculture. Miguel observed that because urban workers' wages were not rising as fast as the rate of inflation, the state might be less likely to subsidize farmers in the future. (Government policies in the late 1980s and early 1990s dramatically confirmed this prediction.)

A number of campesinos reported that they did not have the documents necessary to obtain a loan. Most were young men who had not served in the military. Such men could obtain the documents needed for credit only after paying a small fine, and they were worried that government officials would demand a bribe as well as the fine. Miguel suggested that the men visit the relevant government offices in a group rather than attempt to solve their problems individually.

After the credit discussion ended, Miguel announced that the government buying center for corn in Iquitos was now paying 3.3 intis per kilogram, and one of the villagers said that rematistas in Iquitos were offering 2.2 intis. Everybody agreed that selling to rematistas might be worthwhile, given the cost and inconvenience of transporting the corn to the government buying center.

The next topic discussed at the meeting was agricultural techniques. Miguel reported that a newly available variety of seed corn worked well in restingas. He then discussed the advantages and disadvantage of different types of rice seeds, saying that the most commonly used variety deteriorated after a number of years of use. Miguel concluded his talk by urging villagers to consider new ways of working together. He told them that, in Yanashi, groups of people met with the inspectors from the Ministry of Agriculture who assessed the conditions of prospective borrowers from the Agrarian Bank. This prevented the inspectors from making arbitrary decisions. Miguel also suggested that farmers coordinate their plans when hiring workers during the rice harvest to reduce competition between farmers for laborers during the busiest agricultural season.

After about an hour, Miguel turned the meeting over to Alejandro Gil, the teniente gobernador. The remaining half hour was devoted to a discussion of the activities of two men from a neighboring community who were temporarily living in the Santa Sofía schoolhouse. Miguel did not participate in this part of the meeting.

Conflicts over Access to Natural Resources

The unions become involved in three general types of conflicts over access to land and other natural resources. Campesino communities enter into disputes over land and water with owners of commercial estates, operators of tourist enterprises, and large-scale fishers. Ribereño villages make conflicting claims to newly formed barreales. Individual campesinos disagree with internal land allocation decisions made by teniente gobernadores. When I first came to the Peruvian Amazon, I did not expect campesinos to be involved in many conflicts over natural resources. I assumed that the region's low population density would allow rural people to gain easy access to agricultural plots and hunting and fishing territories. Along with many other outsiders, I failed to recognize the extent to which land in the region varies in its economic desirability. I also underestimated the land requirements of campesino communities.

As discussed earlier, the most valuable agricultural lands are in the floodplains of the major rivers, because yields for major cash crops are higher in barreales and restingas than in alturas. Also, farmers with land along the rivers can take their produce to market much more easily than those living in interfluvial zones or on tributaries, where boats rarely pass. The annual formation and disappearance of barreales makes conflict over access to the best floodplain land inevitable.

Campesino communities often need land that appears "unused" to rural entrepreneurs and government bureaucrats. Apparently uncultivated land in alturas may include important tree crops or be part of an agroforestry cycle. Shifting cultivation methods in alturas require that farmers leave much of the land fallow, and many of the best fishing and hunting spots are around unpopulated oxbow lakes and backswamps away from the major rivers.

The unions pressure the state to provide individual campesinos and rural communities with clearly defined, legally protected rights to land and other natural resources. When conflicts over rights to natural resources arise between campesino communities and powerful outsiders, the unions take whatever legal action they can afford. Union advisers and leaders request that government officials arrange negotiations between the disputing parties and enforce agreements resulting from such meetings.

The campesino organizations sometimes confront formidable adversaries in these struggles. The rural elite can afford to hire good lawyers, and the elites also have close social, political, economic, and family ties with the government bureaucrats who adjudicate disputes. Nonetheless, COPAPMA and FECADEMA prevailed in the 1980s in some conflicts over access to natural resources. They were especially likely to be successful immediately after APRA gained control of the government in 1985.

The elite in Loreto thought that the APRA party might not tolerate blatant abuses of power. Moreover, the campesino organizations were not totally without resources. Rural entrepreneurs rely on campesinos as workers and peaceful neighbors, but when disputes are not resolved satisfactorily, campesinos can engage in work slowdowns and destroy the property of entrepreneurs. Campesinos have only occasionally carried out such actions, but the threat can be worrisome.

The Water Buffalo Project

The most acrimonious disputes between campesino communities and rural elites in the early and mid-1980s concerned a government-sponsored water buffalo project. The history of this controversial project illustrates well how government credit and land tenure policies favor rural elites. My account of the buffalo project is based on interviews with union leaders and advisers, unpublished materials in the files at the Casa Campesina, and an article in a Peruvian journal (Búfalos 1986).

In 1966, researchers associated with the Universidad Nacional de la Amazonía Peruana (UNAP) in Iquitos began examining the feasibility of raising water buffalo in Loreto. Experiments were conducted with 21 animals imported from Brazil. The buffalo fared well, and in 1974 UNAP and the local Ministry of Nutrition agreed to attempt larger-scale experiments. The government imported 106 buffalo from Brazil, which were sold to and raised successfully by an owner of a commercial estate.

The regional government of Loreto established a project in 1981 to give low-cost loans to rural entrepreneurs who agreed to raise buffalo. The project plans listed several justifications for such subsidies. The project would lead to economic development in the Amazon by increasing the income of loan recipients and providing jobs for campesinos hired to care for the animals. Buffalo would serve as traction animals and be a source of red meat, milk, and dairy products.

In early 1982 the regional government purchased 432 buffalo (418 females and 14 males) from a Brazilian firm and sold them to seven rural entrepreneurs. The state also purchased and sold several thousand more buffalo in late 1982 and in 1983. The government budgeted money to purchase another five thousand buffalo in 1984 and 1985, but only a few animals were imported during these years.

Although the Agrarian Bank at first restricted credit to the purchase of animals, eventually it also loaned money to build corrals. Credit terms were extraordinarily favorable: loans were given for 20 years at 18 percent annual interest. This was about one-third of what the bank charged rice and jute growers and well below the annual rate of inflation. Borrowers did not have to pay any interest until the third year and did not have to begin paying off the principal until the fifth year.

The bank's criteria for buffalo loans ensured that only the rural elite could obtain credit. Recipients of loans were required to have rights to a minimum of 2 hectares of pasture for each animal raised. The government's official policy stipulated that each borrower had to raise at least 100 buffalo, but in practice borrowers had to have only a minimum of 40 animals. No campesino—almost by definition—has rights to 80 hectares of land. Only the wealthiest rural residents were able to satisfy the requirements, and fewer than fifty people ultimately were direct beneficiaries of the buffalo project.

The Ministry of Agriculture established regulations that were intended to minimize conflict between buffalo raisers and campesinos. Borrowers were expected to build corrals to prevent their animals from destroying farmers' fields. Buffalo were not to be raised in populated or densely cropped areas.

Despite these policies, the buffalo project led to many land disputes. The large areas of pasture needed for buffalo raising led many project beneficiaries to seek land claimed by campesino communities. The Ministry of Agriculture frequently ignored its rules and gave buffalo raisers title to areas where campesinos grew crops. Some of this land was on islands that had some of the best soil in the Peruvian Amazon. Buffalo also caused problems by destroying crops and injuring campesinos. Few recipients of credit built fences, so when the buffalos exhausted the available pasture, they roamed the countryside seeking other sources of food. Many preferred foraging in crops and fallow fields to looking for food in the forest. In some places, angry campesinos killed buffalo that threatened their crops. Buffalo owners retaliated with legal actions.

Most campesinos' objections to the buffalo project centered on the day-to-day problems caused by land disputes and marauding buffalo. Union leaders were equally upset about the development philosophy the project exemplified. They thought that the government's plan was inspired by development programs in Brazil that were aimed at large landholders. The unions' advisers point out that the buffalo loans were helpful only to already prosperous rural entrepreneurs. The unions objected to the low interest rates on buffalo loans and claimed that many borrowers used their credit for purposes other than raising animals.

The union leaders and advisers also thought that many of the assumptions underlying the buffalo project were unrealistic. Buffalo were not as docile and did not reproduce as quickly as project planners claimed. Since raising buffalo was not labor-intensive, the project created few jobs in the countryside. Traction animals were not needed in Amazonian agriculture. There was no practical way to take fresh buffalo milk from rural areas into the city. Poor urban residents could not afford to buy buffalo meat, and fish were a more abundant source of protein. In any case, the total amount of meat brought into Iquitos did not increase as a result of the buffalo project. Some loan recipients simply stopped raising cattle.

The campesino organizations were not completely consistent in their attitudes toward the buffalo. Some union advisers said they were not opposed to buffalo projects in principle. In Asia many peasants have water buffalo, so small-scale buffalo raising might also be feasible in Amazonia. However, water buffalo in Southeast Asia are confined, sometimes stall-fed, and are used for traction and milk. Their integration into particular intensive Asian agricultural complexes suggests that they might not readily fit into the less intensive and quite different floodplain farming systems of the Peruvian Amazon. An article in *el arrocero* asserted in 1985 that all the buffalo in the area should be sold and the profits used to promote cattle raising among both campesinos and patrones. In another publication (Búfalos 1986), union advisers argued that the Agrarian Bank should stop buffalo loans and instead offer credit to campesinos to raise pigs, chickens, and ducks.

The unions arranged meetings among government officials, buffalo owners, and aggrieved campesinos, and monitored any agreements reached during these meetings. In a number of cases, the Ministry of Agriculture disclaimed responsibility for problems, saying that buffalo owners had not constructed corrals with money loaned to them for that purpose by the Agrarian Bank. When this happened, the unions sought the aid of bank officials. The unions' efforts to promote negotiations had mixed results. In many areas, amicable agreements were established between buffalo owners and their campesino neighbors. In other places, patrones who wanted to raise buffalo were successful in obtaining land claimed by campesinos.

Porvenir is one community where intervention by the campesino organizations turned out to be successful. The owners of the two neighboring fundos, Fernando Montoya and Orlando del Cuadro, were both given rights to barreales farmed by residents of Porvenir. When buffalo belonging to the patrones escaped, damaged fields, and threatened campesinos, the union arranged meetings among the buffalo owners, residents of Porvenir, and representatives of the Ministry of Agriculture. The land tenure conflict was resolved to the satisfaction of the campesinos, and Montoya and del Cuadro constructed corrals that kept the buffalo away from villagers' fields.

The campesino organizations received more opposition in Justicia, a community on the Amazon between Tapirillo and Porvenir. A local patrón who raised buffalo was given rights to land claimed by the community and built corrals for his buffalo on the disputed land. In 1984 some women from Justicia destroyed corral fences that were preventing them from easily reaching their fields. The patrón's complaint to the Ministry of Agriculture received a favorable hearing. Though no one was apparently punished, intervention by the unions in 1985–86 did little to alleviate conflict between the residents of Justicia and the buffalo owner.

Between 1982 and 1986 the unions engaged in a protracted propaganda offensive against the buffalo project. FECADEMA and COPAPMA bombarded government offices with letters of protest, held rallies opposing the project, and issued numerous press releases and publications concerning buffalo. By 1987 the unions were devoting less time to buffalo-related activities, because most of the buffalo that had been raised as part of the project had been slaughtered and sold for meat in the Iquitos market, and few rural entrepreneurs were still borrowing money to raise buffalo.

The failure of the buffalo project cannot be attributed primarily to the protests of the unions. The project was poorly planned and ineptly administered. Some buffalo became sick; others escaped. Most rural entrepreneurs concluded that buffalo were not a worthwhile investment. Many buffalo owners decided not to repay their loans and instead returned the animals to the Ministry of Agriculture. A few of these buffalo were eventually sold on credit to several campesinos who wanted to raise five to ten animals.

Other Conflicts with Entrepreneurs

Amazonian campesinos have a long history of tenure disputes with rural entrepreneurs who extract forest products, grow sugarcane, and raise livestock. Except for the buffalo project and some disputes with commercial foresters, such conflicts occupied only a small portion of the unions' time and rhetoric during the 1980s. The campesino organizations were more preoccupied with the activities of urban-based entrepreneurs such as commercial fishers and operators of tourist enterprises.

Much of the best fishing in the Peruvian Amazon is in oxbow lakes near riverine communities. The unions contend that the residents of such villages should have exclusive fishing rights near their fields and tree crops. The state does not agree with this position, so anyone can fish in an oxbow lake. Campesino fishers from neighboring villages cause few problems; their technology does not allow them to catch large numbers of fish. Villagers object much more to the activities of state-licensed commercial boats, *congeladores,* which have facilities for freezing fish. The unions have been unable to prevent these congeladores from fishing in the community-claimed oxbow lakes. Since the commercial fishers stay in a particular oxbow lake for only a day or two, the unions do not hear about encroachments until long after they leave the area. The state seems to have no plans to change its laws concerning fishing rights.

Tourist enterprises are of increasing economic importance in the Peruvian Amazon. Every year travelers from Europe, North America, and Latin America come to see the wonders of the jungle. Most of these visitors seek a comfortable way to view the people, plants, and animals of the tropical forest, and several entrepreneurs have established profitable businesses that operate tourist camps along the Amazon and Napo rivers. Some of the camps are foreign-owned; others are locally run. The largest enterprise (and the one that many guidebooks say has the best reputation) is the U.S.-owned EXPLORAMA, which operates three camps. Visitors at these tourist camps spent about fifty dollars per day in 1987 for transportation from Iquitos, food, lodging, and guided tours of local flora and fauna. Most tourist camps also provide entertainment by alleged "Indians."

The advisers to the campesino unions dislike the tourist camps. The camps provide little employment to ribereños and degrade Amerindians in their shows. Most of the profits from the enterprises go to wealthy urban residents. Most ribereños, however, are not particularly disturbed by the activities of EXPLORAMA and the other tourist companies. They know little about the camps, and they rarely come into contact with the tourists.

In the 1980s tourist companies were given title to lands used by ribereños for fishing and hunting, and their relations with some campesino communities worsened. After the companies set up their camps, they prohibited campesinos from hunting and fishing on, or even entering, their land because of their desire to conserve the animals and plants of the area. Campesinos, urged on by their advisers, claimed that this deprived them of access to fishing grounds necessary for their subsistence.

The unions have had some success in their confrontations with tourist enterprises. Because some operators of jungle camps lack close ties with local elites, they can be easily threatened. Campesinos living near one proposed location for an EXPLORAMA lodge, for example, demanded compensation (either a share of the profits or free food) in return for abandoning claims to hunting and fishing sites. EXPLORAMA withdrew from the area. In other places compromises have been reached between communities and tourist camps.

Land Conflicts Within and Between Campesino Communities

Union leaders and advisers spent considerable time in the mid-1980s mediating intervillage land tenure disputes. The Ministry of Agriculture had the responsibility for establishing community boundaries in rural areas. When boundary disputes arose, FECADEMA or COPAPMA (if barreales were involved) attempted to arrange a meeting between the teniente gobernadores of the disputing villages and representatives of the ministry.

Campesinos sometimes complained to the unions about internal land allocation decisions in their villages. Such complaints most often occurred when land previously used by one campesino was assigned to another. In such cases a union leader organized and attended meetings between the disputing parties and the teniente gobernador. A representative of the Ministry of Agriculture was sometimes invited to these meetings. Although the unions thought that the ministry should not adjudicate the conflicts, the state was legally required to approve any changes in use rights to particular pieces of land.

Improving Marketing Conditions

The campesino organizations engaged in diverse activities in the 1980s aimed at making small-scale farming more profitable. Much of this work involved applying political pressure through demonstrations, publications, and meetings with public officials. The unions also gave legal aid to campesinos and informed them about the effects of government programs.

Credit

The unions lobbied vigorously for changes in government credit policies. Their publications complained bitterly about cumbersome procedures and the preferential treatment given to large-scale borrowers. Although some changes advocated by the campesino organizations were made during the 1980s, the regional unions' ability to affect the policies of the Agrarian Bank in Loreto was limited. The widest-ranging decisions concerning the availability and allocation of government credit were made on the national level. Furthermore, campesinos have been unwilling to protest credit policies by engaging in direct action, such as a work stoppages. Since most do not take out government loans, only a minority are affected by the actions of the Agrarian Bank. Borrowers who dislike the bank's activities usually register their discontent simply by refusing to take out loans.

In the 1980s, union leaders at the Casa Campesina nonetheless spent large amounts of time on activities related to credit. Many small-scale farmers depended on community leaders and long-time borrowers for information about credit. While these people could be quite helpful, they ordinarily knew only about those policies relevant to their own circumstances. The unions, in contrast, attempted to keep abreast of all the credit policies that affected campesinos. Advisers traveled up and down the rivers of Loreto to tell farmers about the advantages and disadvantages of credit, the mechanisms of getting a loan from the bank, and the effects of changing credit policies. In addition, ribereños with questions about credit could visit the Casa Campesina for help immediately before and after visits to the bank branch in Iquitos.

The campesino organizations were quite effective in helping individual campesinos resolve problems with the Agrarian Bank. Union leaders and advisers sometimes accompanied them on their trips to the bank. For example, in 1987 most small-scale borrowers experienced long delays in getting loans. When campesinos who are impatient with these delays went to the bank with union leaders, they usually received credit quickly. The unions' help in these cases may not have done much to alleviate the overall problem of delayed loans, however, because borrowers without the savvy to consult the campesino organizations often found that their applications received low priority from bank officials.

The unions' attempt to change the rules about access to barreales demonstrates the interrelationship of credit and land tenure. Campesinos could not obtain rice loans without land use rights to the fields they intended to farm. The Ministry of Agriculture gave out certificates guaranteeing temporary use rights to barreales only in October, November, and December. Problems arose when campesinos who had gained access to barreales at other times of the year wanted to obtain credit immediately. This most often occurred when communities made new allocations of barreales after the floods receded in late May and early June. Such problems would be alleviated if the Ministry of Agriculture gave out certificates year-round, but, perhaps because of personnel shortages, it has been unwilling to do this. The unions therefore proposed in 1983 that use rights in barreales be given for two years to local chapters of COPAPMA. The chapters would then have the responsibility for the internal allocation of barreales. Farmers who obtained use rights of barreales in this way would be eligible for credit for two years.

The Ministry of Agriculture and the Agrarian Bank rejected the unions' suggestion rather summarily. The ministry argued that regional land tenure rules required that rights to barreales could be given only to individual campesinos. Groups such as COPAPMA chapters could not hold land communally. Bank officials also asserted that credit could not be given out for two years because barreales disappeared every year. The unions responded that the bank already gave out credit in November for land in barreales that might not exist when the rivers receded in June. The unions' argument may have been logical, but it proved unpersuasive. By the mid-1980s the campesino organizations had given up their efforts to obtain credit and land rights for two years in barreales.

Crop Prices

Campesinos who marketed crops in the 1980s suffered terribly from the extreme price swings on the open market in Iquitos. The unions lobbied against those advocating a free market for all crops and urged the establishment of guaranteed prices for plantains and manioc. The campesino organizations pressed for more frequent and larger upward adjustments of the prices paid by the buying centers for rice, jute, and corn. The unions also protested the payment procedures at the buying centers, pointing out that farmers were not always paid immediately after delivering their crops. Furthermore, they said, the government imposed "discounts" on crops delivered to buying centers. Farmers who delivered their crops were not paid the full guaranteed price. Instead, a fixed percentage was taken off the top by the government to finance the operations of the buying center.

The unions' efforts to secure good guaranteed prices for their crops during the 1980s had mixed success. The government showed no interest in changing its payment procedures and did not set up buying centers for plantains and manioc. Also, the price of jute often lagged behind the rate of inflation, and the corn buying center in Iquitos was often closed. The unions did have some success in influencing the price of rice, the region's most important cash crop and a staple food in many urban households. Members of COPAPMA who were protesting the price they were paid for their rice carried out several strikes during the 1980s in which they refused to bring any products into the markets of Iquitos. The regional government, fearing protests by urban consumers, quickly acceded to the union's demand for increases in the price the buying centers paid for rice.

Marketing Logistics

As discussed earlier, farmers in the Peruvian Amazon have extraordinary difficulty in getting their products to market. The unions therefore lobby for decentralized market facilities to make it easier for campesinos to receive credit and sell crops near their own communities. The campesino organizations are especially interested in increasing the total number of government-sponsored crop collection centers. These *acopios* are both storehouses and delivery centers for crops with state-guaranteed prices. When government agencies provide money for collection centers, the unions often help organize their construction.

There was no acopio near Iquitos in the early 1980s. The collection center that opened in Yanashi in 1985 helped some ribereños, but farmers delivering rice there were given receipts that had to be redeemed in distant buying centers in other parts of Loreto. The unions argued that campesinos should have been paid for their rice at the acopio. They also urged the government to issue receipts for the delivery of corn and jute at the Yanashi storehouse.

The campesino organizations had several other proposals for improving marketing logistics. FECADEMA and COPAPMA suggested that the government regulate the cost of transport and shipping, asked for improvements in the layout of the port in Iquitos, and proposed the establishment of a farmers' market where producers could sell directly to consumers.

The APRA government of Alán García pledged to decentralize government institutions and to improve marketing conditions in the countryside. The government's rhetoric and the unions' lobbying did not do much to improve the economic infrastructure of rural Loreto. One acopio was built upriver from Iquitos at Orellana in 1987, but transportation and shipping costs continued to rise rapidly, and conditions in the port at Iquitos were as miserable as ever.

Technical Aid

Union leaders and advisers do not spend much time providing campesinos with information about agricultural practices. All campesinos know how to raise subsistence crops such as manioc and plantains, and in recent years many have also learned how to raise cash crops such as rice and jute. Farmers also know more about the ecological characteristics of their own pieces of land than do union advisers and leaders living elsewhere. Nevertheless, the unions can provide information to campesinos about the advantages and disadvantages of agricultural innovations. During 1985–86 they routinely informed campesinos in talks and publications about new rice and corn varieties, methods of rat control, and various other agricultural matters. There were, however, only two union agricultural projects that represented a substantial commitment in funds and time. One project, described previously, involved the distribution of rice-threshing machines. The other was an attempt to introduce irrigated rice production to the Peruvian Amazon.

Rice grown under irrigation often provides higher yields than that grown with other production methods. The best yields in barreales in Loreto are about five metric tons per hectare, whereas rice grown in irrigated fields in the high jungles of Peru sometimes yields eight to ten metric tons per hectare. Nevertheless, irrigated rice has never been raised successfully in the area around Iquitos. Most rice is raised in barreales, where irrigation is not possible. Rice can be grown under irrigation only in restingas and on bottomlands (*bajos*) in alturas. In 1986 COPAPMA started a pilot project with irrigated rice in San Rafael, an upland village located a short distance downriver from Iquitos. The unions had been active in San Rafael while that community had been engaged in land tenure struggles with neighboring patrones. The community's alturas include some bajos suitable for irrigated rice.

COPAPMA's irrigated rice project was an opportunistic response to adverse circumstances. Humberto, a campesino from the high jungle, was spending time in Iquitos because of political problems in his own community and judicial procedures against him in Iquitos. He was an intelligent, outgoing 25-year-old and had little to do in the city. The campesino organizations thought that they could take advantage of Humberto's agricultural expertise and forced stay in Iquitos to begin the project.

The San Rafael project required some startup funds to buy a pump and to rent the machines used in canal building and land leveling. CO-PAPMA had to pick its way through a bureaucratic maze to obtain these funds. The union sought money from the Ministry of Agriculture and the Corporación de Desarrollo de Loreto (the Development Corporation of Loreto, or CORDELOR), which is largely funded by taxes on oil companies and is the principal regional government agency. The Ministry of Agriculture receives some of its financial support from CORDELOR, including that for the Programa Regional de Arroz (the Regional Rice Program).

In early 1986 CORDELOR agreed to provide 200,000 intis (about $12,500) for an experimental ten-hectare irrigated rice project in San Rafael. Rental machinery valued at 156,000 intis would be provided free; the remaining 44,000 intis would be a loan to COPAPMA. The money for the project would come from funds CORDELOR had already transferred to the Programa Regional de Arroz. The program, however, at first refused to allocate any money to COPAPMA, so the union proposed that CORDELOR fund the project directly. CORDELOR would not do this, but it did arrange to transfer additional funds to the Programa Regional de Arroz for the project. COPAPMA and the program agreed to this suggestion with some reluctance. The union leaders and advisers thought that they were losing control of the project and that the Ministry of Agriculture might make important decisions without consulting the campesinos.

Before any money was transferred, CORDELOR insisted on getting the approval of its representatives in Yurimaguas on the assumption that the bureaucrats in the high jungle were more knowledgeable about irrigated rice cultivation than CORDELOR personnel in Iquitos. The Yurimaguas office cut down the size of the project, approving 100,000 intis for a five-hectare experiment.

The San Rafael project never flourished. The machinery was not delivered to San Rafael for many months. In June 1986 Humberto returned to his home in the high jungle. He was disappointed with the delays in the project and wanted to see his wife and children and work on his fields.

He returned to Iquitos in 1987 after the machinery arrived, but the project did not turn out well. Humberto could only visit Iquitos for short periods, and the farmers' unfamiliarity with irrigated rice cultivation led to many mistakes. The project was eventually abandoned.

Politics and Human Rights

Many of the unions' activities involve efforts to influence government policies concerning land tenure, credit, and prices. Because some political parties are more committed to the rural poor than others, the unions occasionally express preferences in elections. For example, in the early 1980s the unions made no secret of their desire to replace Fernando Belaúnde and his Acción Popular party with either APRA or the Izquierda Unida. Nevertheless, the unions ordinarily do not endorse candidates and tend to take a skeptical attitude toward whatever party holds power. The unions' aloofness from conventional politics stems partly from a reluctance to become overly identified with any one party or faction, but they also recognize that no matter who is in power, adverse relations between campesinos and local elites (including government bureaucrats) are likely to continue.

The unions frequently became involved in conflicts over governance and human rights during the 1980s. The regional government vacillated in the extent to which it would allow campesino organizations to participate in state decision making. The government refused to recognize FECADEMA, and allowed the producer organizations to participate in some meetings at the Agrarian Bank and the Ministry of Agriculture but not others.

The unions devoted much of their rhetoric in 1985–86 to asserting their right to participate in government decision making. A typical complaint appeared in *el arrocero* in February 1986:

> The government ought to comply with its own laws that have to do with coordinating with organizations that represent campesinos, as is stated in our Political Constitution of the State in Article 158. [But] CORDELOR approved a plan of development for 1986 without recognizing our problems and our suggestions. They made a plan without the participation of our organization [COPAPMA], and that is bad. (My translation)

The unions also attempted to take action when campesino communities were threatened with a loss of autonomy. Occasionally (twice in early 1986) the regional authorities tried to impose a teniente gobernador on a community without an election. The regional authorities also tried at least once to remove a teniente gobernador because of his alleged communism. When the regional authorities attempted to interfere with local decision making, the campesino organizations tried to mobilize residents of the affected village, encouraging them to complain to higher authorities and to refuse to accept the actions of the regional government.

The unions sometimes took action when a particular community was not satisfied with a local schoolteacher. Campesinos had very little control over the assignment of schoolteachers to their villages. A few schoolteachers left their communities for protracted periods, missed classes because of drunkenness, or were otherwise irresponsible or incompetent. In such circumstances, the unions strongly urged the relevant authorities to seek a replacement.

The unions' most controversial and potentially dangerous activities concerned human rights issues. In parts of Peru, guerrilla groups work together with narcotics traffickers. The government in these areas has declared martial law and summarily jailed (and allegedly murdered) campesinos thought to be revolutionaries, drug traffickers, or both (*narcosenderistas*). Human rights groups assert that the government has jailed many innocent citizens in the sierra and high jungle of Peru.

When Belaúnde was president in the early 1980s, the regional government regularly called union leaders terrorists or communists and used their supposed leftist sympathies as an excuse for not responding to the complaints of FECADEMA and COPAPMA. The unions around Iquitos were, however, allowed to organize without being overtly repressed. Moreover, government agencies adopted a more conciliatory attitude toward the unions after APRA came to power in 1985.

Despite the improved political climate, union leaders became deeply involved in human rights issues in the mid-1980s. A number of campesinos in the area around Yurimaguas and Lagunas in the high jungle were arrested for their putative role in guerrilla and narcosenderista organizations. Nine of the alleged revolutionaries (including Humberto of the irrigated rice project) were brought to Iquitos and imprisoned. Most of the accused had been active in campesino organizations in the high jungle. The leaders of FECADEMA and COPAPMA thought that the prisoners were unjustly accused and took an active role in their defense, obtaining legal aid for the accused, helping the prisoners communicate with their families and friends, and providing subsistence for those campesinos who were out of jail awaiting trial. The union leaders felt a strong sense of solidarity with the imprisoned campesinos from the high jungle. They thought that if guerrilla activity increased in the low jungle, the local government would be likely to use a supposed narcosenderista threat as a pretext for repressing the unions and their leaders.

Prospects

The campesino organizations face numerous obstacles in their efforts to improve the lives of the ribereños. Union leaders and advisers emphasize that the interests of campesinos directly oppose those of merchants, moneylenders, millers, and other powerful individuals in the Peruvian Amazon. The unions' rhetoric sometimes overestimates the strength of their opposition, however. From the perspective of the power brokers of Lima, most of the individuals who oppose the unions are middle class. When national leaders advocate policies explicitly aimed at the rural poor (as was the case during the early days of the APRA government), minor rural patrones can do relatively little to suppress the activities of campesino organizations.

The unions can suffer when development agencies withdraw support or when economic conditions worsen. During the mid-1980s the unions' activities were affected greatly by financial constraints. When CAAAP withdrew its support around the end of 1984, the unions sought, with mixed success, to seek other financial support for their advisers. In 1987 COPAPMA's income dropped when rice yields were low due to early floods, which disrupted harvesting in barreales. The unions had to reduce their paid staff further, and they canceled the annual FECADEMA-COPAPMA meeting.

Development agencies and political organizations can exert a tremendous influence on union activities. When a Dutch church-related organization that was providing funds to COPAPMA emphasized technical aid in the late 1980s, the rice producers' union largely abandoned its political activities. FEDECANAL's focus on human rights and the struggle over access to natural resources reflect its support from local political groups.

Despite their tremendous problems, the unions seem likely to survive, though not necessarily in their present form. Poor rural Amazonians cannot improve their material circumstances without collective action. Before the unions were established, campesinos had no protection against mistreatment by members of the local elite, and they appreciate the help the unions have given them in their struggles over access to natural resources and credit. Ribereños have also seen that religious groups, development agencies, and political organizations have been willing to provide technical and financial support for campesino organizations. The unions would obviously be affected dramatically if the national government changed hands via a military coup (of whatever political stripe) or a guerrilla-led revolution. However, even in such circumstances campesinos would have collective interests opposed to those of other Amazonians. A new kind of general-purpose campesino organization might well be formed.

12. Prospects for Sustainable Development

Many discussions of Amazonian ecology and economics (e.g., Anderson 1990a; Hecht and Cockburn 1989) condemn government policies that favor entrepreneurs such as cattle ranchers, loggers, miners, and oil drillers. While such policies have unquestionably led to deforestation and increased socioeconomic stratification in parts of Brazil, they are not the only obstacles to sustainable, equitable Amazonian development. Even though the Iquitos area has hardly any large-scale enterprises and little deforestation, few ribereños have been able to improve their material circumstances much in recent years. Some of their difficulties are Peru-specific. The country's faltering economy has limited investment in tropical lowlands, and state agricultural policies have done little to help Amazonian campesinos. Other economic, ecological, and sociopolitical problems faced by ribereño farmers, however, are similar to those encountered by the rural poor in floodplain areas in neighboring countries.

State Agricultural Policies in the Peruvian Amazon

Peru has lacked the resources to provide much support for either large-scale enterprises or small-scale farmers in its Amazonian regions. The only significant state-sponsored efforts aimed at ribereños in recent years have involved credit and guaranteed prices for certain crops. These promising programs, which were ended in the early 1990s, allowed some farmers to increase cash cropping and reduce their dependence on the owners of commercial estates and rural and urban moneylenders.

State agricultural policies in the Peruvian Amazon have changed greatly since I began conducting research near Iquitos. When I made my first trip to the region in July 1984, most ribereño farmers strongly opposed state economic policies. The bulk of government agricultural credit was given to rural and urban entrepreneurs. Those villagers who were able to obtain credit received small loans and had to pay high interest rates. Government buying centers for rice, jute, and corn were often closed, and regional bureaucrats tended to support owners of commercial estates and other members of the rural elite in their conflicts with campesino communities.

When I returned to the region in July 1985, ribereño farmers were much less hostile to state agricultural policies. The newly elected APRA government was explicitly looking for ways to improve economic conditions in rural areas. Plans were announced to expand agricultural credit and lower interest rates. The state was buying rice, jute, and corn from farmers at guaranteed prices that usually kept pace with inflation. Campesino unions were frequently successful in their disputes with members of the local elite over access to land and other natural resources.

Economic conditions deteriorated all over Peru in the late 1980s. The rate of inflation soared, and the gross domestic product dropped. International lending agencies shunned Peru because of the APRA government's explicit policy of paying only a small portion of its annual interest on outstanding debts. There were allegations of corruption at the highest level of the government, with large sums of money said to be funneled outside of the country. The Sendero Luminoso stepped up its guerrilla activities, and drug traffickers gained control of certain parts of the high jungle.

As a result, the APRA government was unable to carry out many of its plans for improving economic conditions in rural parts of the Peruvian Amazon. A proposed decentralization of buying centers and government lending agencies never occurred, the state was unable to provide much agricultural credit in 1988 and 1989, fewer and fewer farmers were able to borrow money from the Agrarian Bank, and because of inflation, loans covered only a small portion of most farmers' production costs.

The 1990 Peruvian presidential election was won by Alberto Fujimori, who opposed many of APRA's populist economic policies. Fujimori's government quickly instituted austerity programs designed to end hyperinflation and regain support for Peru from its creditors. Inflation rates dropped sharply, and the international financial community gradually lessened its isolation of Peru. The free-market policies of the new government, however, had an immediate adverse effect on the rural Amazonian poor: the state essentially stopped supporting ribereño farmers. All agricultural products had to be sold on the open market; state buying centers for rice, corn, and jute were abolished. The amount of credit available to small-scale farmers was cut drastically, so few ribereños were able to obtain crop loans.

Obstacles to Sustainable, Equitable Development in Floodplain Amazonia

Ribereño farmers who attempt to grow cash crops face formidable obstacles even in relatively good times, such as the mid-1980s. Floods annually threaten crops grown in fertile low-lying areas. Farmers have difficulty selling crops because of wild price fluctuations and the distance between most villages and Iquitos. Rural elites dispute campesinos' claims to desirable land. Many segments of the population lack access to financial and technical aid offered by the Peruvian government and international development agencies.

Crop Losses from Unpredictable Flooding

The floodplains along the major whitewater Amazonian rivers have sometimes been regarded as potential sites for increased cash cropping (e.g., Denevan 1984; Hiraoka 1989). It is true that soils are fertile there and are amenable to intensive agriculture. Riverine locations ensure that products can be taken to market by boat. However, the experiences of ribereños near Iquitos show that the cultural ecology of floodplain farming in parts of Amazonia can limit long-term agricultural productivity. Farmers have difficulty formulating plans because they cannot predict the location and availability of barreales. Rice fields are lost when floods fail to cover barreales in April, and rice harvests are lost when floods cover barreales prematurely in October. Even crops grown in all but the very highest parts of restingas are destroyed by floods once or twice every decade, and when this happens ribereño households are likely to find themselves without a sufficient supply of staples such as manioc and plantains.

The most prosperous farmers have annual use rights to several fields on land of varying susceptibility to flooding. Access to barreales and playas enables them to plant risky but potentially profitable cash crops such as rice and cowpeas in the most suitable soils, while access to high restingas and alturas enables them to grow manioc and plantains in places that rarely or never flood. Yet the impermanence of barreales and the periodic inundation of restingas can prevent even the most skillful farmers from steadily accumulating savings from the sale of floodplain crops.

Marketing Problems

Amazonian farmers often have difficulty selling their crops. Because of the small, dispersed population of the lowland forest, many rural residents live far from major marketing centers. Crop prices in these centers fluctuate as shipments of particular products arrive. Farmers who make long trips to a market may be forced to sell their products at unusually low prices.

The importance of price supports for floodplain farmers in such circumstances cannot be overestimated. The ecology of riverine agriculture makes cash cropping a risky endeavor in the best of times; price supports provide the assurance that farmers lucky enough to have good harvests can make a decent profit. The campesino unions of the Peruvian Amazon therefore bitterly fought attempts to eliminate state buying centers. When these centers were nevertheless abolished in the early 1990s, many farmers immediately reacted by reducing the amount of land they devoted to rice, corn, and jute, and their household economies became even more subsistence-oriented.

Competition over Rights to Land and Other Natural Resources

Advocates of sustainable, equitable development often stress the importance of establishing indigenous Amazonians' rights to land and other natural resources. They emphasize the need for Brazilian Amerindians and caboclos to protect their land from invasion by cattle ranchers and gold and uranium miners. But the many disputes over rights to natural resources in the Iquitos area show that tenure can be of paramount importance even in areas where there are few large-scale commercial enterprises. Campesino communities have been involved in disputes over access to land and water with estate owners, commercial fishers, loggers, and operators of tourist enterprises. Campesino unions have had to mediate many tenure conflicts within and between ribereño villages.

The reason these struggles over access to natural resources occur despite the low population density of the Peruvian Amazon is that not all land and water are equally valuable. Barreales have been desired by both ribereño rice growers and estate owners who raise water buffalo; alturas near rivers are sought by loggers, owners of tourist enterprises, and ribereño agroforesters and hunters; and commercial fishers using oxbow lakes can threaten an important part of the subsistence base of floodplain communities. Much land between rivers, in contrast, is desired by neither ribereño farmers nor entrepreneurs. These interfluvial zones, which comprise most of the Peruvian Amazon, are populated almost exclusively by Amerindians.

Uneven Development Support for the Rural Population

Although many writers have observed that Amazonian development programs usually favor the prosperous, few have discussed inequities in the distribution of aid to the rural poor. In the lowland Peruvian Amazon, government credit and technical aid programs have gone disproportionately to communities along major rivers near the towns and cities of the departments of Loreto and Ucayali. Farmers living in villages such as Porvenir, Santa Sofía, and Tapirillo may not receive much aid either from the state or nongovernmental development organizations, but they are luckier than their counterparts who live away from the Amazon.

Agricultural development programs in the Peruvian Amazon have focused on crops grown in floodplains. Residents of altura villages, largely ignored by the Agrarian Bank and often without much agricultural income, have been more likely than inhabitants of floodplain villages to borrow money from and work for owners of commercial estates. Because of this, the semifeudal social and economic relations typical of the Peruvian Amazon in the years immediately after the end of the rubber boom survive in an attenuated form in some ostensibly independent altura villages.

The most striking inequity of agricultural development programs has been their almost complete neglect of the female half of the ribereño population. Despite a well-developed feminist critique of studies that ignore the economic role of women (see Bossen 1989), few discussions of sustainable development in Amazonia consider the differential impact of policy decisions on men and women. Women are rarely even considered as potential recipients of economic and technical aid in rural areas near Iquitos. Agricultural credit has been given almost entirely to men. The campesino unions, whose regional and local leaders are almost all male, have encouraged women's participation in some health and education projects funded by international development agencies, but the unions' agricultural programs—involving the distribution of rice threshers, experiments with irrigation, and advice about credit—have all been aimed at men.

Grassroots Organizations

Cooperatives, unions, collectives, and community stores are proliferating throughout Latin America. Advocates of financial and technical aid to these energetic grassroots organizations argue that state development programs aimed at the poor often involve cumbersome bureaucracies and show little understanding of local economic and political conditions. They regard assistance to grassroots groups as a way to "strengthen the poor in the short run so that they can mobilize through organized collective action and confront the fundamental causes of their poverty in the long run" (Annis and Hakim 1988a:1). Such support is to be given with no strings attached to organizations created and controlled by poor people.

The various peasant unions of Amazonia show that donors almost inevitably end up influencing grassroots organizations. The union of rubber tappers of the state of Acre in Brazil, for example, has been involved for some years in land conflicts with cattle ranchers. The Acre rubber tappers became internationally famous after Chico Mendes, one of the union leaders, was brutally murdered in December 1988. Mendes had gained support for his movement from environmental organizations based in North America and Europe. Accounts of the union sometimes note the difficulties the rubber tappers had in reconciling the political goals of members with the conservation goals of some of the largest donors (e.g., Hecht and Cockburn 1989:182–83; Revkin 1990:205), but most writers who extol the alliance of rubber tappers and environmentalists downplay such conflicts.

The campesino unions of the Iquitos area show how the provision of aid can diminish the autonomy of Amazonian unions involved in less dramatic conflicts. COPAPMA, FECADEMA, and FEDECANAL have helped many campesino communities gain rights to natural resources and have also lobbied for changes in state agricultural policies. These organizations could easily be portrayed as providing a voice for previously powerless rural Amazonians, but such a depiction would be simplistic. The activities of COPAPMA, FECADEMA, and FEDECANAL have been the consequence of dialogues between campesino members and union advisers. Some advisers are foreigners funded by European church-related development agencies; others are Peruvian volunteers associated with local political movements. Because the advisers are a source of funds and technical expertise, their views can influence union activities. The campesino leaders, however, are hardly the pawns of the advisers. Many have well-considered political views and are knowledgeable about details of particular land tenure disputes.

The split between FEDECANAL and COPAPMA in the late 1980s illustrates how outside advisers influence union actions. The European-funded advisers to COPAPMA wanted to concentrate primarily on offering technical aid to rice farmers, but the more politically oriented Peruvian advisers to FEDECANAL preferred to maintain the unions' focus on struggles over access to natural resources. While these disagreements were not the immediate cause of FEDECANAL's withdrawal from the Casa Campesina, they fueled the growing tension between the two unions which preceded the split. Many members of COPAPMA wanted the union to continue its efforts to resolve land tenure disputes, but they cared more about maintaining financial support from the European development agencies.

The Resilience of Ribereño Household Economies

Socioeconomic and political analyses of Peru in the 1990s have been unremittingly gloomy and at times apocalyptic. A series of articles and editorials in the *New York Times* in April 1992 exemplifies the dismal view of Peru presented by the media of the industrial countries. Peru was in the news because President Alberto Fujimori, supported by the military, had dissolved the Congress. One reporter, Nathaniel Nash, wrote that "the most graphic pictures of poverty and hopelessness fail to capture [the country's] social cauldron" (April 12). He quoted a "senior Western official" as saying that "Peru is the most ungovernable country in South America, and one of the most ungovernable in the world." In an opinion piece the same day, the famous Peruvian novelist and sometime politician Mario Vargas Llosa wrote that the economic crisis had reduced incomes to "pitiful extremes." In another opinion piece on April 13, Leslie Gelb referred to the "hellish realities" of Peru. The tenor of the *Times*'s coverage could perhaps be seen most clearly when the reporter Thomas Friedman stated that Peru is an "impoverished country whose courts are widely believed to have been corrupted by drug traffickers and whose capital is under attack by vicious Maoist guerrillas" (April 15).

The seemingly interminable and intractable sociopolitical crises in Peru make it hard to be optimistic about the prospects for the Iquitos area. The economic situation of the inhabitants of riverine villages, however, seems much less desperate than that of many other Peruvians. Living in a backwater has some advantages; even in the early 1990s the region was not much affected by either the Sendero Luminoso or the narcotics trade. The cultural ecology and household economies of ribereño communities are sufficiently subsistence-oriented to cushion them from the worst effects of Peru's crises. Because ribereño farmers produce almost all of their food, they are less affected by hyperinflation than city dwellers. Unlike many farmers in the sierra, Amazonian agriculturalists have access to sufficient land to grow enough food to feed their families. Cooperative work groups enable ribereños to raise many crops without using hired laborers. The diversity of crops and fields ensures reliable food production in years of normal flooding.

For a brief period in the mid-1980s, sustainable, equitable development seemed possible in the ribereño villages near Iquitos. Even then the risks and uncertainties associated with floodplain farming prevented most ribereños from increasing their incomes. But communities were winning struggles over rights to natural resources, and the state was promising to expand credit and decentralize marketing outlets.

When I returned from my most recent fieldwork in the Iquitos area in 1987, I was still mildly optimistic about the prospects for improved economic conditions in floodplain villages. The events of the early 1990s, however, have been sobering. Environmentalists may rejoice that the Peruvian government has been too poor and distracted to encourage large-scale development in its tropical lowlands. They may also celebrate the ways in which the cultural ecology of ribereño households enables them to weather even the most severe economic downturns. The inhabitants of floodplain villages themselves may be less sanguine about their future in the hinterland of a troubled country.

Appendix 1
Household Socioeconomic Surveys

Figure 6.1 and some of the tables in this book are based on a household socio-economic survey that Miguel Pinedo and I carried out between November 1985 and April 1986. We collected information from 28 households in Porvenir, 23 in Santa Sofía, and 31 in Tapirillo. We did not survey 9 households in Porvenir, 2 in Santa Sofía, and 3 in Tapirillo. Miguel and I would have liked to have included two of the unsampled households (one in Santa Sofía and one in Tapirillo) in the survey. The other omissions were deliberate. Because we wanted to restrict our sample to households whose members were primarily local farmers and fishers, we did not survey the following households:

1. Households in which the principal wage earners earned most of their money from full-time, salaried employment (four households of schoolteachers and three households in Porvenir in which men worked on the commercial estate of Fernando Montoya).

2. Households that had moved into a community very recently (three households in Porvenir).

3. Households in which the residents had been away from the community for most of the year (one household in Porvenir).

4. Households in which most income came from work as a boat owner or storekeeper (one household in Tapirillo).

Figure 6.1 and some of the book's tables are thus based on 82 of the 84 households that obtained most of their food and income from local farming and fishing in 1985–86. The omission of other types of households is important only in parts of chapters 6 and 7. Figure 6.1 gives the age-sex structure of the three villages and several tables present information about household structure, ethnicity, and marriage patterns. The figure and tables are based on 85 percent (82 of 96) of the households in Porvenir, Santa Sofía, and Tapirillo. The demography, ethnicity, and family structure of the 14 missing households probably resemble those of others in the three villages, though I have no way of knowing whether this is the case. Table 7.6 gives estimates of gross household incomes from crops, animals, and wage labor in the three villages. The inclusion of the missing households would have had little effect on the estimates for Santa Sofía and Tapirillo. The estimate of income from wage labor in Porvenir, however, would be somewhat higher than that given in the table, and the estimates of income from other sources would be somewhat lower.

As every anthropologist knows, surveys are—to say the least—an imperfect way to find out about behavior. Some responses to our inquiries about past economic activities were rough guesses, and some people interviewed were unable to answer all our questions. Most of the people we interviewed were adult males, so we doubtless missed some of the contributions of women and children to household economies. The numbers in the tables based on the survey should be regarded as our best estimates. In some cases (e.g., Tables 7.3 and 7.4) these estimates are probably reasonably accurate; in other cases (e.g., Table 7.6) they are ballpark figures.

Appendix 2
Cost-Benefit Analyses

Tables 7.1 and 7.2 are based on a spreadsheet analysis of the profitability of rice plots in barreales under various conditions. Some of the assumptions about labor inputs and cash outlays used in constructing the spreadsheet were made in a study (Elaboración de Costo de Producción 1986) carried out by the late Jan Vogelzang for the Comité de Productores de Arroz de la Provincia de Maynas (COPAPMA). Other assumptions are the result of my own research.

The spreadsheet analysis considers the interaction of the following variables:

hectares of rice planted in barreal
yield per hectare
percentage of rice remaining after drying
price paid by government buying center per kilogram of dried rice
cost per kilogram for drying the rice
labor inputs per hectare for cleaning, weeding, and pest control
kilograms of rice harvested per labor-day
available household labor for cleaning, weeding, pest control, and harvesting
wage labor rate per day for tasks other than harvesting
payment to wage laborers per kilogram of rice harvested
amount of seeds planted per hectare
cost of seeds
amount of pesticide and herbicide applied per hectare
costs of pesticides and herbicides
cost of renting a fumigator
cost of constructing a temporary roofed structure for storing rice
cost of transporting hired workers to fields
cost per sack used in transporting rice
kilograms of rice per sack
cost per metric ton for loading, shipping, and unloading rice
cost per metric ton for transporting rice by truck from the Iquitos port to the
    buying center

cost of travel to Iquitos to obtain loans
size of first loan portion
time between receipt of first loan portion and repayment
size of second loan portion
time between receipt of second loan portion and repayment
size of third loan portion
time between receipt of third loan portion and repayment
interest rate on each loan portion.

Glossary

Acción Popular. A center-right political party that held power in Peru between 1980 and 1985. Acción Popular was led by Fernando Belaúnde Terry during this period.

aguajales. Shallow swamps dominated by aguaje palms (*Mauritia flexuosa*).

aguardiente. A strong liquor made from sugarcane.

alturas. Tropical forest uplands away from floodplains. Often called *terra firme* by anthropologists and ecologists.

APRA (Alianza Popular Revolucionaria Americana). A center-left political party that governed Peru between 1985 and 1990. APRA was led by Alán García during this period.

backswamps. Low areas in the tropical forest that are inundated much of the year but that support dense vegetation. Backswamps are called *tahuampas* in the Peruvian Amazon.

barreales. Mud deposits that appear annually in floodplains when rivers fall. Barreales, which are above water for four to six months of the year, have the most fertile soils in the Peruvian Amazon.

CAAAP (Centro Amazónico de Antropología y Aplicación Práctica). An organization that sponsors research in the Peruvian Amazon and carries out small-scale development projects concerned with agriculture, education, and public health. CAAAP receives financial support from the Catholic church and various European groups.

cetical. A floodplain land type associated with the cetico tree (*Cecropia latifolia*). Ceticales are common in low restingas.

cocha. An oxbow lake. Cochas are important fishing sites.

colectivo. A small motorized boat that carries passengers and cargo. Ribereños who live in villages within about 80 kilometers of Iquitos use these river buses to travel to the city.

COPAPMA (Comité de Productores de Arroz de la Provincia de Maynas). The Iquitos-based branch of the national rice producers' union. COPAPMA is a grassroots campesino organization that is concerned with a variety of political, economic, and social issues.

CORDELOR (Corporación de Desarrollo de Loreto). The principal government agency in the department of Loreto. CORDELOR is largely funded by taxes on oil companies.

ECASA (Empresa de Comercialización de Arroz). A state organization that bought rice from Peruvian farmers at a guaranteed price. ECASA was abolished in 1991 when the government led by Alberto Fujimori instituted a series of austerity measures.

FECADEMA (Federación de Campesinos de Maynas). An Iquitos-based multi-purpose campesino organization that attempted in the 1970s and 1980s to improve economic and health conditions in ribereño villages.

FEDECANAL (Federación Departamental de Campesinos y Nativos de Loreto). An Iquitos-based grassroots organization of ribereños and Amerindians that seeks to improve economic and health conditions in rural areas. FEDECANAL was established in 1987 when FECADEMA merged with a similar organization representing Amerindians.

fundo. A commercial estate owned and operated by a patrón. Residents of a fundo receive goods on credit in exchange for their labor on the estate's enterprises.

habilitador. A contractor who lends money to rural residents in exchange for exclusive rights to buy their forest products, agricultural crops, or fish.

inti. Former unit of Peruvian currency. The inti replaced the sol in 1986. The inti was worth 1,000 soles.

Izquierda Unida. A loose coalition of leftist political parties of Peru. Many, but not all, leaders of the campesino unions supported the Izquierda Unida in the mid-1980s.

lancha. A large boat that carries passengers and cargo. Lanchas make regularly scheduled trips along major rivers.

masato. A manioc beer that is consumed throughout Amazonia.

minga. A cooperative work party. The term *minga* is most often applied to festive work parties in which farmers issue an invitation to their neighbors to work on a particular task. The host family is expected to provide extraordinary food and drink but has little or no obligation to attend future work parties called by guests. The term *minga* is also sometimes applied to exchange labor groups, in which farmers work on each other's fields on a rotating basis. The food and drink served to guests are not much better than ordinary, and the amount of work that each group member provides for another is reciprocated almost exactly.

patrón. Formerly the owner-operator of a fundo. The term *patrón* is now used more generally to refer to a variety of rural and urban entrepreneurs and moneylenders.

playas. Sand deposits that appear annually in floodplains when rivers fall. Playas are usually lower than barreales and are above water for less of a year.

regatón. A merchant who travels to riverine communities to sell basic consumer goods and buy products of the field or forest. Today, regatones usually go to communities that are seldom visited by colectivos or lanchas.

rematista. A small-scale wholesaler in a town or city who buys products from incoming boats and sells them to stores, vendors, and larger-scale wholesalers (*mayoristas*).

restingas. Natural levees. Although restingas are sometimes inundated, they are the highest parts of the floodplains.

ribereño. A non-Amerindian born and raised in a rural part of the Peruvian Amazon.

sol. Former unit of Peruvian currency. The sol was replaced by the inti in 1986. One inti was worth 1,000 soles.

teniente gobernador. The highest political position in a ribereño village. The teniente gobernador represents the village in many of its dealings with the outside world.

transportista. The owner-operator of a colectivo.

UNAP (Universidad Nacional de la Amazonía Peruana). The only university in Iquitos.

la Voz de la Selva. A radio station affiliated with the Catholic church which aims its broadcasts at the rural population of the department of Loreto.

References Cited

Adams, Dale, Douglas Graham, and J. D. Von Pischke, eds.
1984   Undermining Rural Development with Cheap Credit. Boulder, Colo.: Westview Press.

Aguero, Oscar
1985   El Milenio en la Amazonía Peruana: Los Hermanos Cruzados de Francisco da Cruz. Amazonía Peruana 12:133–45.

Allen, William
1968   A Ceramic Sequence from the Alto Pachitea, Peru. Masters thesis, Department of Anthropology, University of Illinois.

Anderson, Anthony
1990a   Deforestation in Amazonia: Dynamics, Causes, and Alternatives. In Alternatives to Deforestation: Steps Toward Sustainable Use of the Amazon Rain Forest, A. Anderson, ed., 3–23. New York: Columbia University Press.

Anderson, Anthony, ed.
1990b   Alternatives to Deforestation: Steps Toward Sustainable Use of the Amazon Rain Forest. New York: Columbia University Press.

Annis, Sheldon, and Peter Hakim
1988a   Introduction: What Is Grassroots Development? In Direct to the Poor: Grassroots Development in Latin America, S. Annis and P. Hakim, eds., 1–3. Boulder, Colo.: Lynne Rienner.

Annis, Sheldon, and Peter Hakim, eds.
1988b   Direct to the Poor: Grassroots Development in Latin America. Boulder, Colo.: Lynne Rienner.

Aramburú, Carlos
1986   Población y Producción en la Amazonía Peruana. In Priorización y Desarrollo del Sector Agrario en el Perú, A. Figueroa Arévalo and J. Portocarrero Maisch, eds., 325–48. Lima: Pontificia Universidad Católica del Perú, Departamento de Economía.

Babb, Florence
1989   Between Field and Cooking Pot: The Political Economy of Market-women in Peru. Austin: University of Texas Press.
Barlett, Peggy
1982   Agricultural Choice and Change: Decision Making in a Costa Rican Community. New Brunswick, N.J.: Rutgers University Press.
Barth, Fredrik
1969   Introduction. *In* Ethnic Groups and Boundaries, F. Barth, ed., 9–38. Boston: Little, Brown and Company.
Beckerman, Stephen
1979   The Abundance of Protein in Amazonia: A Reply to Gross. American Anthropologist 81:533–60.
1987   Swidden in Amazonia and the Amazon Rim. *In* Comparative Farming Systems, B. L. Turner II and S. Brush, eds., 55–94. New York: Guilford Press.
Belaúnde Terry, Fernando
1965   Peru's Own Conquest. Lima: American Studies Press.
Bergman, Roland
1980   Amazon Economics: The Simplicity of Shipibo Indian Wealth. Syracuse, N.Y.: Syracuse University, Department of Geography.
Boehm, Christopher
1978   Rational Preselection from Hamadryas to Homo Sapiens: The Place of Decisions in Adaptive Process. American Anthropologist 80:265–96.
Boserup, Ester
1965   The Conditions of Agricultural Growth: The Economics of Agrarian Change under Population Pressure. Chicago: Aldine.
1981   Population and Technological Change: A Study of Long-Term Trends. Chicago: University of Chicago Press.
Bossen, Laurel
1989   Women and Economic Institutions. *In* Economic Anthropology, S. Plattner, ed., 318–50. Stanford, Calif.: Stanford University Press.
Boussard, J., and M. Petit
1967   Representation of Farmer's Behaviour Under Uncertainty with a Focus-Loss Constraint. Journal of Farm Economics 49:869–80.
Browder, John, ed.
1989   Fragile Lands of Latin America: Strategies for Sustainable Development. Boulder, Colo.: Westview Press.
Brown, Paul
1987   Population Growth and the Disappearance of Reciprocal Labor in a Highland Peruvian Community. *In* Research in Economic Anthropology, vol. 8, B. Isaac, ed., 225–42. Greenwich, Conn.: JAI Press.

Búfalos
1986   Búfalos: Un Programa Regional de Despojo a los Campesinos de la Selva. Amazonía Indígena 11:17–24.

Bunker, Stephen
1985   Underdeveloping the Amazon: Extraction, Unequal Exchange, and the Failure of the Modern State. Urbana: University of Illinois Press.
1991   Review of Fragile Lands of Latin America: Strategies for Sustainable Development, John Browder, ed. American Anthropologist 93:485–87.

Cancian, Frank
1979   The Innovator's Situation: Upper-Middle-Class Conservatism in Agricultural Communities. Stanford, Calif.: Stanford University Press.

Carvajal, Gaspar de
1988   [1500s] Discovery of the Orellana River. *In* The Discovery of the Amazon, J. Toribio Medina, ed., 167–235. New York: Dover.

Casement, Roger
1912   The Putomayo Indians. Contemporary Review 102:317–28.

Castonguay, Luis
1987   Vocabulario Regional del Oriente Peruano. Iquitos: Centro de Estudios Teológicos de la Amazonía (CETA).

Censo
1940   República de Perú, Censo Nacional de Población de 1940, vol. 10. Departamentos: Loreto, Amazonas, San Martín, Madre de Dios. Ministerio de Hacienda y Comercio, Dirección Nacional de Estadística.
1961   Sexto Censo de Población: Primer Censo Nacional de Vivienda. Lima: Dirección Nacional de Estadística y Censos.
1972   Censos Nacionales de Población, II de Vivienda. Lima: Oficina de Estadistíca y Censos.
1981   Censos Nacionales de Población, III de Vivienda. Lima: Instituto Nacional de Estadística.

Chagnon, Napoleon, and Raymond Hames
1979   Protein Deficiency and Tribal Warfare in Amazonia: New Data. Science 203:910–13.

Chaumeil, Jean-Pierre
1981   Historia y Migraciones de los Yagua de Finales del Siglo XVII Hasta Nuestras Días. Lima: Centro Amazónico de Antropología y Aplicación Práctica (CAAAP).

Chayanov, A. V.
1966   [1920s] The Theory of Peasant Economy. Translated from the Russian and German editions. Homewood, Ill.: R. Irwin.

Chibnik, Michael
1978   The Value of Subsistence Production. Journal of Anthropological Research 34:561–76.

1981a   The Evolution of Cultural Rules. Journal of Anthropological Research 37:256–68.

1981b   Small Farmer Risk Aversion: Peasant Reality or Policymakers' Rationalization? Culture and Agriculture 10:1–5.

1990   Double-Edged Risks and Uncertainties: Choices About Rice Loans in the Peruvian Amazon. *In* Risk and Uncertainty in Tribal and Peasant Economies, E. Cashdan, ed., 279–302. Boulder, Colo.: Westview Press.

1991   Quasi-Ethnic Groups in Amazonia. Ethnology 30:167–82.

Chibnik, Michael, and Wil de Jong

1989   Agricultural Labor Organization in Ribereño Communities of the Peruvian Amazon. Ethnology 28:75–95.

Chirif, Alberto, and Carlos Mora

1980   La Amazonía Peruana. *In* Historia del Peru, vol. 12: Procesos e Instituciones, 219–321. Lima: Editorial Juan Mejía Baca.

Clay, Jason

1988   Indigenous Peoples and Tropical Forests: Models of Land Use and Management from Latin America. Cultural Survival Report 27. Cambridge, Mass.: Cultural Survival.

Cochrane, T. T., and P. A. Sanchez

1982   Land Resources, Soils, and Their Management in the Amazon Region: A State of Knowledge Report. *In* Amazonia: Agriculture and Land Use Research, S. Hecht, ed., 137–209. Cali, Colombia: Centro Internacional de Agricultura Tropical (CIAT).

Cohen, John Michael

1975   Journeys Down the Amazon. London: Charles Knight.

Cohen, Ronald

1978   Ethnicity: Problem and Focus in Anthropology. Annual Review of Anthropology 7:379–403.

Collier, Richard

1968   The River That God Forgot: The Story of the Amazon Rubber Boom. New York: Dutton.

Collins, Jane

1989   Small Farmer Responses to Environmental Change: Coffee Production in the Peruvian High Selva. *In* The Human Ecology of Tropical Land Settlement in Latin America, D. Schumann and W. Partridge, eds., 238–63. Boulder, Colo.: Westview Press.

Comité Nacional de Productores de Arroz

1986   Mimeographed report on estimated rice production in 1985 in the various departments of Peru.

Coomes, Oliver

1992   Making a Living in the Amazon Rain Forest: Peasants, Land, and Economy in the Tahuayo River Basin of Northeastern Peru. Ph.D. thesis, Department of Geography, University of Wisconsin, Madison.

Cowell, Adrian
1990   The Decade of Destruction: The Crusade to Save the Amazon Rain
        Forest. New York: Henry Holt and Company.
d'Ans, André Marcel
1982   L'Amazonie Péruvienne Indigène. Paris: Payot.
Davis, Shelton, and Robert Mathews
1976   The Geological Imperative: Anthropology and Development in the
        Amazon Basin of South America. Cambridge, Mass.: Anthropology
        Resource Center.
Davis, William
1973   Social Relations in a Philippine Market. Berkeley: University of Cali-
        fornia Press.
Dean, Warren
1987   Brazil and the Struggle for Rubber: A Study in Environmental History.
        Cambridge: Cambridge University Press.
de Jong, Wil
1987   Organización del Trabajo en la Amazonía Peruana: El Caso de las
        Sociedades Agrícolas de Tamshiyacu. Amazonía Indígena 7 (13): 11–
        17.
1992   Unpublished manuscript. New York Botanical Garden.
Delboy, Emilio
1942   Memorandum Sobre la Selva del Perú. Lima: Sanmarti y Cia.
Denevan, William
1976   The Aboriginal Population of Amazonia. *In* The Native Population of
        the Americas in 1492, W. Denevan, ed., 205–34. Madison: University
        of Wisconsin Press.
1984   Ecological Hetereogeneity and Horizontal Zonation of Agriculture in
        the Amazon Floodplain. *In* Frontier Expansion in Amazonia, M.
        Schmink and C. Wood, eds., 311–36. Gainesville: University of Florida
        Press.
Denevan, William, and Christine Padoch, eds.
1988   Swidden-Fallow Agroforestry in the Peruvian Amazon. Advances in
        Economic Botany 5. New York: New York Botanical Garden.
de Soto, Hernando
1989   The Other Path: The Invisible Revolution in the Third World. New
        York: Harper and Row.
Diener, Paul, Kurt Moore, and Robert Mutaw
1980   Meat, Markets, and Mechanical Materialism: The Great Protein Fi-
        asco in Anthropology. Dialectical Anthropology 5:171–92.
Dobkin de Rios, Marlene
1972   Visionary Vine: Psychedelic Healing in the Peruvian Amazon. San Fran-
        cisco: Chandler.

1984   Hallucinogens: Cross-Cultural Perspectives. Albuquerque: University of New Mexico Press.

Dobyns, Henry
1966   Estimating Aboriginal American Population: An Appraisal of Techniques with a New Hemispheric Estimate. Current Anthropology 7: 395–416.

Durham, William
1979   Scarcity and Survival in Central America: Ecological Origins of the Soccer War. Stanford, Calif.: Stanford University Press.

Eden, Michael
1978   Ecology and Land Development: The Case of Amazonian Rainforest. Transactions of Institute of British Geographers 3:444–63.
1990   Ecology and Land Management in Amazonia. London: Belhaven Press.

Elaboración de Costo de Producción
1986   El Arrocero [Iquitos, Peru] 21:7–10.

Erasmus, Charles
1955   Culture Structure and Process: The Occurrence and Disappearance of Reciprocal Farm Labor. Southwestern Journal of Anthropology 12: 444–69.

Fearnside, Philip
1987a   Rethinking Continuous Cultivation in Amazonia. BioScience 37: 209–14.
1987b   Causes of Deforestation in the Brazilian Amazon. *In* The Geophysiology of Amazonia: Vegetation and Climate Interactions, R. Dickinson, ed., 37–53. New York: Wiley.

Ferrando, Delicia
1985   Situación Demográfica. *In* La Selva Peruana: Realidad Poblacional, 33–57. Lima: Asociación Multidisciplinaria de Investigación y Docencia en Población (AMIDEP).

Foresta, Ronald
1991   Amazon Conservation in the Age of Development. Gainesville: University of Florida Press.

Foster, George
1962   Traditional Cultures. New York: Harper and Row.

Foweraker, Joe
1981   The Struggle for Land: A Political Economy of the Frontier of Brazil from 1930 to the Present Day. New York: Cambridge University Press.

Freund, Rudolf
1956   The Introduction of Risk in a Programming Model. Econometrica 24:253–63.

Fritz, Samuel
1922   Journal of the Travels and Labours of Father Samuel Fritz in the River

of the Amazons Between 1686 and 1723. Compiled by George Edmundson. London: Hakluyt Society.

Fuentes, Hildebrando
1908   Loreto: Apuntes Geográficos, Históricos, Estadísticos, Políticos, Sociales. Vol. 2. Lima: Imprenta de la Revista.

Furneaux, Robin
1969   The Amazon: The Story of a Great River. London: Hamish Hamilton.

Gentry, Alwyn, and José López-Parodi
1980   Deforestation and Increased Flooding in the Upper Amazon. Science 210:1354–56.

Gill, Lesley
1987   Peasants, Entrepreneurs, and Social Change: Frontier Development in Lowland Bolivia. Boulder, Colo.: Westview Press.

Gladwin, Hugh, and Michael Murtaugh
1980   The Attentive-Preattentive Distinction in Agricultural Decision Making. *In* Agricultural Decision Making: Anthropological Contributions to Rural Development, P. Barlett, ed., 115–36. New York: Academic Press.

Gonzalez-Vega, Claudio
1984   Cheap Agricultural Credit: Redistribution in Reverse. *In* Undermining Rural Development with Cheap Credit, D. Adams, D. Graham, and J. D. Von Pischke, eds., 120–32. Boulder, Colo.: Westview Press.

Goodman, David, and Anthony Hall, eds.
1990   The Future of Amazonia: Destruction or Sustainable Development. New York: St. Martin's Press.

Gourou, Pierre
1966   The Tropical World: Its Social and Economic Conditions and Its Future Status. New York: Wiley.

Gow, Peter
1991   Of Mixed Blood: Kinship and History in Peruvian Amazonia. Oxford: Oxford University Press.

Grohs, Waltraud
1974   Los Indios del Alto Amazonas del Siglo XVI al XVIII: Poblaciones y Migraciones en la Antigua Provincia de Maynas. Bonner Amerikanistische Studien, no. 2. Bonn.

Gross, Daniel
1975   Protein Capture and Cultural Development in the Amazon Basin. American Anthropologist 77:526–49.

Guillet, David
1980   Reciprocal Labor and Peripheral Capitalism in the Central Andes. Ethnology 19:151–67.

Handelman, Don
1977   The Organization of Ethnicity. Ethnic Groups 1:187–200.
Hanks, Lucien
1972   Rice and Man: Agricultural Ecology in Southeast Asia. Chicago: Aldine.
Hardenburg, Walter
1912   The Putomayo: The Devil's Paradise. London: T. Fisher Unwin.
Harris, Marvin
1977   Cannibals and Kings: The Origins of Culture. New York: Random House.
1979   Cultural Materialism: The Struggle for a Science of Culture. New York: Random House.
1984   Animal Capture and Yanomamo Warfare: Retrospect and New Evidence. Journal of Anthropological Research 40:183–201.
Hawkins, John
1984   Inverse Images: The Meaning of Culture, Ethnicity, and Family in Postcolonial Guatemala. Albuquerque: University of New Mexico Press.
Hecht, Susanna
1985   Environment, Development, and Politics: Capital Accumulation and the Livestock Sector in Eastern Amazonia. World Development 13: 663–84.
Hecht, Susanna, and Alexander Cockburn
1989   The Fate of the Forest: Developers, Destroyers, and Defenders of the Amazon. London: Verso.
Hernández, Toribio
1946   História de la Fundación del Pueblo de Tamshiyacu. Unpublished manuscript in the library of Centro de Estudios Teológicos de la Amazonía (CETA), Iquitos, Peru.
Herndon, William
1952   [1854] Exploration of the Valley of the Amazon. Compiled by H. Basso. New York: McGraw-Hill.
Hiraoka, Mário
1985a   Cash Cropping, Wage Labor, and Urbanward Migrations: Changing Floodplain Subsistence in the Peruvian Amazon. In The Amazon Caboclo: Historical and Contemporary Perspectives, E. Parker, ed., 199–242. Studies in Third World Societies No. 32. Williamsburg, Va.: College of William and Mary.
1985b   Changing Floodplain Livelihood Patterns in the Peruvian Amazon. Tsukuba Studies in Human Geography [Japan] 9:243–75.
1985c   Mestizo Subsistence in Riparian Amazonia. National Geographic Research 1:236–46.
1986   Zonation of Mestizo Riverine Farming Systems in Northeast Peru. National Geographic Research 2:354–71.

1989   Agricultural Systems on the Floodplains of the Peruvian Amazon. *In* Fragile Lands of Latin America: Strategies for Sustainable Development, J. Browder, ed., 75–101. Boulder, Colo.: Westview Press.

1992   *Caboclo* and *Ribereño* Resource Management in Amazonia: A Review. *In* Conservation of Neotropical Forests: Working from Traditional Resource Use, K. Redford and C. Padoch, eds., 134–57. New York: Columbia University Press.

Hirschman, Albert
1984   Getting Ahead Collectively: Grassroots Experiences in Latin America. New York: Pergamon.

Johnson, Allen
1972   Individuality and Experimentation in Traditional Agriculture. Human Ecology 1:145–59.

1982   Reductionism in Cultural Ecology: The Amazon Case. Current Anthropology 23:413–28.

Katzin, Margret
1960   The Business of Higglering in Jamaica. Social and Economic Studies 9:297–331.

Kelly, Arlene
1984   Family, Church, and Crown: A Social and Demographic History of the Lower Xingu River Valley and the Municipality of Gurupá. Ph.D. thesis, University of Florida.

Kroeger, Axel, and Françoise Barbira-Freedman
1988   Cultural Change and Health: The Case of South American Rain Forest Indians. *In* Tribal Peoples and Development Issues, J. Bodley, ed., 221–36. Mountain View, Calif.: Mayfield.

Kuczynki-Godard, Máximo
1944   La Vida en la Amazonía Peruana: Observaciones de un médico. Lima: Libreria Internacional del Perú.

Kunreuther, Howard, and Gavin Wright
1979   Safety-First, Gambling, and the Subsistence Farmer. *In* Risk, Uncertainty, and Agricultural Development, J. Roumasset, J. Boussard, and I. Singh, eds., 213–30. New York: Agricultural Development Council.

Lamb, F. Bruce
1985   Rio Tigre and Beyond: The Amazon Jungle Medicine of Manuel Córdova. Berkeley: North Atlantic Books.

Lathrap, Donald
1970   The Upper Amazon. London: Thames and Hudson.

Lin, William, G. Dean, and C. Moore
1974   An Empirical Test of Utility versus Profit Maximization in Agricultural Production. American Journal of Agricultural Economics 56:497–508.

Lipton, Michael
1979   Agricultural Risk, Rural Credit, and the Inefficiency of Inequality. *In* Risk, Uncertainty, and Agricultural Development, J. Roumasset, J. Boussard, and I. Singh, eds., 341–62. New York: Agricultural Development Council.

Luna, Luis Eduardo
1984a   The Concept of Plants as Teachers Among Four Mestizo Shamans of Iquitos, Northeastern Peru. Journal of Ethnopharmacology 11:135–56.
1984b   The Healing Practices of a Peruvian Shaman. Journal of Ethnopharmacology 11:123–33.

McNeil, Mary
1964   Lateritic Soils. Scientific American 211 (November): 96–102.

Marcoy, Paul [Laurent Saint Cricq]
1875   Travels in South America. Vol. 2. London: Blackie and Son.

Marzal, Manuel
1984   Las Reducciones Indígenas en la Amazonía de Virreinato Peruano. Amazonía Peruana 10:7–45.

Meggers, Betty
1954   Environmental Limitations on the Development of Culture. American Anthropologist 56:801–24.
1971   Amazonia: Man and Culture in a Counterfeit Paradise. Chicago: Aldine.
1985   Aboriginal Adaptation to Amazonia. *In* Key Environments: Amazonia, G. Prance and T. Lovejoy, eds., 307–27. Oxford: Pergamon.
1988   The Prehistory of Amazonia. *In* People of the Tropical Rain Forest, J. Denslow and C. Padoch, eds., 53–62. Berkeley: University of California Press.

Meggers, Betty, and Clifford Evans
1983   Lowland South America and the Antilles. *In* Ancient South Americans, J. Jennings, ed., 287–335. San Francisco: W. H. Freeman.

Miller, Darrel
1985   Highways and Gold: Change in a Caboclo Community. *In* The Amazon Caboclo: Historical and Contemporary Perspectives, E. Parker, ed., 167–98. Studies in Third World Societies No. 32. Williamsburg, Va.: College of William and Mary.

Moore, M. P.
1975   Co-operative Labour in Peasant Agriculture. Journal of Peasant Studies 2:270–91.

Moran, Emilio
1981   Developing the Amazon. Bloomington: Indiana University Press.
1982   Ecological, Anthropological, and Agronomic Research in the Amazon Basin. Latin American Research Review 17:3–42.

1993   Through Amazonian Eyes: The Human Ecology of Amazonian Populations. Iowa City: University of Iowa Press.

Myers, Thomas

1973   Toward the Reconstruction of Prehistoric Community Patterns in the Amazon Basin. *In* Variation in Anthropology, D. Lathrap and J. Douglas, eds., 233–52. Urbana: Illinois Archaeology Survey.

1992   Agricultural Limitations of the Amazon in Theory and Practice. World Archaeology 24:82–97.

Netting, Robert, Richard Wilk, and Eric Arnould, eds.

1984   Households: Comparative and Historical Studies of the Domestic Group. Berkeley: University of California Press.

Nicholaides, J. J., III, D. E. Bandy, P. A. Sanchez, J. H. Villachica, A. J. Coutu, and C. S. Valverde

1984   Continuous Cropping Potential in the Upper Amazon Basin. *In* Frontier Expansion in Amazonia, M. Schmink and C. Wood, eds., 337–65. Gainesville: University of Florida Press.

Nugent, Stephen

1993   Amazonian Caboclo Society: An Essay on Invisibility and Peasant Economy. Providence, R.I.: Berg.

Orlove, Benjamin

1977   Alpacas, Sheep, and Men. New York: Academic Press.

Ortiz, Sutti

1979   The Effect of Risk Aversion Strategies on Subsistence and Cash Crop Decisions. *In* Risk, Uncertainty, and Agricultural Development, J. Roumasset, J. Boussard, and I. Singh, eds., 231–46. New York: Agricultural Development Council.

Pace, Richard

1992   Social Conflict and Political Activism in the Brazilian Amazon: A Case Study of Gurupá. American Ethnologist 19:710–32.

Padoch, Christine

1986   The Campesinos of Santa Rosa: History and Ethnicity in an Amazonian Community. Paper presented at the annual meeting of the American Anthropological Association, Philadelphia.

1988a   Aguaje (*Mauritia Flexuosa* L. f.) in the Economy of Iquitos, Peru. *In* The Palm—Tree of Life: Biology, Utilization, and Conservation, M. Balick, ed., 214–24. Advances in Economic Botany 6. New York: New York Botanical Garden.

1988b   The Economic Importance and Marketing of Forest and Fallow Products in the Iquitos Region. *In* Swidden-Fallow Agroforestry in the Peruvian Amazon, W. Denevan and C. Padoch, eds., 74–89. Advances in Economic Botany 5. New York: New York Botanical Garden.

1988c   People of the Floodplain and Forest. *In* People of the Tropical Rain

Forest, J. S. Denslow and C. Padoch, eds., 127–41. Berkeley: University of California Press.

Padoch, Christine, and Wil de Jong

1987   Traditional Agroforestry Practices of Native and Ribereño Farmers in the Lowland Peruvian Amazon. *In* Agroforestry: Realities, Possibilities, and Potentials, H. L. Gholz, ed., 179–94. Dordrecht, The Netherlands: Martinus Nijhoff.

1989   Production and Profit in Agroforestry: An Example from the Peruvian Amazon. *In* Fragile Lands of Latin America: Strategies for Sustainable Development, J. Browder, ed., 102–13. Boulder, Colo.: Westview Press.

1990   The House Gardens of Santa Rosa: Diversity and Variability in an Amazonian Agricultural System. Economic Botany 45:166–75.

Padoch, Christine, Jomber Chota Inuma, Wil de Jong, and John Unruh

1985   Amazonian Agroforestry: A Market-Oriented System in Peru. Agroforestry Systems 3:47–58.

Padoch, Christine, and Miguel Pinedo-Vásquez

1991   Floodtime on the Ucayali. Natural History (May): 48–57.

Park, Thomas

1992   Early Trends Toward Class Stratification: Chaos, Common Property, and Flood Recession Agriculture. American Anthropologist 94:90–117.

Parker, Eugene

1981   Cultural Ecology and Change: A Caboclo Várzea Community in the Brazilian Amazon. Ph.D. thesis, University of Colorado, Boulder.

Parker, Eugene, ed.

1985   The Amazon Caboclo: Historical and Contemporary Perspectives. Studies in Third World Societies No. 32. Williamsburg, Va.: College of William and Mary.

Peck, Robert

1990   Promoting Agroforestry Practices Among Small Producers: The Case of the Coca Agroforestry Project in Amazonian Ecuador. *In* Alternatives to Deforestation: Steps Toward Sustainable Use of the Amazon Rain Forest, A. Anderson, ed., 167–80. New York: Columbia University Press.

Pinedo-Vásquez, Miguel

1986   Annually Flooded Lands of the Peruvian Amazon: Use and Tenure. Paper presented at the annual meeting of the American Anthropological Association, Philadelphia.

Plattner, Stuart

1989   Economic Behavior in Markets. *In* Economic Anthropology, S. Plattner, ed., 209–21. Stanford, Calif.: Stanford University Press.

Prance, Ghillean

1989   Economic Prospects from Tropical Rainforest Ethnobotany. *In* Fragile

Lands of Latin America: Strategies for Sustainable Development, J. Browder, ed., 61–74. Boulder, Colo.: Westview Press.

Price, David

1989   Before the Bulldozer: The Nambiquara Indians and the World Bank. Cabin John, Md.: Seven Locks Press.

Provinse, John

1937   Cooperative Ricefield Cultivation Among the Siang Dyaks of Central Borneo. American Anthropologist 39:77–102.

Raimondi, Antonio

1929   [ca. 1874] El Perú. Lima: Imprenta Torres Aguirre.

1942   [1862] Apuntes sobre la Provincia Litoral de Loreto. Iquitos: Imprenta El Oriente.

Ramos, Alcida

1984   Frontier Expansion and Indian Peoples in the Brazilian Amazon. *In* Frontier Expansion in Amazonia, M. Schmink and C. Wood, eds., 83–104. Gainesville: University of Florida Press.

Regan, Jaime

1983   Hacia la Tierra sin Mal: Estudio de la Religión del Pueblo en Amazonía. Iquitos: Centro de Estudios Teológicos de la Amazonía (CETA).

1988   Mesianismo Cocama: Un Movimiento de Resistencia en la Amazonía Peruana. América Indígena 48:127–38.

Renard-Casevitz, France-Marie

1980   Contrasts Between Amerindian and Colonist Land Use in the Southern Peruvian Amazon (Matsiguenga Area). *In* Land, People, and Planning in Contemporary Amazonia, F. Barbira-Scazzocchio, ed., 249–55. Cambridge: University of Cambridge Centre of Latin American Studies.

Revkin, Andrew

1990   The Burning Season: The Murder of Chico Mendes and the Fight for the Amazon Rain Forest. Boston: Houghton Mifflin.

Rogers, Everett

1969   Modernization Among Peasants: The Impact of Communication. New York: Holt, Rinehart & Winston.

Roosevelt, Anna

1980   Parmana: Prehistoric Maize and Manioc Subsistence Along the Amazon and Orinoco. New York: Academic Press.

1987   Chiefdoms in the Amazon and Orinoco. *In* Chiefdoms in the Americas, R. Drennan and C. Uribe, eds., 153–85. Lanham, Md.: University Press of America.

1989   Resource Management in Amazonia Before the Conquest: Beyond Ethnographic Projection. *In* Resource Management in Amazonia: Indigenous and Folk Strategies, D. Posey and W. Balée, eds., 30–62. Advances in Economic Botany 7. New York: New York Botanical Garden.

1991   Moundbuilders of the Amazon: Geophysical Archaeology on Marajo Island, Brazil. San Diego: Academic Press.

Roosevelt, Anna, R. A. Housely, M. Mimazio da Silveira, S. Maranca, and R. Johnson

1991   Eighth Millennium Pottery from a Prehistoric Shell Midden in the Brazilian Amazon. Science 254:1621–24.

Roseberry, William

1983   Coffee and Capitalism in the Venezuelan Andes. Austin: University of Texas Press.

1989   Anthropologies and Histories: Essays in Culture, History, and Political Economy. New Brunswick, N.J.: Rutgers University Press.

Ross, Eric

1978a   The Evolution of the Amazon Peasantry. Journal of Latin American Studies 10:193–218.

1978b   Food Taboos, Diet, and Hunting Strategy: The Adaptation to Animals in Amazon Cultural Ecology. Current Anthropology 19:1–36.

Rumrrill, Róger

1983   Iquitos, Capital de la Amazonía Peruana. Iquitos: Róger Rumrrill.

San Román, Jesús

1975   Perfiles Históricos de la Amazonía Peruana. Lima: Ediciones Paulinas.

San Román, Jesús, José Barletti, and Jorge Gadea, eds.

no date   [ca. 1970] Estudio Socio-económico de los Ríos Amazonas y Napo. Vol. 1: Visión de los Caseriós, Muestra y Aspectos Demográficos y Migratorios de los Dos Ríos. Iquitos: Centro de Estudios Teológicos de la Amazonía (CETA).

Saul, Mahir

1983   Work Parties, Wages, and Accumulation in a Voltaic Village. American Ethnologist 10:77–96.

Schmink, Marianne, and Charles Wood

1992   Contested Frontiers in Amazonia. New York: Columbia University Press.

Schmink, Marianne, and Charles Wood, eds.

1984   Frontier Expansion in Amazonia. Gainesville: University of Florida Press.

Schwartzman, Stephan

1989   Extractive Reserves: The Rubber Tappers' Strategy for Sustainable Use of the Amazon Rainforest. In Fragile Lands of Latin America: Strategies for Sustainable Development, J. Browder, ed., 150–65. Boulder, Colo.: Westview Press.

Shibutani, Tamotsu, and Kian Kwan

1965   Ethnic Stratification. New York: Macmillan.

Shoemaker, Robin
1981   The Peasants of El Dorado: Conflict and Contradiction in a Peruvian Frontier Settlement. Ithaca, N.Y.: Cornell University Press.

Smith, Anthony
1990   Explorers of the Amazon. New York: Viking.

Smith, Carol
1975   Production in Western Guatemala: A Test of Von Thünen and Boserup. *In* Formal Methods in Economic Anthropology, S. Plattner, ed., 5–37. Washington, D.C.: American Anthropological Assocation.

Sponsel, Leslie
1983   Yanomama Warfare, Protein Capture, and Cultural Ecology: A Critical Analysis of the Arguments of the Opponents. Interciencia 8:204–10.
1986   Amazon Ecology and Adaptation. Annual Review of Anthropology 15:67–97.

Stocks, Anthony
1978   The Invisible Indians: A History and Analysis of the Relations of the Cocamilla Indians of Loreto, Peru, to the State. Ph.D. thesis, Department of Anthropology, University of Florida.
1984   Indian Policy in Eastern Peru. *In* Frontier Expansion in Amazonia, M. Schmink and C. Wood, eds., 33–61. Gainesville: University of Florida Press.
1987   Tropical Forest Development in Peru. Development Anthropology Network 5 (2):1–8.

Stoll, David
1982   Fishers of Men or Founders of Empire: The Wycliffe Bible Translators in Latin America. London: Zed Press.

Swetnam, John
1978   Interaction Between Urban and Rural Residents in a Guatemalan Marketplace. Urban Anthropology 7:137–53.

Taussig, Michael
1987   Shamanism, Colonialism, and the Wild Man: A Study in Terror and Healing. Chicago: University of Chicago Press.

Toribio Medina, José, ed.
1988   [1894] The Discovery of the Amazon. New York: Dover.

Trager, Lillian
1981   Customers and Creditors: Variations in Economic Personalism in a Nigerian Market System. Ethnology 20:133–46.

van den Berghe, Pierre, and George Primov
1977   Inequality in the Peruvian Andes: Class and Ethnicity in Cuzco. Columbia, Mo.: University of Missouri Press.

Villarejo, Avencio
1979   Así es la Selva: Estudio Monográfico de la Amazonía Peruana. Iquitos: Centro de Estudios Teológicos de la Amazonía (CETA).

Wagley, Charles
1953   Amazon Town: A Study of Man in the Tropics. New York: Macmillan.

Webb, Richard, and Graciela Fernández Baca
1990   Perú en Números. Lima: Cuánto.

Werlich, David
1978   Peru: A Short History. Carbondale, Ill.: Southern Illinois University Press.

Werner, David
1977   Donde no hay Doctor. Palo Alto, Calif.: Hesperian Foundation.

Wilk, Richard, ed.
1989   The Household Economy. Boulder, Colo.: Westview Press.

Wilson, Patricia, and Carol Wise
1986   The Regional Implications of Public Investment in Peru, 1968–1983. Latin American Research Review 21:93–116.

Zavaleta, Luis, Richard Simmons, and Richard King
1984   Incentivos y Asignación de Recursos para el Fomento de Productos Agrícolas en el Perú: Arroz y Trigo. Desarrollo Rural en las Americas 16:71–90.

Index

Acción Popular party, 197, 215
Acopios (crop collection centers), 212, 213
Acre state, Brazil, 224
Advisers, union: assistance to elected officials, 199; and campesinos' credit problems, 210; criticisms of water buffalo project, 205, 206; financial support for, 217; and independence of unions, 224–25; opposition to tourist camps, 208, 209; visits to villages, 201–2
Agoutis, 25, 129
Agrarian Bank, xv, 60, 62, 71, 78, 80, 95, 119, 120, 130, 155, 159, 167, 173; advice of campesino unions concerning, 201–2, 210; assessing riskiness of loans of, 187–89; availability of loans from, 175, 220; and catastrophic medical costs, 91–92; contraction of credit by, 190–91; contracts of, 176–78; coverage of production and marketing costs, 179, 181; credit applications to, and landownership, 75–76; credit programs of, xiii; defaults on loans from, 178–80, 185–86; diversion of loans from, to

household maintenance, 174, 181–82, 184, 188, 189; effects of loans on production, 184–85; extension of credit for plantains and manioc, 156–57; loans to transportistas, 168; neglect of alturas by, 223; processing of loans by, 175–76, 184–86; profile of borrowers from, 182–84; profitability of loans from, 179, 180; reform of, 189–90, 210–11; relations with campesino unions, 215; subsidies to water buffalo project, 204–6
Agroforestry, 7; cycles of, 111–12; income from, 112; location of housing and, 73; ownership of land and, 75
Aguaje, 63, 114, 156
Aguardiente (cane liquor), 34–35, 42, 45, 79, 80, 92, 139, 140
Air service, 48, 58
Alcohol: control of Indian labor with, 34–35; effect on agricultural labor, 137
Alcoholism, 92
Alianza Popular Revolucionaria Americana (APRA), 192; agrarian program of, 156–57, 190, 220;

and improvement of market logistics, 212–13; relations with campesino unions, 198–99, 215–17; and resource disputes, 203–4

Alturas. *See* Uplands

Amazonía Peruana (journal), 195

Amazon River, 86; access to markets along, 79–80; changes in course of, 101; fish migrations on, 24; mission settlements along, 29, 30; precolumbian settlements along, 26, 28; ribereño settlements along, 72; rise and fall of, 14, 16, 62, 67, 76, 101, 102; tourist camps on, 208; transportation on, 58–60; water content of, 21–22; water levels of, 21

Amerindians: changes in ethnicity among, 32; citizenship of, 34; colonial authority over, 33; colonization by Europeans, 28–29; contact with European explorers, 28; cultural divisions among, 31; and deforestation, 1; demography of, 8–9; displacement by development, 5; epidemics among, 31–32; ethnic classification of, 47–48, 84–87; in forest products industry, 43; grassroots organization of, 195, 197, 198; language of, 31, 37, 42; missions' effect on ecology of, 32–33; opposition to nature reserves, 4; ownership of land by, 74, 85, 222, 223; in postindependence economy, 35, 37–38; precolumbian societies of, 26–28; relations with merchants, 34–35, 37; reserves for, 5; and ribereñoization, 46–48, 100; in rubber economy, 38, 41–42; settlement by missionaries, 12, 29–32; settlement patterns of, 73;

subsistence systems of, 4; as tourist attractions, 208

Amerindian surnames, 107–10

Amnesties, loan, 178, 180

Ancestry, in definition of ethnic identity, 83, 86–87

Andes Mountains: and Amazon flooding patterns, 21; cooperative labor in, 135, 139; development in, 4, 7; as obstacle to development, 3; sediments from, 22

Armadillos, 25, 129

Army, Peruvian, 48–49, 166–67

El arrocero (newspaper), 199, 206, 215

Ayni (direct labor exchange), 139

Ayuahuasca, 90

Bajos (bottomlands), growth of rice in, 213–15

Balata, 44, 99

Barbasco, 44

Barreales, 22, 23; access to, as determinant of economic activity, 79, 181; agricultural methods in, 111, 113; allocation to cash crops, 153, 154; growth of rice in, 116–20, 125, 147, 158, 171, 175–81, 185, 186, 190, 213; growth of secondary crops in, 121; location of villages near, 73; maintaining access to, 163; ownership of, xiii, 75–77, 185, 203, 206–7, 209–11, 222; unpredictable flooding of, 221

Barth, Fredrik, 83

Beckerman, Stephen, 19

Belaúnde Terry, Fernando, 3, 198, 215, 216

Belém, Brazil, 39

Belén, Peru: agricultural marketplace of, 62; annual flooding of, 16; migration of villagers to, 166, 170

Bergman, Roland, 114, 115, 120, 128
Birth control, 154
Birth rates, 55, 59, 102
Boats. *See* Colectivos; Lanchas; Transportation
Borja, Peru, 29, 36
Boserup, Ester, 7, 8
Brazil, 54, 86, 87, 156, 167; air service to, 58; Amazonian colonists from, 42; Amazonian development programs, 2–3, 205; Amerindian population of, 8; environmental destruction in, 2–3, 6; GNP of, 3; patrones from, 42; rubber tappers of, 224; in rubber trade, 39; trade with Peruvian Amazon, 34–37, 44; water buffalo imports from, 204
Brazil nuts, 112
Breadfruit, 121
Bunker, Stephen, 4–5

CAAAP. *See* Centro Amazónico de Antropología y Aplicación Práctica
Caballococha, Peru, 60, 87, 99, 100, 170
Caboclos, 9
Caihua, 122
Cajamarca, Peru, 99
Callao province, Peru, 53
Cambas, 9
Campesino unions, xiii–xiv, 93; advocacy in resource disputes, 99, 194, 202–9, 222, 225; advocacy of higher crop prices, 211–12, 222; affiliation of author's research with, xv–xvii; challenge of land tenure system, 75; counteracting of rural poverty, 11; and credit reform, 189–90,

210–11; establishment of, 194–97; estimates of cost of living, 70; favoring of extractive reserves by, 6; financial (in)dependence of, 217, 224–25; ideology of, 198–99; and improvement of market logistics, 212–13; inequality of women in, 199–200, 223; influence of, 193; and institutionalization of labor groups, 141; involvement in human rights issues, 216–17; organizational structure of, 199–201; political participation by, 215–16; prospects for, 217–18; and ribereño access to resources, 164; technical aid by, 213–15; visits of advisers to locals, 201–2; Yanashi conference, 192–93
Cancian, Frank, 174
Capironal, Peru, 76–77
Capybaras, 25, 129
Casa Campesina, 196, 197, 200, 204, 210, 225
Caserios, 45–46
Catalán, Peru, 100
Catholic church, xiv, 67; rural development projects, 194–98; rural following of, 90. *See also* Missionaries; Missions
Cattle: and destruction of rain forest, 3; economic importance of, 80; in village economies, 98, 99, 101, 102
Caymans, 25, 129
Cedar, 43, 44
Centro Amazónico de Antropología y Aplicación Práctica (CAAAP), xiv, xvi; development projects of, 194–95; retreat from confrontation, 196–97, 217
Centro de Investigación de la Amazonía Peruana (CIAP), xv

Certificado de domicilio, 75
Certificates, land-use, 74–77, 100,
    210–11
Ceticales, 23
Chaumeil, Jean-Pierre, 32
Chicha (corn liquor), 34–35
Chickens: commercial production of,
    79, 159, 160, 162, 171, 175;
    income from, 125, 126, 155;
    prices for, 67, 69
Child bearing, 106
Children: as agricultural laborers,
    138; as hedge against economic
    risk, 154; upward mobility of,
    158, 166, 170
Cholera epidemic (1990s), 92
Cholos, 84–85
CIAP. *See* Centro de Investigación de
    la Amazonía Peruana
Clothing, peasant, 78
Coca: growth of, 4; income from, 57;
    trade in, xii, 53, 54, 162–63
Cocamas, the, 97, 100, 107; contact
    with European explorers, 28;
    epidemics among, 32; mission
    settlements of, 32; post-
    independence settlements of, 35,
    36; precolumbian settlements of,
    26–27
Cocamillas, the, 32, 84–85
Colectivos (river buses), 59, 63–65,
    71, 79, 102, 123, 128, 156, 167–
    68, 186
Colombia, 54, 87
Colonialism: administration of, 12,
    33; economy of, 28–29, 33–34
Colonization: and destruction of rain
    forest, 2–3; geographic obstacles
    to, 3–4; government subsidies to,
    36; and population groups, 9,
    42–43

Comité de Productores de Arroz
    de la Provincia de Maynas
    (COPAPMA), 193; advocacy in
    resource disputes, 203, 207, 209,
    211; advocacy of higher crop
    prices, 212; clientele of, 196, 197;
    and credit reform, 211; establish-
    ment of, 196; financial hardships
    of, 217; financial (in)dependence
    of, 217, 224–25; growth of, 196;
    ideology of, 198–99; and improve-
    ment of market logistics, 212;
    involvement in human rights
    issues, 216–17; organizational
    structure of, 200, 201; participa-
    tion in political process, 215, 216;
    technical aid by, 213–14; thresher
    program of, 157–58
Commercial estates. *See* Fundos
Communal medical supply, 91, 92
Communal work days, 88
Community studies, 11, 12
Compadrazgo, 45–46, 90
Congeladores (commercial fishing
    boats), 208
Constitution, Peruvian, and
    landownership, 75
Consumer price index, 70
Contamana, Peru, 99
Cooperative work groups, 77, 78, 93;
    advantages/disadvantages of, 142–
    44, 155; conditions of labor of,
    140–41; and credit, xiii; and
    demand for wage labor, 130;
    depression of wages and prices by,
    151; ecology of, 151; in extractive
    economies, 135, 149–50; food for,
    126, 139; historical antecedents
    of, 144; importance of, xiii;
    incidence of, 139–40, 141;
    institutionalization of, 141, 146;

occasions for, 137–40, 144–49, 160, 162; participation in, 140; persistence of, in cash economy, 134–35, 150–51; reliance on, vs. hired labor, 134–35; and rice cultivation, 116; socioeconomic relations of, 137, 150–51; types of, 134

COPAPMA. *See* Comité de Productores de Arroz de la Provincia de Maynas

CORDELOR. *See* Corporación de Desarrollo de Loreto

Coriander, 122

Corn (maize), 10, 14, 33, 38, 45, 114; commercial production of, 58, 116, 120, 132, 150, 157, 171, 201; continuous cropping of, 20; growing of, 111–13, 119, 124–25, 140; marketing of, 60–62, 119, 120, 202, 211, 212, 220, 221; prices for, 67, 68; reduction of acreage in, 222; relative importance of, 122–24; as subsistence crop, 160; varieties of, 202; yields from, 119, 120

Corporación de Desarrollo de Loreto (CORDELOR), 214, 215

Correría, 40–43

Cortemañanas, 140

Cowpeas, 114, 121, 171; commercial production of, 221; growing of, 113; relative importance of, 122, 124

Credit, informal, 175, 178, 179, 182, 187, 188

Credit programs: access to, as determinant of economic activity, 80; advice of campesino unions on, 201–2, 210; applications for, and landownership, 75–76; assessing riskiness of loans, 187–89; availability of loans, 175, 220; beneficiaries of, xiii; and cash cropping, 50, 61, 150, 156, 219; and catastrophic medical costs, 91–92; changes in, 176, 188; contraction of, 190–91, 220–21; contracts of, 176–78; coverage of production and marketing costs, 179, 181; diversion of loans to household maintenance, 174, 181–82, 184, 188, 189; and economic risk, 14–15, 155; effect on production, 184–85; environmental factors and demand for loans, 181; experimental, 156–57; and exploitation of rain forest, 2, 3; and hiring of wage labor, 130, 142, 147, 150, 177, 181, 186; impact of inflation on, 71; and incentives vis-à-vis rice production, 116, 119; inequitable development and, 5; inequities in, 173, 175, 176, 189, 191, 205, 219–20, 223; and land-use patterns, xiv; loan defaults, 178–80, 185–86; processing of loans, 175–76, 184–86; profile of borrowers, 182–84; profitability of loans, 179, 180; purpose of, 175; reform of, 189–90, 210–11; relationship of land tenure to, 210–11; risk aversion and demand for loans, 174, 180–82; and rural poverty, 10, 11; subsidies to water buffalo project, 204–6; wisdom of, 173–74

Cultural evolution, 155–56

Curanderos (shamans), 90, 91

DDT, 44

Death rates, 55–56

Debt peonage system, 34–35, 37
Deforestation, 1; extent of, 6–7; and
    flooding, 102
de Jong, Wil, xiii, 9, 123, 135,
    140, 147
Development: abandonment of, 190,
    220–21; agricultural credit in,
    173, 191; equitability of, 5–6, 10–
    11, 205; grassroots organizations,
    193–95, 224; and missionization,
    32–33; outside agencies for, 194–
    98, 217, 223–25; unevenness of,
    2–4, 223. *See also* Campesino
    unions; Credit programs; Sustain-
    able agriculture; Sustainable
    development
Disease: devastation of Amerindian
    populations by, 31–32; incidence
    of, 92
Domestic animals, 125–27, 155,
    204–7
Domestic servants, 78
Drug traffic, xii, 4, 53, 54, 57, 162–
    63, 216, 217, 220, 225, 226
Ducks, 126

ECASA. *See* Empresa de
    Comercialización de Arroz
Ecuador, 48–49, 54, 167
Education: and community control,
    216; and integration of Peruvian
    economy, 49; in ribereño villages,
    89–90; and upward mobility, 166,
    170, 171
Eggs, income from, 126
Empresa de Comercialización de
    Arroz (ECASA), 60–61, 117
Encomienda agreements, 63, 65
Encomienda system, 28–29
Entrepreneurs: in agricultural
    marketing chain, 63; and competi-
    tion over resource rights, 1–2, 87–

88, 194, 204–9, 222–23; connec-
    tion of rural communities to, 13;
    economic power of, 194; eligibility
    for loans, 175, 189, 220; exploita-
    tion of rain forest by, 2; inequi-
    table development and, 5; and
    mission economies, 32; opposition
    to nature reserves, 4; participation
    in campesino organizations, 198,
    201; role in village economy, 80
Esperanza, Peru, 98
Estates, commercial. *See* Fundos
Ethnic identity, 47–48, 82–87; and
    surnames, 107–10
European surnames, 107–10
Exchange labor groups, 134, 135,
    139; advantages/disadvantages of,
    142–44; conditions of labor of,
    140–41; in extractive economies,
    149; historical antecedents of,
    144; incidence of, 140, 141;
    institutionalization of, 141, 146;
    occasions for, 137, 138, 144–49;
    persistence of, in cash economy,
    150–51; socioeconomic relations
    of, 137
Experimentation, agricultural, 156–
    58, 213–15
EXPLORAMA, 208, 209
Explorers, 2, 12, 27, 28
Extractive reserves, 5–7

Family market basket index, 70
Family planning, 154
Fariña, 102, 115
Farmers' market, 68, 70, 212
Fearnside, Philip, 20
FECADEMA. *See* Federación de
    Campesinos de Maynas
FEDECANAL. *See* Federación
    Departamental de Campesinos y
    Nativos de Loreto

Federación de Campesinos de
Maynas (FECADEMA), 193;
advocacy in resource disputes,
203, 207, 209; clientele of, 196;
establishment of, 194; financial
(in)dependence of, 217, 224–25;
growth of, 196; ideology of, 198;
and improvement of market
logistics, 212; involvement in
human rights issues, 216–17;
merger of, 197; organizational
problems of, 195; organizational
structure of, 200; organization
of producer groups, 195–96;
participation in political process,
215, 216
Federación Departamental de
Campesinos y Nativos de Loreto
(FEDECANAL): clientele of, 197;
establishment of, 197; financial
(in)dependence of, 217, 224–25;
organizational structure of, 200
Fernando Lores district, Peru, 47
Fertilizers, 5–7, 20
Festive work parties, 134, 135;
advantages/disadvantages of, 142–
43; in extractive economies, 149;
food for, 139; historical anteced-
ents of, 144; incidence of, 139–40;
occasions for, 137–40, 145, 147–
49, 162; participation in, 140;
persistence of, in cash economy,
150–51; socioeconomic relations
of, 137
Fish: commercial production of, 49,
159–61, 171; in floodplains, 24;
marketing of, 62, 63; migrations
of, 24; ornamental, 49; prices for,
68; as staple food, 79, 116, 127
Fishing, 24; continuation of traditional practices in, 152; as
determinant of settlement patterns, 72; disputes over access to,
203, 208–9, 222–23; economic
importance of, 79; for home
consumption, 161, 162; income
from, 127–29, 131, 133; maintaining access to, 163; methods
of, 128; response to changing
conditions in, 152; in ribereño
village economies, 77; as subsistence activity, 100; yields of, 128
Foods: diversification of sources of,
153; favoring of staple crops, 153,
154; staple, 78–79, 114–16, 127
Forest products: economic importance of, 79, 80; income from, 58;
marketing of, 62; prices for, 68
Franciscans: and Jesuit expulsions,
33; and Peruvian independence,
34; settlements in Amazonia by,
29–31
Fritz, Samuel, 30
Fujimori, Alberto, 225; closure of
government buying centers, 61;
credit policies of, 190–91, 220;
lowering of inflation by, 70
Fundos (commercial estates): decline
of, 46, 50, 150; domination of
alturas, 223; hiring of ribereños
by, 130, 131; impact on cooperative labor, 144, 150; importance
to village economies, 80; land
disputes between campesinos and,
206–7; and land redistribution,
98–99; ownership of land by, 74,
76, 194; persistence in remote
areas, 50; in rubber economy, 40–
42, 45; socioeconomic organization of, 38, 45; ties of village
economies to, 97–101

Game animals, 129
García, Alán, 157, 198, 199, 212

Gasoline, price of, 167
Gold, 28
Goodyear, Charles, 39
Government buying centers, 60–62, 116, 117, 119, 120, 177, 178, 196, 202, 211–12, 220–22
Gow, Peter, 48, 86
Gross, Daniel, 20–21
Guaba, 121
Guerrilla warfare, xii, 53, 54, 190, 216, 217, 220, 225, 226
Guillet, David, 135, 149, 151
Gurupá, Brazil, 193

Habilitadores (contractors), 62, 65, 78, 80, 135, 178, 187, 188
Hermanos de la Cruz (Brothers of the Cross), 90
Herndon, William, 35, 36
Highways, Amazonian, 3
Hiraoka, Mário, 23–25; on fishing yields, 128; on plantain cultivation, 115; on protein consumption, 127; on ribereño standard of living, 78; on secondary crops, 120
Hired labor. *See* Jornaleros
Households: agricultural labor by, 138, 142, 146–49, 155, 181, 189; allocation of land to, 77; cash-cropping, 161–63; domestic cycles of, 106; economic organization of, 77–79; income sources of, 131–33; lessening of risk by, 153–55; long-term goals of, 152; long-term risk aversion by, 162–64; maintenance of urban and rural residences, 81; mixed-economy, 159–61; short-term goals of, 152, 158–63; size and composition of, 102–6, 164–65; subsistence-oriented, 159, 160

Housing, ribereño, 46, 73, 74
Huallaga River: mission settlements along, 29; precolumbian settlements along, 28; ribereño settlements along, 72; transportation on, 58–59
Huánuco, Peru, 29
Human rights, 216–17
Hunting, 25; disputes over access to, 203, 208–9, 222; economic importance of, 79; income from, 129; maintaining access to, 163; in ribereño village economies, 77

Illiteracy, 88
Income: diversification of sources of, 153, 156; mean, 132–33; sources of, 57–58, 112, 116, 119, 121–22, 124–33
Indiana, Peru, 89–91
Indians. *See* Amerindians
Infant mortality, 55, 56
Inflation: and austerity policy, 220; impact on rural economy, 70–71; and returns to rice production, 188; size of loans and, 179, 189, 220
Informal sector, 53, 130
Insecticides, 44
Instituto Lingüistico del Verano (Summer Institute of Linguistics), 198
Insurance: agricultural credit as, 174, 181–82, 184, 188, 189; labor groups' programs of, 141, 143
Iquitos, Peru, 29, 157, 161, 169, 199, 213–15; access to, as determinant of village economy, 79–80; agricultural marketplace of, 62, 63, 66–67, 116, 211; campesino organizations of, 170, 195–97, 200, 216; cosmopolitan nature of,

43; as credit center, 176, 184, 210; drug trade in, 57; education in, 88–90; fish and meat sales in, 128–29, 159, 161, 206, 207; government buying center at, 60–61, 119, 178, 202, 212; livestock prices in, 126; loans to entrepreneurs of, 175; medical care in, 91; migration of villagers to, 102, 106, 152, 165–67, 170–72; population of, 36, 43, 47, 49, 54, 56; port facilities of, 212, 213; in postindependence economy, 35, 36, 38; in rubber economy, 40, 41, 43, 97; sale of cash crops in, 50, 51, 58, 70, 77, 78, 101–2, 114, 117, 121–23, 150, 151, 159, 161, 162; ties of villages to, 81–82, 94, 95, 101; and tourism, 208; as trading center, 2; transit connections, 48, 58–60, 80, 156, 167–68, 186; wage labor in, 130, 131
Irrigation project, 213–15
Izquierda Unida (United Left), 198, 215

Jaguars, 129
Jesuits, 97; expulsion of, 33, 34; settlements in Amazonia by, 12, 29–32
Johnson, Allen, 156
Jornaleros (hired workers): advantages/disadvantages of, 142, 143; and credit policies, 130, 142, 147, 150, 177, 181, 186; and jute cultivation, 121; recruitment of, 138, 146–49, 162; and rice cultivation, 116–18, 130; substitution of family labor for, 181, 189; wages paid to, 130
Justicia, Peru, 207

Jute, 10, 16; commercial production of, 49, 50, 58, 94, 95, 120–21, 150, 156, 157, 171, 175, 179, 181–82; economic importance of, 80, 122; marketing of, 60–62, 71, 211, 212, 220, 221; producer groups for, 196, 200; reduction of acreage in, 222; yields from, 121

Kuczynki-Godard, Máximo, 45, 46

Labor, division of, 77–78
Lagunas, Peru, 31, 60, 84–85, 216–17
Lanchas, 58–59, 63, 79–80
Land tenure: communal, 74, 85, 211; disputes over, xiv–xvii, 1–2, 74, 75, 87–88, 98–99, 101, 194, 202–3, 205–7, 222–23, 225; on floodplains, xiii; relationship of credit programs to, 210–11; system of, 74–77
Language, and ethnic identity, 84
Law enforcement, 88
Leche caspi, 44, 45, 99
Levees, natural. *See* Restingas
Liberation Theology, 198
Libertad, Peru, 101
Life expectancy, 55, 56
Lima, Peru, 80, 171, 195, 197; connections to Amazonia, 48, 49, 58; government aid to, 54
Literacy, 88
Livestock, 125–27, 155, 204–7
Loans, government. *See* Credit programs
Loreto department, Peru: agriculture in, 38; campesino organizations of, 193–97, 200–201; and collapse of rubber industry, 43; connections to outside, 48; contraction of credit in, 190–91; distribution of

development aid in, 223; economic contribution of, 53; economic infrastructure of, 212–13; education in, 88–90; ethnic identity in, 84–85; ethnicity of, 47; exports from, 49; governance of, 87–88; government buying centers in, 60–61; household economies of, 78–79; and population, 37, 54–57; in post-independence economy, 36–37; religious affiliation in, 90; rubber economy in, 38, 39; sale of crops on open market, 62–70; settlement patterns of, 72–73; sources of income in, 57–58; standard of living of, 74, 165–66; transit in, 58–60, 167–68; water buffalo project in, 204–7

Mahogany, 43, 44
Malaria, 92
Manatí, Peru, 76–77, 99, 100
Manaus, Brazil, 2
Mangua, Peru, 101
Manioc (*yuca*), 14, 16, 33, 38, 45, 190; commercial production of, 49, 58, 114–16, 131, 132, 151, 156–57, 159, 162, 171, 201; growing of, 111–13, 115, 124–25, 130, 140, 149; marketing of, 63, 70, 211, 212; prices for, 66–69; relative importance of, 122–24; as staple food, 78–79, 114, 116, 127, 150, 221; as subsistence crop, 153–55, 159, 160; yields from, 115
Marañon River, 29; mission settlements along, 29; precolumbian settlements along, 28; ribereño settlements along, 72; rise and fall

of, 14, 16, 67, 101; transportation on, 58–59
Marcoy, Paul, 35, 36
Marketing chains, xii, 62–70
Marketplace: access to, as determinant of economic activity, 79–80; government-subsidized, 60–62, 116, 117, 119, 120, 177, 178, 196, 202, 211–12, 220–22; impact of inflation on, 70–71; intermediaries in, 62–63, 65; logistical problems of, 212–13, 222; open, 62–70, 116, 220–21; sale of cash crops in, 51; socioeconomic relations within, 65–66
Marriage: age of, 106; community-of-origin patterns, 107; and definition of ethnic boundaries, 84, 85; sanctioning of, 90; surname patterns, 107–10
Martial law, 216
Marupa, Peru, 159
Masato, 79, 139, 140, 142, 143
Maynas region: campesino organizations of, 200; colonial economy of, 31, 33, 34; missionization of, 29; population distribution, 56; postindependence economy of, 35–38; religious affiliation in, 90; standard of living of, 74
Mayoristas (large-scale wholesalers), 63, 65
Medical care, 91–92
Meggers, Betty, 19, 27
Mendes, Chico, 224
Merchants: relations with Indians, 34–35, 37; in rubber economy, 41
Mestizos: as ethnic designation, 86; and ribereñoization, 46, 47; in rubber economy, 41; settlement of riverine communities, 99–100

Migration: and population age, 102; and population growth, 54–56, 99; rural-urban, 81

Mijanos (fish migrations), 24

Military service, as economic opportunity, 166–67

Mingas. *See* Cooperative work groups; Festive work parties

Ministry of Agriculture: and approval of loans, 176, 182, 184, 186, 190, 202; assignment of land rights by, 74–76, 88, 100, 205, 209, 211; and irrigated rice project, 214; relations with campesino unions, 215; and water buffalo project, 205–7

Ministry of Nutrition, 204

Miraflores Island, 98

Missionaries: accounts of pre-columbian societies by, 27; expulsion of, 33, 34; and Peruvian independence, 34; settlements in Amazonia by, 12, 29–32

Missions: administration of, 31; alteration of Amerindian ecology by, 32–33; economy of, 31, 33; epidemics in, 31–32

Moran, Emilio, 19, 20

Moyobamba, Peru, 36

Mud bars. *See* Barreales

Napo River, 86; mission settlements along, 29; rise and fall of, 67; tourist camps on, 208

Narcosenderistas, 216, 217

National Institute for Agricultural Research and Promotion, 20

National Institute of Statistics, 53, 55–56

Nauta, Peru, 97, 157; as credit center, 184; government buying center at,

60; in postindependence economy, 35, 36

New York Botanical Garden, xii

Ocelots, 129

Ocho de Mayo, Peru, 101

Ocopa, Peru, 33, 34

Oil, 44; boom in, 165–66; income from, 57; price of, 167

Omaguas, Peru, 35, 36, 97

Omaguas, the, 97; contact with European explorers, 28; mission settlements of, 30, 32; post-independence settlements of, 35, 36; precolumbian settlements of, 26–27; use of rubber by, 38

Onions, 122

Orellana, Francisco de, 28

Orellana, Peru, 213

Oxbow lakes, fishing rights in, 208, 222–23

Pacas, 25, 129

Pace, Richard, 193

Pacific coast of Peru, 51–53; political instability in, 53, 190; rice production in, 201

Padoch, Christine, xii, xiv, 9, 47, 48

Papayas, 121; commercial production of, 159, 162, 171; prices for, 67, 69

Pará, Brazil, 37

Park, Thomas, 7, 8

Patrones: abandonment of fundos, 46; approval of loans for, 176, 190, 191; descent of ribereños from, 158; and drug trade, 57; economic power of, 194; land disputes between campesinos and, 206–7; loans from, 179, 182; relations with, as hedge against

risk, 164; role in economy, 37, 80;
in rubber economy, 40–42; sexual
liaisons of, 46; ties of villagers to,
94, 95, 97–101
Peach palm, 112, 121
Peanuts, 113, 122, 171
Peripheral zones, 10
Peruvian Agrarian Reform (1970s),
75, 99
Petroleum. *See* Oil
Petroperu, 57
Pevas, Peru, 60
Pigs: commercial production of, 160;
income from, 125–27, 155
Pineapples, 112, 121
Pinedo-Vásquez, Miguel, 51, 60;
familiarity with villages, 94; role
in research, xiv–xvii, 94–95, 127,
147, 168, 179; work as union
adviser, 201–2
Plantains, 14, 16, 38, 45, 190;
commercial production of, 49, 58,
102, 114–16, 131, 132, 151, 156–
57, 159, 171, 201; growing of,
111–15, 124–25, 130, 148–49;
marketing of, 63, 70, 211, 212;
prices for, 66–69; relative importance of, 122–24; as staple food,
78–79, 114, 116, 127, 150, 221;
as subsistence crop, 153, 154,
159, 160; yields from, 114–15
Playas, 22, 23; agricultural methods
in, 111, 113; growth of secondary
crops in, 121, 171
Political economy, in analysis of
sustainable development, 4–5
Population density, 20–21, 73
Population distribution, 51, 53,
56–57
Population groups, 8–9, 42–43,
46–48
Population growth, 54–56

Portugal: colonization of Amazonia,
29, 32; exploration by, 2; slaving
raids, 30, 32
Portugal, Peru, 121
Porvenir, Peru, 13–14, 30, 152, 158;
agricultural credit in, 173, 176–
89; agricultural methods of, 111,
112; cooperative labor in, 134;
diet in, 127; differences from other
villages, 96; distribution of
development aid in, 223; education in, 89, 90; fishing in, 127–29;
growth of crops, by land type,
124–25; history of, 97–99;
household size and composition,
102–6; hunting in, 129; land
disputes in, 87–88, 98–99, 206–7;
livestock of, 125–27; marriage
patterns of, 107–10; mean income
level of, 132–33; medical care in,
91–92; military service in, 166–67;
mixed-economy households of,
159–61; mobility of residents of,
81, 82; population distribution in,
56; primary cash crops of, 116–
20; primary food crops of, 114–
15; recruitment of agricultural
labor in, 135, 140, 141, 144, 147,
149; relative importance of crops
of, 122–24; relative importance of
income sources of, 131–33;
remittance income in, 131; as
research subject, 94–95; sanitation
in, 92; secondary crops of, 120–
22; transit connections, 60, 186;
visits of union advisers to, 201;
wage labor in, 130, 131
Prices: in encomienda agreements,
63; inflation-adjusted, 70; selling,
66–70, 177, 211–12, 222; and
trading partnerships, 65

Price supports: and cash cropping, 50, 60, 61, 116, 119, 120, 219; and economic risk, 14–15; and rural poverty, 10

Primary schools, 88–89, 171

Protein: and faunal resources, 20–21; from staple foods, 116, 127, 206

Protestantism, evangelical, 90; and campesino organizations, 198

Pucallpa, Peru, 49, 59, 169

Pueblos jovenes (squatter settlements), 54, 166

Puerto Rico, Peru, 99, 100

Quechua language, 31, 37, 42

Quito, Ecuador, 29, 31, 33, 34

Raimondi, Antonio, 36–38

Rainfall, average, 17

Reducciones: administration of, 31; alteration of Amerindian ecology by, 32–33; economy of, 31, 33; epidemics in, 31–32; population of, 30, 32, 33; settlement of, 30

Regatones: in agricultural marketing chain, 62–63, 65, 80; economic power of, 194, 217; role in economy, 37, 45; in rubber economy, 41

Regional analyses, 11–14

Regional Office of Statistics (Loreto department), 66, 70

Religious affiliation, 90

Rematistas (small-scale wholesalers), 63, 65–69, 119, 130, 199, 202

Remittances, income from, 131, 133

Requena, Francisco, 33

Requena, Peru, 30, 56, 60, 80

Restingas, 22, 23; access to, as determinant of economic activity, 79, 122–23, 187; agricultural methods in, 111–13; growth of

corn in, 119, 120, 125, 171, 202; growth of manioc in, 115, 125, 147, 171; growth of plantains in, 114–15, 125, 147, 171; growth of rice in, 117, 125, 186, 213; growth of secondary crops in, 121; high, allocation to subsistence crops, 154, 155, 160; location of villages near, 73; low, allocation to cash crops, 153, 154; maintaining access to, 163; ownership of, 75, 203; planting of crops on, 67; soil quality of, 23–24; unpredictable flooding of, 221–22

Rice, 10, 14, 114; and annual flooding, 17; commercial production of, 49, 50, 58, 79, 94, 95, 102, 116, 119, 120, 131–33, 150, 151, 156, 159, 162, 170, 171, 221; commercial production of, extension of credit for, 157, 175–90, 201, 210–11; commercial production of, risk of credit for, 155, 187–89; continuous cropping of, 20; economic importance of, 79, 80, 122–24; growing of, 8, 111–13, 116–19, 124–25, 130, 138, 144, 147, 167; harvesting with thresher, 156–58, 213; irrigated, 213–15; marketing of, 60–62, 71, 117, 120, 211, 212, 220, 221; producer groups for, 196, 200–201; reduction of acreage in, 222; selling price of, 177; and unpredictable flooding, 221; varieties of, 202; yields from, 117–20, 177, 180, 185, 186, 213

Risk: definition of, 153, 188; of loan defaults, 178–80, 185–86

Risk aversion: and demand for agricultural credit, 174, 180–82;

in food production, 153–55; long-term, 162–64

Risk taking, xiv; in agricultural financing, 156–57; in agricultural techniques, 156–58

Rondônia state, Brazil, 7, 9

Roosevelt, Anna, 20–21, 24–25, 27

Roseberry, William, 11–12

Rosewood oil, 49

Ross, Eric, 20–21, 32

Rotenone, 44

Rubber: boom in, 2, 12, 26, 38–43, 85, 87, 97, 100, 107, 110, 150; collapse of industry, 43, 100–101; cultivation of plantations, 39–40; demographic impact of, 42–43; exploitation of rain forest for, 2; industrial applications of, 39; prices for, 39, 40; recruitment of labor force, 40–42; and settlement patterns, 12; wartime demand for, 44

Rubber tappers union (Acre, Brazil), 224

Saint Cricq, Laurent. *See* Marcoy, Paul

Sand bars. *See* Playas

Sanitation, 92

San Joaquín de Omaguas mission, 30–32, 97, 98. *See also* Omaguas, Peru

San Jorge, Peru, 23; diet in, 127; fishing in, 127, 128; plantain cultivation in, 115; standard of living of, 78

San Martín department, Peru, 42, 100, 135

San Rafael, Peru, 213–15

San Román, Jesús, 195

San Salvador de Omaguas, Peru, 98

Santa Rosa, Peru, 30; agricultural credit in, 181; agricultural methods of, 112; description of, 136; ethnicity of, 47; recruitment of agricultural labor in, 135, 140

Santa Sofía, Peru, 13–14, 30, 32, 152, 158; agricultural credit in, 173, 179–85, 187–89; agricultural methods of, 111; allocation of land to, 76–77, 88; annual flooding of, 16, 17; cooperative labor in, 134; diet in, 127; differences from other villages, 96; distribution of development aid in, 223; economic opportunity in, 170–72; education in, 89, 90; ethnic identity in, 86–87; fishing in, 127–29; growth of crops, by land type, 124–25; history of, 99–100; household economic strategies, 159, 160; household size and composition, 102–6; hunting in, 129; livestock of, 125–27; marriage patterns of, 107–10; mean income level of, 132–33; military service in, 166–67; mobility of residents of, 81, 82; population distribution in, 56; primary cash crops of, 116–20; primary food crops of, 114–15; recruitment of agricultural labor in, 135, 139, 147, 149; relative importance of crops of, 122–24; relative importance of income sources of, 131–33; remittance income in, 131; as research subject, 94, 95; sanitation in, 92; secondary crops of, 120–22; visits of union advisers to, 201–2; wage labor in, 130, 131

Sarsaparilla, 37

Secondary schools, 89–90, 158, 166, 168, 170, 171, 188

Sendero Luminoso (Shining Path), xii, 54, 162, 220, 225

Shimbillo, 121, 162

Shining Path. *See* Sendero Luminoso

Shipibo, the, 114, 115, 120

Sierra, 51–53; government aid to, 53–54; land redistribution in, 99; political instability in, 53, 190

Slavery: precolumbian, 28; raiding expeditions, 30, 32

Soccer clubs, 92–93

Soil quality: and agricultural intensification, 7, 8, 20; in floodplains, 23–24; in uplands, 19–20

Spain: colonial administration of, 12, 33; colonization of Amazonia, 28–29; end of colonialism of, 34; exploration by, 2, 12, 28

Spanish language, 37, 42, 47, 84, 85, 87, 170

Standard of living, 74, 78; improvement of, 165–66

Star apples, 121, 162

Steamboats, 36

Stocks, Anthony, 30, 84–86

Subhabilitadores (subcontractors), 62, 63, 65

Subsistence production: impact of missionization on, 32–33; as priority over cash cropping, 153, 154; in short-term household strategies, 159–61; in village economy, 100

Sugarcane, 45, 80

Surnames, as indicator of ethnic stratification, 107–10

Sustainable agriculture: and economic stratification, 9–11; and poverty, 10–11

Sustainable development: and agricultural intensification, 7–8; equitability in, 5–6; obstacles to, 221–23; and political economy, 4–5; prospects for, 226; and state agricultural policies, 219–21; strategies of, 4; and subsistence systems, 4, 5

Sweet peppers, 122

Tagua, 44, 45, 100, 101

Tahuampas, 23

Tamshiyacu, Peru, xiii, 29, 47; agroforestry cycles of, 111–12; description of, 136; education in, 89–90; history of, 135; medical care in, 91; recruitment of agricultural labor in, 135, 140, 141, 146–48; secondary crops of, 120

Taperiba, 121

Tapira Chica, Peru, 101

Tapirillo, Peru, 13–14, 30, 47, 152, 158; agricultural credit in, 173, 179–85, 187–89; agricultural methods of, 111; annual flooding of, 16–17; cash-cropping households of, 161–63; cooperative labor in, 134; diet in, 127; differences from other villages, 96; distribution of development aid in, 223; economic opportunity in, 169–70; education in, 89, 90; ethnic identity in, 86; fishing in, 127–29; growth of crops, by land type, 124–25; history of, 100–102; household size and composition, 102–6; hunting in, 129; livestock of, 125–27; marriage patterns of, 107–10; mean income level of, 132–33; military service in, 166–67; mobility of residents of, 81,

82; population distribution in, 56; primary cash crops of, 116–20; primary food crops of, 114–15; recruitment of agricultural labor in, 135, 139–41, 147, 149; relative importance of crops of, 122–24; relative importance of income sources of, 131–33; remittance income in, 131; as research subject, 94–95; sanitation in, 92; secondary crops of, 120–22; thresher program in, 157–58; transit connections, 167; visits of union advisers to, 201; wage labor in, 130, 131

Taxation: and exploitation of rain forest, 2, 3, 6–7; inequitable development and, 5

Teachers, 89, 216

Technical aid, 156–58, 213–15, 217, 225

Temperature, average monthly, 17

Teniente gobernador: allocation of land rights and, 75, 76, 87–88, 163, 203, 209; interference of regional government with, 216; responsibilities of, 87–88; scheduling of work parties by, 139; selection of, 87

Threshers, gasoline-operated, 156–58, 213

Titles, land, 74, 75

Tomatoes, 114, 121, 122, 159; commercial production of, 162, 171; prices for, 67, 69; relative importance of, 122–24

Tourism, 100, 208–9

Trading partnerships, 65–66

Transportation: access to, as determinant of economic activity, 79–80; of cash crops to market, 49–51, 61, 63, 64, 66, 71, 101–2, 117, 123, 150, 212, 213; and community isolation, 12–13; economic opportunities in, 167–68, 186; and exploitation of rain forest, 3–4; and integration of Peruvian economy, 48–50; and mobility patterns, 81–82; and oil exploration, 57; in regional economy, 58–60; and rural poverty, 10; as stimulus to colonization, 36

Transportistas, 59, 63, 65, 77, 167–68

Tropical fruits, 7, 38; commercial production of, 160–62; economic importance of, 79; in village economies, 101, 102

Ucayali department, Peru: distribution of development aid in, 223; economic contribution of, 53; ethnicity of, 47; population growth in, 54

Ucayali River, 86, 99; mission settlements along, 29, 30; precolumbian settlements along, 26, 28; ribereño settlements along, 72; rise and fall of, 14, 16, 67; transportation on, 58–59; transport of Amazonian products on, 49

Umarí, 112, 114, 147–48

UNAP. *See* Universidad Nacional de la Amazonía Peruana

Universidad Nacional de la Amazonía Peruana (UNAP), xv, xvi, 204

Uplands (alturas): access to, as determinant of economic activity, 79, 187; agricultural methods of, 111–12; allocation to subsistence crops, 153–55, 160; cooperative labor in, 139; elevation of, 17; faunal resources of, 20–21;

growth of corn in, 119; growth of manioc in, 115, 125, 147; growth of plantains in, 114, 125; growth of rice in, 117, 213–15; hunting in, 129; livestock of, 127; maintaining access to, 163; neglect by development programs, 223; ownership of, 75, 203, 222; secondary crops of, 120; and settlement patterns, 17, 73; soil quality of, 19–20

Upward mobility, 158, 165–72

Urbanization, 56–57

Urubamba River, 86

Uvilla, 112

Vendors, in agricultural marketing chain, 68–70, 119

Voz de la Selva (radio station), 67, 192

Vulcanization, 39

Wage labor: advantages/disadvantages of, 142, 143, 155; coordination of hiring, 202; and credit policies, 130, 142, 147, 150, 177, 181, 186; economic importance of, 80, 95; and economic opportunity, 169; impact on cooperative labor, 144, 151; income from, 129–31, 133; and jute cultivation, 121; occasions for, 137–38, 146–49, 160, 162; reliance on, vs.

cooperative groups, 134–35; in ribereño village economies, 77, 78; and rice cultivation, 116–18, 130; socioeconomic relations of, 34–35, 37, 137, 138; substitution of family labor for, 181, 189

Wagley, Charles, 193

Warfare: guerrilla, xii, 53, 54, 190, 216, 217, 220, 225, 226; precolumbian, 28

Water buffalo project, 204–7

Watermelons, 114, 121, 159, 171; relative importance of, 122–24

Wickham, Henry, 39

Women's roles: in ribereño households, 77; in union organizations, 199–200, 223

Wood: export from Amazonia, 43–44, 49; income from, 58

World War I, 44

World War II, 44, 48

Yaguas, the, 32, 87, 99, 100, 109, 170

Yanallpa, Peru, 30; changing of crop patterns in, 123; description of, 136; history of, 135; recruitment of agricultural labor in, 135, 140, 141

Yanashi, Peru, 192–93, 202, 212

Yuca. See Manioc

Yurimaguas, Peru, 20, 31, 56, 214, 216–17

About the Author

Michael Chibnik is Professor and former Chair of Anthropology at the University of Iowa. He received his doctoral degree in anthropology from Columbia University in 1975 and later was a postdoctoral fellow in quantitative anthropology and public policy at the University of California, Berkeley. Chibnik taught at Jersey City State College and Columbia University before joining the faculty at Iowa in 1978. He has also worked as a consultant for the National Academy of Sciences and the Xerox Corporation.

Chibnik's research has focused on household economies, cultural ecology, grassroots organizations, and agricultural decision making. He has conducted fieldwork in the Peruvian Amazon, Belize, Guatemala, and various parts of the United States. His research has been supported by grants from the National Science Foundation, the National Institute of Mental Health, the Midwest Universities Consortium for International Activities, and the University of Iowa.

Chibnik edited *Farm Work and Fieldwork: American Agriculture in Anthropological Perspective* (Cornell University Press, 1987). He has contributed articles to many journals, including *Amazonía Indígena, Amazonía Peruana, American Ethnologist, Annual Review of Anthropology, Culture and Agriculture, Journal of Anthropological Research,* and *Practicing Anthropology.* He has also written chapters for *Farm Work and Fieldwork* and other edited books.